Running ESXi on a Raspberry Pi

Installing VMware ESXi on Raspberry Pi 4 to run Linux virtual machines

Thomas Fenton
Patrick Kennedy

Apress®

Running ESXi on a Raspberry Pi: Installing VMware ESXi on Raspberry Pi 4 to run Linux virtual machines

Thomas Fenton
Ridgefield, WA, USA

Patrick Kennedy
Austin, TX, USA

ISBN-13 (pbk): 978-1-4842-7464-4
https://doi.org/10.1007/978-1-4842-7465-1

ISBN-13 (electronic): 978-1-4842-7465-1

Managing Director, Apress Media LLC: Welmoed Spahr
Acquisitions Editor: Aaron Black
Development Editor: James Markham
Coordinating Editor: Jessica Vakili

Distributed to the book trade worldwide by Springer Science+Business Media New York, 233 Spring Street, 6th Floor, New York, NY 10013. Phone 1-800-SPRINGER, fax (201) 348-4505, e-mail orders-ny@springer-sbm.com, or visit www.springeronline.com. Apress Media, LLC is a California LLC and the sole member (owner) is Springer Science + Business Media Finance Inc (SSBM Finance Inc). SSBM Finance Inc is a **Delaware** corporation.

For information on translations, please e-mail booktranslations@springernature.com; for reprint, paperback, or audio rights, please e-mail bookpermissions@springernature.com.

Apress titles may be purchased in bulk for academic, corporate, or promotional use. eBook versions and licenses are also available for most titles. For more information, reference our Print and eBook Bulk Sales web page at http://www.apress.com/bulk-sales.

Any source code or other supplementary material referenced by the author in this book is available to readers on GitHub via the book's product page, located at www.apress.com/978-1-4842-7464-4. For more detailed information, please visit http://www.apress.com/source-code.

Printed on acid-free paper

I dedicate this book to my mother, the noted author and historian Cleta Fenton. My father Darrell Fenton, who is the most honest man I have ever known. And, most importantly, my granddaughter Eleanor Jane Fenton, who brings so much joy to my life.

I would also like to publicly thank David Harriman and Josh Fenton for the work they did on the book. Their wordsmithing made the book much more readable.

– Tom Fenton

I dedicate this book to my parents and family for always supporting me and my nieces Gracen and Emerson and nephew Pierce for bringing joy while working on this. Also, a quick thanks to the STH (ServeTheHome.com) team, our audience, and those in the industry for supporting our efforts over the past 12 years.

– Patrick Kennedy

Table of Contents

About the Authors

Tom Fenton has worked with virtualization for over two decades. He's held staff and senior-level positions at VMware, IBM, ControlUp, and other high-tech companies. He wrote the first training course for Horizon, VMware's virtual desktop product. He is a frequent contributor to StorageReview.com, *Virtualization & Cloud Review* magazine, and other blogs and websites. He lives in the Pacific Northwest and enjoys skiing, snowboarding, hiking, and trail riding.

Patrick Kennedy after the better part of a decade working in a management consulting firm with many technology clients started ServeTheHome.com. Over the past 12+ years, STH has grown to be the place to learn about new server, storage, and networking technologies as Patrick and the STH team look at the latest solutions.

Patrick is a Silicon Valley, California, guy now roaming the hill country surrounding Austin, Texas.

About the Technical Reviewer

Darren Hirons is Lead Solutions Engineer at VMware. He has over 20 years of experience working with a wide variety of VMware products and other datacenter technologies. His focus more recently has been in the end user computing space, where he helps customers architect solutions to address business challenges.

Acknowledgments

We freely acknowledge that the work and information in this book has been greatly shaped by the VMware ESXi on Arm community whose legions are far too numerous to mention. Their work and dedication to this project can be found in the many forums that they contribute to. A special shout-out needs to go to William Lam, a Senior Staff Solution Architect at VMware, for documenting so much about VMware technologies and, in particular, ESXi on Arm on his website `https://williamlam.com/`. William's tireless work with the community is simply amazing!

Preamble

All of the author's proceeds from this book will go to Mount Hood Kiwanis Camp (`https://mhkc.org/`). This scenic camp sits on 22 acres of the US Forest Service land at the base of Mount Hood. It offers summer and winter camps that help empower children and adults with disabilities through overnight, outdoor, recreational programming. Both of us have had outstanding experiences with the Kiwanis organization over the years and gladly support this camp.

CHAPTER 1

Setting the Framework for ESXi on Arm on Pi

In this chapter, in order to set the stage for the rest of the book, we will look at the datacenter before virtualization was available. We will then discuss virtual machines (VMs) and the classifications of the types of hypervisors that are commonly in use. We will also give you a little background of VMware, the company that developed ESXi. As ESXi is an integral part of the vSphere family, we will also touch on some of the other vSphere products.

The Datacenter Before Virtualization

Before delving into topics like ESXi, Arm servers, and virtual machines (VMs), we need to go back and talk about what the datacenter looked like in 2001, right before virtualization became a mainstay. This was an exciting time; the Internet was just becoming widely used, and multitiered architecture was the *de facto* standard for delivering applications and services.

A typical three-tier architecture (see Figure 1-1) was composed of a presentation tier, a domain logic tier, and a data storage tier. By separating an application into these layers of abstraction, any single tier could, in theory, be modified without affecting any of the others. For availability

© Thomas Fenton and Patrick Kennedy 2022
T. Fenton and P. Kennedy, *Running ESXi on a Raspberry Pi*,
https://doi.org/10.1007/978-1-4842-7465-1_1

and performance reasons, each layer within this architecture could be composed of multiple servers delivering the services needed for the respective layer.

Figure 1-1. *Three-Tier Architecture*

During this time, a widely accepted best practice in datacenters was to have one physical server run a single service. The servers and operating systems (OSs) that ran on them didn't have quality of service (QoS) features that would prevent an application from overconsuming resources on a server, which in turn prevented other active applications from running effectively.

Furthermore, we didn't want any applications or OSs to bring down an entire multitiered application due to a software or hardware failure. Because it was impractical to "rightsize" the physical components for each physical server to match the load that was required of them by the services they were providing, this led to *server sprawl* (see Figure 1-2) – an overabundance of servers only using a small fraction of compute capacity that they were capable of.

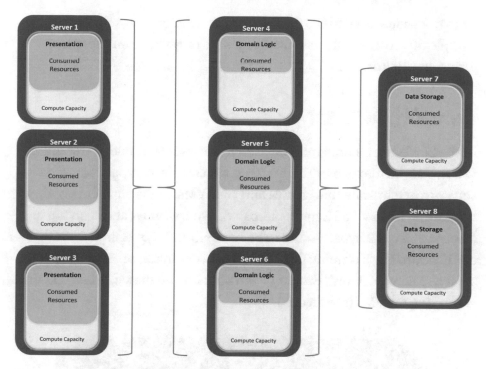

Figure 1-2. *Server Sprawl*

As the demand for computer servers exploded, it became apparent to even the most casual observer that the current datacenter was unsustainable; a new technology and/or datacenter methodology was needed, and fortunately, a new technology was coming on the scene at this exact time.

x86 operating system virtualization allowed multiple instances of an x86 operating system to run on a physical x86 server. These instances are now known as virtual machines, or VMs for short.

Introduction to Virtual Machines (VMs)

VM technology is not new; in fact, IBM supported the use of VMs back in the mid-1960s on their mainframe computers, and, later on, Unix systems supported something akin to VMs. However, these VM technologies were not widely used in the datacenter for a variety of reasons, including complexity, cost, and the fact that they were only viable on expensive proprietary hardware.

Type 2 Hypervisor

In the 2000s, a few companies devised hypervisor technology, a solution to run VMs on inexpensive commodity x86 servers. A hypervisor is the software or hardware that creates and runs VMs. In the early days of this revelation, we first had Type 2, or hosted, hypervisors that run on top of a base OS. Type 2 hypervisors can be basically thought of as just another application that is running VMs. In fact, you could run other applications, such as Microsoft Word, Excel, or even Solitaire, on the same base OS that is running the VMs (see Figure 1-3).

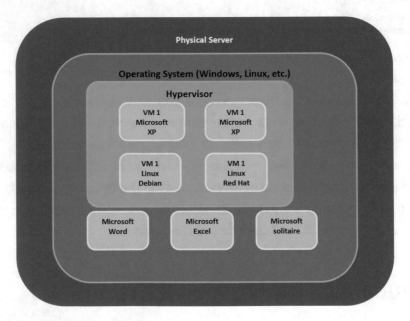

Figure 1-3. *Type 2 Hypervisor*

While Type 2 hypervisors were initially convenient to use, they posed various issues because of the fact that they run on top of an existing OS. These issues ranged from compatibility issues with the hypervisor when the base OS was changed or updated to the inability of the hypervisor provider to modify the base OS to optimize it for hypervisor use, rather than general application use.

Currently, the most popular Type 2 hypervisors, and the OSs that they run on top of, are VMware Workstation (MS Windows), VMware Fusion (macOS), KVM (Linux), Oracle VirtualBox (Linux, Windows, Solaris), and Parallels (Mac).

Type 1 Hypervisor

To overcome the limitations of the Type 2 hypervisors, companies created Type 1 hypervisors for x86 systems. Whereas a Type 2 hypervisor runs as an application on a base OS, a Type 1 hypervisor runs natively on the hardware, thereby supplanting the need for a base OS (see Figure 1-4). Type 1 hypervisors are also referred to as native, or bare metal, hypervisors as they run natively on the bare metal of a server.

The advent of Type 1 hypervisors radically changed the datacenter as it allowed multiple instances of OSs to run on a single physical server to safely, securely, and fully utilize the resources of the server. But server consolidation was just the beginning of the benefits that VMs and hypervisors brought to the datacenter. Later in this book, you will learn about some other benefits they offer.

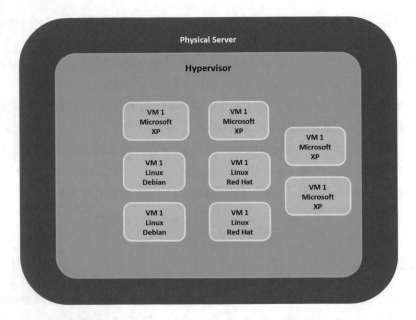

Figure 1-4. *Type 1 Hypervisor*

A hypervisor not only provides a place for VMs to run, it also provides
the means to create and manage them. VMs can be created from scratch by
installing an OS on them, or they can be cloned from an existing VM. The
management functions that hypervisors provide vary greatly depending
on the hypervisor, but they all provide compute resource management and
security for the VMs that they manage.

A VM is composed of various configuration and data files that describe
the VM and hold the data that makes up the VM. For example, a VMware
VM is composed of a VM configuration file, BIOS or EFI configuration file,
VM swap file, log file, data disk, as well as other files. Usually, each VM is
kept in a separate folder.

The most popular Type 1 hypervisors are VMware ESXi, Microsoft
Hyper-V, and XenServer.

VMware

VMware was founded in 1998 in Palo Alto, CA, by five individuals, including Mendel Rosenblum who was, at the time (and still is), a professor of computer science at Stanford University. Since their founding, VMware has become a leader of enterprise-level virtualization; and their Type 1 hypervisor, ESXi, is currently the most popular hypervisor in the enterprise.

VMware's first product was VMware Workstation, a Type 2 hypervisor launched in 1999 that ran on top of a Windows x86 system. While Workstation was designed to run on desktop systems, VMware also launched two products for the server market in 2001: GSX (a Type 2 hypervisor) and ESX (a Type 1 hypervisor). GSX quickly fell to the wayside as ESX became the *de facto* standard in enterprise datacenters. In 2004, ESX was renamed to ESXi, with the "i" standing for *integrated* (around this time VMware shrunk the code to ~32MB and moved many of the management functions of ESX to vCenter Server).

Throughout the years, VMware has continued to develop new technologies and acquire companies for their technologies. One of VMware's more notable acquisitions was Propero, a virtual desktop infrastructure (VDI) provider, in 2007; this acquisition later morphed into VMware Horizon, their very popular VDI solution. Also, in 2012, they acquired Nicira Inc., the creator of network virtualization products, who later became known as VMware NSX.

While VMware's acquisitions have primarily focused on companies within the virtualization space, they have also branched out and acquired technologies in other fields. As a prime example, in 2018, they acquired Heptio, a company deeply steeped into Kubernetes (K8s).

Of course, not all of VMware's current technologies and products were inherited from acquisitions; some of their great technologies have also been developed in-house. For instance, in 2014, they released vSAN, a software-defined storage (SDS) solution for VMware ESXi, which is currently one of the highest-selling SDS solutions in the datacenter.

VMware vSphere

When ESX was first released, it quickly became adopted by enterprise-class users. It also soon became apparent that its various instances running in the datacenter needed another program to oversee and manage them. To tackle this job, VMware created vSphere, a platform composed of not only ESXi but also other products and technologies to provide reliability, performance, business continuity (BC), and disaster recovery (DR) for a datacenter. Some of the products and features currently under the banner of vSphere include

- vCenter Server – A central management portal for controlling and managing ESXi hosts.

- VMware vSphere Client – An HTML5-based GUI for vCenter Server, replacing the vSphere Web Client that was Flash-based and before that the C# client.

- vSphere vMotion – A feature that allows a user to move a running VM from one ESXi host to another without incurring any downtime.

- vSphere Storage vMotion – A feature that allows a user to move a running VM from the storage on which it resides onto another storage location.

- VMware vSphere Distributed Switch (VDS) – A virtual network switch that can span multiple ESXi hosts.

- vSphere High Availability (HA) – A technology that monitors and restarts VMs if needed.

- Fault Tolerance (FT) – A technology that mirrors a VM across different physical servers. If one of the physical servers fails, the VM running on the other physical server will continue to operate unimpeded.

- VMware Distributed Resource Scheduler (DRS) – A feature that balances the compute resource usage of VMs between the ESXi hosts in a cluster.

- VMware Storage Distributed Resource Scheduler – A feature that balances the storage resource usage of VMs between the ESXi hosts in a cluster.

VMware is continuing to develop the above-listed features and technologies and to integrate new features into their products.

vCenter Server

While ESXi handles running VMs on a physical server, vCenter Server tells the ESXi hosts what to do and acts as a central administration point (see Figure 1-5). vCenter Server can be accessed in a few different ways: graphically via the vSphere Client; from a command line; or programmatically using APIs or PowerCLI, VMware's extension to PowerShell.

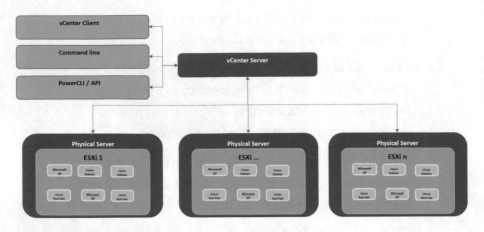

Figure 1-5. *vCenter Server*

As VMs are simply a collection of files, any ESXi server is capable of running vCenter Server as long as it has access to these files. In order to enable this functionality, VMware created a shared file system called VMware Virtual Machine File System (VMFS) and called the location on which a VMFS resides a *datastore*.

vCenter Server can be used to instantiate (start) a VM being stored on a datastore to any of the ESXi servers that are attached to it (Figure 1-6). Also, because the VMs are just software constructors, they can be configured or reconfigured as needed, for instance, if a VM needs more virtual CPU (vCPU) cores or more memory.

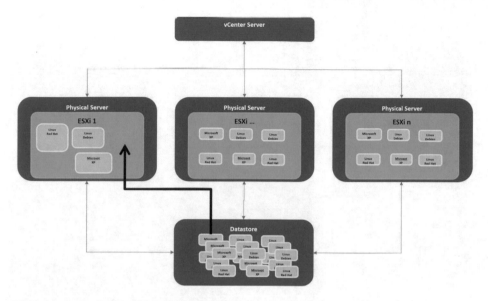

Figure 1-6. *Instantiating a VM*

vMotion

vCenter Server 1.0 was released in 2003 and enabled one of VMware's most defining features – vMotion, a tool that allows a running VM to be moved from one ESXi server to another (Figure 1-7). Although the vMotion action itself occurs between two ESXi servers, the integration of vCenter Server allowed for cross-server coordination. vMotion made it possible for the files that make up a VM to be stored on a datastore that multiple ESXi hosts could access, rather than on local storage that only a single ESXi host could access.

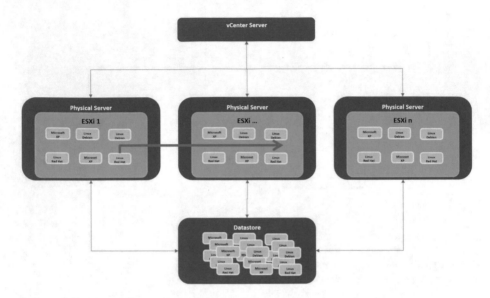

Figure 1-7. *vMotion*

The impact that vMotion had on VMware and the datacenter as a whole cannot be overstated; it allowed VMware to sell virtualization as a business continuity (BC) solution as well as for server consolidation.

From a BC standpoint, vMotion allows applications to be evacuated while still running from one host to another without disruption. This allows servers to be brought down for maintenance or replacement without affecting the day-to-day operation of a business. Datacenters can rebalance the VMs running on an ESXi host to make sure that their physical resources are being consumed uniformly. VMware even came up with a scheme, using vMotion, to consolidate VMs on a minimal number of servers and then power off servers during the night or at other times when they were unneeded.

Storage vMotion

Later, VMware came out with Storage vMotion, a tool that allows VMs to be moved from one datastore to another without incurring any downtime for the VMs (Figure 1-8). This allows storage arrays to be replaced or maintained without application downtime since the VMs that they run on are unaffected by this change. When a datastore starts to run out of capacity, vMotion can be used to free up capacity on it without disrupting applications that are running. Another benefit that Storage vMotion provides is that critical VMs can be more performant or reliable as needed.

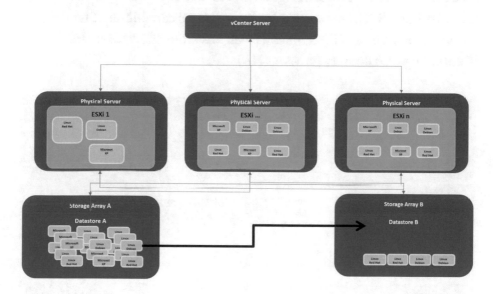

Figure 1-8. *Storage vMotion*

vCenter Server Appliance

VMware originally released vCenter Server as a Windows application that required a separate Windows instance and a separate database, but they followed it with vCenter Server Appliance (VCSA). VCSA is a virtual appliance with Linux as its base OS and comes with a preinstalled Postgres database. A virtual appliance is a VM that has an application preinstalled on it and can be quickly deployed and configured.

VCSA comes in three different versions: *Essentials*, *Foundation*, and *Standard* (Figure 1-9). Essentials is a very low-priced option, but also has a limit of three dual-proc servers and does not have all the features included in Standard. Foundation is designed for smaller environments as it only supports four ESXi hosts and is also limited in its capabilities. Standard supports thousands of ESXi hosts as well as advanced features such as vCenter High Availability (vCenter HA).

Features	Essentials	Foundation	Standard
Management service	X	X	X
Database server	X	X	X
VMware vCenter APIs	X	X	X
Inventory service	X	X	X
vCenter Single Sign-On	X	X	X
vCenter Server Appliance Migration Tool	X	X	X
vRealize Orchestrator			X
vCenter High Availability (VCHA)			X
vCenter Server Backup & Restore			X
Enhanced Linked Mode (ELM)			X
ESXi Host Management (max)	3 Hosts (2CPU MAX)	4 Hosts	2000 Hosts

Figure 1-9. *VCSA Versions*

Summary

Server virtualization has taken over the datacenter, and the pioneer of it is VMware. They have hypervisors that run on top of operating systems (Type 2) or directly on server (Type 1). VMware vSphere is a family of products and features that enable a virtualized datacenter. The remainder of this book will focus on VMware's hypervisor ESXi but will also touch on other technologies such as vMotion.

In the next chapter, we will look at Arm processors, Raspberry Pi (RPi) systems, and ESXi on Arm.

CHAPTER 2

ESXi on Arm on Pi and the Post-virtualized Datacenter

In the first chapter, we showed how a multitiered application in the datacenter prior to virtualization required different physical servers, with each server running a single application (Figure 1-2). Once virtualization was introduced, however, that same datacenter could run the same multitiered applications using VMs, consolidating them from eight underutilized servers to three fully utilized servers (Figure 2-1).

In this chapter, we'll give an overview of the Arm architecture and the Raspberry Pi. Then we'll discuss ESXi on Arm currently in the datacenter and go over some of the limitations of ESXi on Arm on Pi.

Figure 2-1. *Server Consolidation*

© Thomas Fenton and Patrick Kennedy 2022
T. Fenton and P. Kennedy, *Running ESXi on a Raspberry Pi*,
https://doi.org/10.1007/978-1-4842-7465-1_2

Arm

x86 is a set of instructions that was developed by Intel to be used for their microprocessors. This architecture uses a complex instruction set computer (CISC) philosophy and was substantially upgraded when Intel developed a CISC 64-bit microprocessor architecture (this is known as x64). Although the majority of current desktop and datacenter servers are x64 systems, there are other microprocessor architectures currently in use, and ARM (or Arm) is quickly gaining popularity.

Arm was designed as a reduced instruction set computer (RISC) architecture. There are many differences between CISC and RISC architectures, and proponents of both sides, but those discussions are far beyond the scope of this book.

RISC is not new – it has been around since the mid-1980s – but it has recently found new fame as Arm systems are becoming more prevalent in datacenters and in home and personal devices. Arm processors tend to be less expensive and consume less power than CISC-based systems.

These factors are why many cell phones use Arm processors. Apple recently released Arm-based desktop and laptop systems. Public cloud providers have also been using Arm systems for years, and all the large computer manufacturers have released, or have announced plans to release, Arm-based servers for the datacenter.

Raspberry Pi

The Raspberry Pi (RPi, or simply Pi) is a small inexpensive single-board Arm computer that was originally designed to help teach computer skills. Hobbyists soon flocked to them however, and an increasing number of products were designed around them; eventually, enterprises started to use them in unconventional uses like edge devices and VDI clients.

The first widely available Pi system was the Model B (Figure 2-2) released in 2012. It was quite rudimentary, with only 256MB of RAM and a 700MHz Arm11 processor. It was rated at 0.213 GFLOPS.

www.raspberrypi.org

Figure 2-2. *RPi Model B*

The latest Pi, the Pi 4B+, was released in 2019 and supports up to 8GB of RAM with a quad-core Arm Cortex-A72 processor that operates at 1.5GHz. It has two 4K micro-HDMI ports, two USB 3.0 ports, two USB 2.0 ports, a micro-SD card slot, 2.4GHz and 5.0GHz IEEE 802.11ac wireless, Bluetooth 5.0, BLE, and one GbE port. It is powered via a 3A, 5V USB-C connector and also has a 40-pin general-purpose input-output (GPIO) connector. A Pi 4 Model B with 8GB of RAM is priced at around $80 and rated at 13.5 GFLOPS (Figure 2-3).

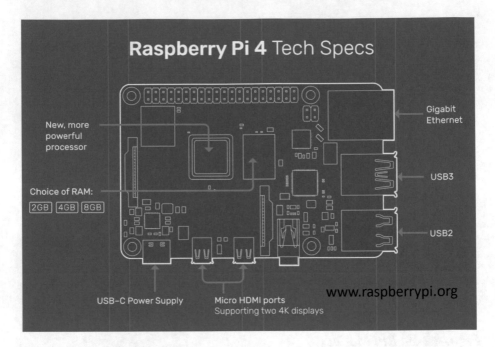

Figure 2-3. *RPi 4 Tech Specs*

ESXi on Arm on Pi

Rumors circulated for years that VMware was working on ESXi for Arm. On October 6, 2020, Kit Colbert, the VP and CTO of VMware, confirmed these rumors and announced that VMware was releasing an ESXi on Arm Fling. Although the announcement itself generated a great deal of interest, the fact that it ran on a Pi escalated the enthusiasm as it allowed people to work on a truly inexpensive platform.

ESXi on Arm is not an officially supported VMware product. Instead ESXi on Arm is a *Fling*, a term used to describe software created by VMware for the benefit of VMware customers. Flings are used to gauge the adoption and usefulness of a product or technology before evaluating whether or not to make it a full-fledged official VMware product. ESXi on Arm proved to be a home run for VMware, gaining over 10,000 downloads shortly after it was released.

VMware has discussed use cases for ESXi on Arm in the datacenter (vSAN witness nodes, Arm servers, SmartNICs, etc.). They have also discussed edge and IoT uses like wind turbine monitoring, discrete video surveillance, and even stand-alone Arm-based point of sale (POS) devices.

The supported hardware for ESXi on Arm includes datacenter servers such as the Lenovo ThinkSystem HR350A (Ampere eMAG) (Figure 2-4), near-edge devices like the SolidRun HoneyComb LX2 (Figure 2-4), and far-edge devices including the Raspberry RPi 4B – 4GB or 8GB model (Figure 2-5).

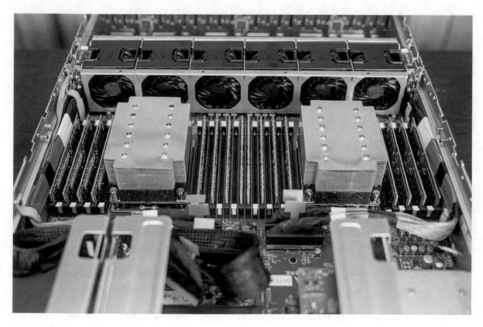

Figure 2-4. *Edge Device*

Figure 2-5. RPi 4B

ESXi on Arm Currently in the Datacenter

ESXi on Arm has some interesting use cases at both the home and enterprise levels, but VMware invested significant time, money, and engineering resources, and it is capable of running on far more powerful hardware than a Pi. Having ESXi on a Pi is just a benefit for its development.

VMware has always been enterprise-driven; their products are designed to modernize large enterprise-sized datacenters, and ESXi on Arm is no exception. VMware has access to the architects of some of the world's largest datacenters. VMware correctly foresaw that Arm processors would become a major component not only for core server usage but also to make Arm and x64 servers in general more efficient. They have achieved this by offloading network and storage functions to lower-priced Arm processors, which frees up a server's main processor for more valuable work.

Cloud Providers and Arm Servers

Cloud providers have been a major user of Arm servers. Not only do they purchase Arm servers from various companies, they also design their own Arm-based servers. Cloud providers take advantage of the Arm architecture and streamlined instruction set to optimize the efficiency of their workload.

Amazon Web Services (AWS) has been making Arm processors available to the general public since 2018, when they introduced a Graviton1 processor EC2 (A1) instance at AWS re:Invent in November 2018. This instance was based on a 16-core 64-bit Arm Cortex-A72 processor running at 2.3Ghz. AWS followed it up in 2019 with a Graviton2 instance that they claimed offered seven times the performance of A1 instances.

The Graviton2 is powered by an Arm Neoverse N1 processor, which scales from 8 to 16 cores per chip and 128 cores per socket. Arm claims that their N1 processor has 30% greater performance per watt than the Cortex-A72 processor.

Oracle has announced that they are using the Ampere Altra 80-core processor (Arm Neoverse N1) in their Arm-based cloud instances. Microsoft, as of writing this, has not shown their Arm cloud hardware, but they have previously shown demos of Windows on Arm running on servers. Google has been using Arm-based processors internally for years.

Datacenter Arm Servers

There are many server companies that have Arm-based servers. The major server suppliers like Dell and Lenovo offer Arm-based servers, as well as companies that are focused exclusively on Arm-based servers.

To get a better feel for the range of Arm systems that ESXi supports, let's compare the hardware of the Raspberry Pi 4 Model B with its four cores and 8GB of RAM with the Lenovo ThinkSystem HR350A, a 2U rack server designed for datacenter usage that, at the time of this writing, is being demoed to select customers. It has a 32-core 64-bit ARMv8 CPU running at 3.3GHz and has support for 512GB of RAM. For storage, it supports two NVMe drives in the chassis and six external storage bays.

Supercomputers

In June of 2020, when the annual TOP500 supercomputer rankings were released by TOP500.org, Japan's Fugaku Arm-based supercomputer was at the top of the list. To achieve the number one spot, it performed 416 petaflops on the High-Performance Linpack (HPL) benchmark, beating the previous holder of the title by an outstanding 280%.

Fugaku runs an unmodified version of Red Hat Enterprise Arm Linux. It has 158,976 Fujitsu A64FX processors running at 2.2GHz. Each processor contains 48 Arm cores for a total of slightly more than 7.5 million cores. The A64FX also includes specialized vector units and high-bandwidth memory (HBM) to achieve this level of performance.

Japan is not the only country using A64FX processors in supercomputers. US-based Sandia National Laboratories announced that they have begun the installation of a Fujitsu PRIMEHPC FX700 system. The EUC is also seeing the benefits of the Arm architecture, and its members are working on a supercomputer based on an EUC-developed Arm processor.

ESXi on Arm and the Future of the Datacenter

The future of Arm in the datacenter looks promising as new products and topologies that use existing products are beginning to emerge. Many of the products will need to be monitored and managed, and VMware will use its incredible presence in the datacenter to do just that – and will back much of this on VMware's ability to have ESXi run on Arm.

SmartNIC/DPU

At VMworld 2020, VMware announced Project Monterey. This was an underreported announcement, but one with a major impact. As VMware Chief Executive Pat Gelsinger said during VMworld, Monterey is a *"major rearchitecture of vSphere itself."* The importance of this rearchitecture cannot be understated as vSphere is the umbrella under which ESXi, vCenter Server (its management plane), and basically all of VMware's virtualized datacenter platforms (both on-premise and cloud-based) all reside.

Kit Colbert wrote a blog at the end of September of 2020 that clarified some details pertaining to Project Monterey. Specifically, he specified that Monterey uses SmartNICs to offload a traditional server's network and network storage workload from a server's CPU (Figure 2-6) to a SmartNIC's CPU (Figure 2-7).

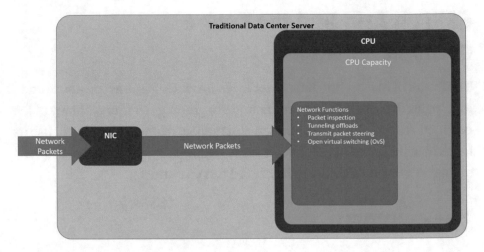

Figure 2-6. *NIC in Traditional Server*

The obvious workloads for SmartNICs are ones that relate to the operation and security of general network information. By using SmartNICs, these services can be performed without impacting the server's CPU as only the network information that is relevant to that server is processed by the server's CPU (Figure 2-7).

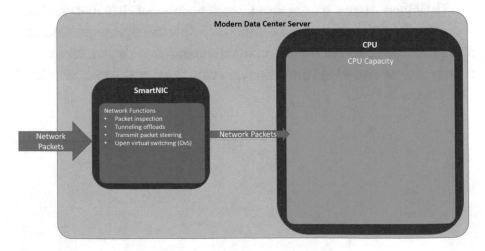

Figure 2-7. *SmartNIC in Server*

SmartNICs can also deal with network storage by taking on the task of compression, encryption, block queuing, packet assembly, and even NVMe over Fabrics (NVMe-oF) that previously took place on the server (see Figure 2-8). By having the SmartNIC accomplish these tasks, the storage data can be passed along to the server rather than having the server take up the CPU cycles required to perform these tasks (see Figure 2-9).

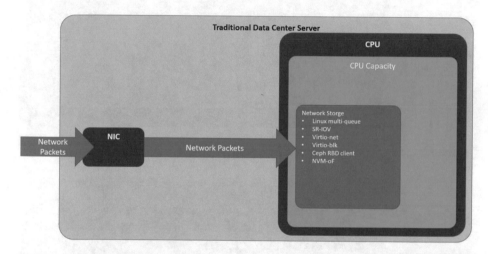

Figure 2-8. *Network Function in Traditional Sever*

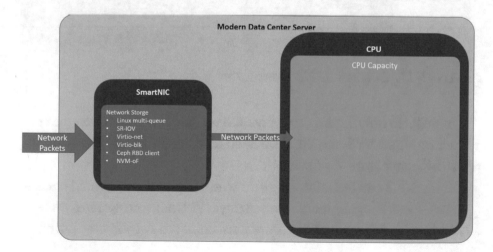

Figure 2-9. *Network Function with SmartNIC*

Less obvious workloads for SmartNICs are ones that deal with the performance of network information. By having the SmartNIC perform latency-sensitive work, the work can be completed more quickly than at a near-line rate (Figures 2-10 and 2-11).

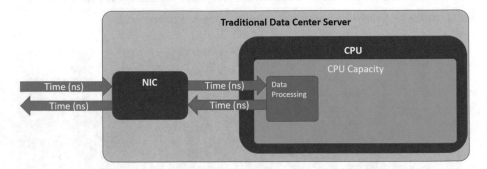

Figure 2-10. *Traditional NIC Latency*

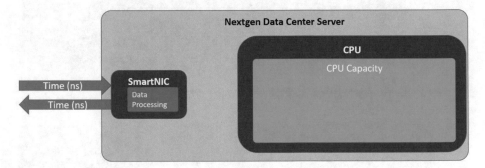

Figure 2-11. *SmartNIC Network Latency*

In order to fully understand why ESXi on Arm is an important part of VMware's vision for SmartNICs, we need to first look at the underlying physical architecture of a SmartNIC.

SmartNICs can be built using application-specific integrated circuits (ASICs), Field-Programmable Gate Arrays (FPGAs), and systems on a chip (SoCs). ASICs and FPGAs are performant; however, they have limited flexibility, and it's difficult to add additional functionality to them if needed. SoCs are extremely flexible, but they lack the speed of ASICs and FPGAs.

To provide both flexibility and performance, some SmartNICs use SoCs for control-plane functions due to their inherent flexibility and FPGAs or ASICs for data-plane functions for increased performance. The primary advantage of using an FPGA over an ASIC is that an FPGA can be reprogrammed when a new functionality is developed and/or needed, whereas ASICs are hardwired and can be more difficult to update (Figure 2-12).

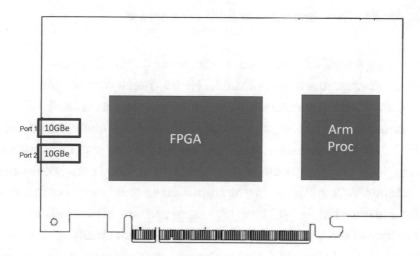

Figure 2-12. *Arm/FPGA SmartNIC*

In a server with a SmartNIC, there are two instances of ESXi running on it: one for the server's main CPU(s) and VMs and another for the SmartNIC and the VMs that handle the offload work that the SmartNIC is taking on (Figure 2-13).

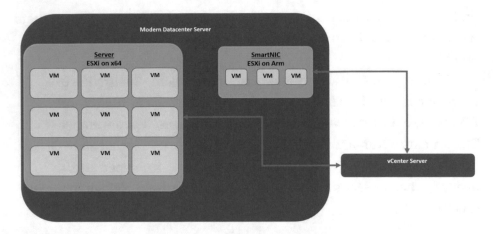

Figure 2-13. *Two Instances of ESXi on a Server*

By using SmartNICs, the datacenter can be further disaggregated into the infrastructure and application layers, thereby creating another layer of abstraction by separating the NICs from the server itself. When the network workload is separated from the servers, a reduction on the servers' CPU usage can be seen as the SmartNICs take over tasks such as encryption and compression of general network and network storage traffic. SmartNICs will also have an improved security model as threats will be addressed at the NIC level and managed via policies rather than managed individually at the server or VM level. Finally, system administrators will have visibility at the NIC, rather than the server, level for the network.

Computational Storage

A new term is starting to emerge to describe the ability of a VM/device/ server/hypervisor to process data directly on the same device as the storage – *computational storage*. Arm's Director of Storage Solutions, Neil Werdmuller, recently wrote:

> *Computational storage is emerging as a critical piece of the data storage puzzle because it puts processing power directly on the storage device, giving companies secure, quick and easy access to vital information.*

I have seen a few computational storage appliances in use, including Dell PowerStore products, and other Arm-based computational storage appliances.

Dell PowerStore Storage Appliances

Computational storage, based on vSphere, has already appeared in x86 systems. It is interesting to see how it was implemented as it may give insight into how it will be implemented on Arm systems.

In 2020, Dell Technologies released a new midrange storage platform – PowerStore. This product line is based on the latest technology as it supports NVMe drives, and its operating system (PowerOS) uses containers to deliver its features. Physically, it is a 2U rack appliance, with four x64 Intel processors. Another unique feature is that one of its varieties, the X Series, runs two separate instances of ESXi (Figure 2-14).

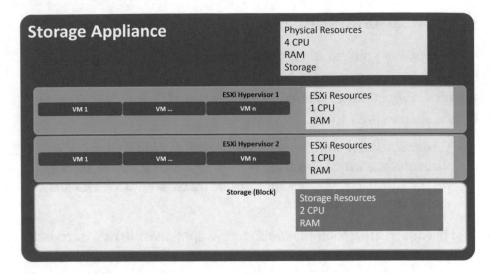

Figure 2-14. *Dell PowerStore Storage Appliance*

In a traditional datacenter, both physical and virtual machines connect to a storage array to process data. The systems are connected over fiber or Ethernet, usually through a switch. Although these networks are very fast, even a nanosecond of delay becomes unacceptable for some workloads (Figure 2-15).

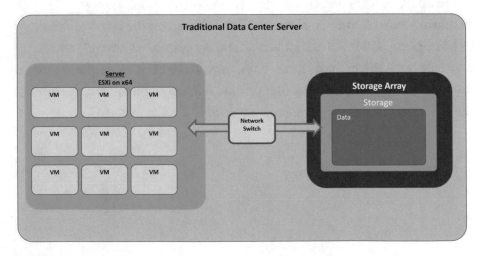

Figure 2-15. *Delay When Connecting Servers to Storage*

By having the hypervisor on the same physical system as the storage, the network and its latency are both removed (Figure 2-16).

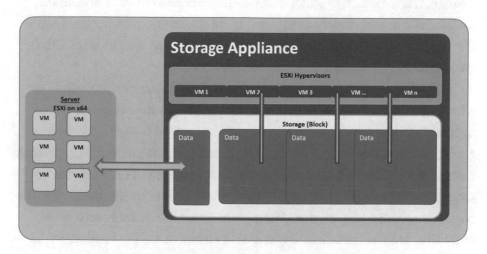

Figure 2-16. *Reduced Delay When VMs are on Storage*

At the time of this writing, the PowerStore X Series currently uses x64 processors, but there are also companies using Arm processors on their Arm-based storage arrays.

Arm-Based Computational Storage

Computational storage appliances can combine storage and VMs on the same physical server. This assumes that Arm processors can effectively deliver storage – and they can. In fact, two companies that provide storage arrays that can be powered by Arm processors are SoftIron and QNAP.

SoftIron

SoftIron's enterprise-grade storage arrays were designed from the metal up to the use Arm processors. SoftIron leverages Arm processors' lower cost, power efficiency, and SoC architecture to streamline the transfer of data from physical storage devices. SoftIron's flagship product Ceph is an open source SDS (software-defined storage) that delivers block, file, and object storage. It is a mature product that was first released in 2012 and since then has been extensively developed by all the major commercial Linux distributions (e.g., Canonical, Red Hat, and SUSE) as well as Intel, Cisco, and SanDisk.

SoftIron has compared the performance of its Arm storage solution with x64 storage. Indeed, it has impressive performance improvements over x64 storage especially where object sizes are 64 – 4096K. To their credit, SoftIron does concede that x64-based systems currently do perform better with 40Gbe and faster networks. Their arrays not only provide storage, but they also perform data transcoding directly on the device (they have not specified if they use VMs, containers, or another mechanism to do this, but computationally intensive activities are performed on the array). One needs to remember that SoftIron uses an older A1100 Arm processor on their devices and that this may account for the performance of the device.

QNAP

QNAP is a well-regarded manufacturer of NAS appliances, ranging from a single-disk appliance for home use to a 24-bay active-active dual-controller unit designed for enterprise use. QNAP uses either x64 or Arm processors depending on the appliance. Some of their Arm-based appliances, such as the TS-1635AX NAS (Figure 2-17), supply storage as well as containers and VMs. This device uses Linux, rather than ESXi, to manage VMs and containers. Due to the market that it is addressing, and cost that ESXi would likely impose (VMware has yet to reveal any pricing for ESXi on Arm if it becomes a product), it is unlikely that QNAP would run ESXi on this class of storage device. I included this device as it is an operation array that has a hypervisor on it.

https://www.qnap.com/

Figure 2-17. QNAP 1635AX NAS

Given that we already have Arm systems that can provide storage and VMs on the same appliance, and that Dell PowerStore runs ESXi on its x64-powered storage arrays, it is not a far reach to assume that in the near future we will see VMs being managed via ESXi on Arm.

Limitations of Using a Pi for ESXi

While being able to run ESXi on a low-priced device such as a Pi is a boon for enterprises and enthusiasts alike, it does come with some limitations in terms of software and hardware compatibility.

ESX's biggest limitation is the fact that it is a Fling; as such, VMware has not made any commitments with regard to eventual production or even its continued availability – or to continue to support the Pi if it does go into production. Furthermore, because VMware does not officially support it, anyone troubleshooting will need to work through issues on their own or consult one of the online support communities.

Executables

A key point to remember is that ESXi on Arm will only run VMs that have OSs that are compiled for Arm processors, which represents a very small subset of all the software able to run on x86 systems. You will not be able to run Windows desktop or server OSs on it. Android devices run on Arm processors; however, they will not run as a guest on ESXi on Arm.

One potential avenue to address this is through emulation software. While per-core licensing makes this troublesome, there are successful examples of this. Qualcomm showed their emulation technology for Windows devices. Perhaps the best-known example at this point is the Apple M1 Rosetta software that allows programs compiled for x86 to run on Apple silicon Macs. There are many challenges running this in the VMware ecosystem, but something like this could happen.

There are many great and unique projects that use the Pi, but if you plan on running them as VMs on the device, it is unlikely to run successfully or smoothly as the ESXi hypervisor abstracts the hardware away from it. That said, popular versions of Linux for Arm64 run without any issues, including Ubuntu, CentOS, Fedora, and Debian, as well as lesser-known ones such as Photon OS. Raspberry Pi OS will run on it as well as FreeBSD. The ESXi on Arm community is strong, and more and more OSs are becoming available to run on it every week.

You will not be able to vMotion a running VM from an ESXi server running on an x64 server to an ESXi on Arm host, nor will you be able to start an x64 VM on an Arm server. VMware offers many pre-built virtual applications (vApps), but as these are all (so far) designed for x64 servers, they will not run on Arm servers.

Pi Hardware

There are a myriad of third-party hardware attachments for the Pi that people use for all sorts of interesting purposes. These range from small LED displays to GPS receivers. However, it is extremely unlikely that any of these tools will work on a Pi with ESXi installed on it since the required drivers and connectors aren't exposed to ESXi or passed through to the VMs that run on it.

Overcommitment of Physical Resources

ESXi supports the *overcommitment* of physical resources (e.g., CPU, RAM, and storage), meaning that the running VMs are configured to "have" more physical resources dedicated to them than exist on the actual physical machine.

For example, if five VMs with 2GB of RAM, two vCPUs, and 100GB of storage were running on a Pi with 8GB of RAM, four CPU cores, and 256GB of storage, the VMs in this scenario would be overcommitted (Figure 2-18). In many cases, this will work fine as the physical resources will not be accessed at the same time. In the rare occurrence that all of the VMs do, in fact, try to access their maximum allocated resources simultaneously, then the hypervisors have various means to elegantly deal with them.

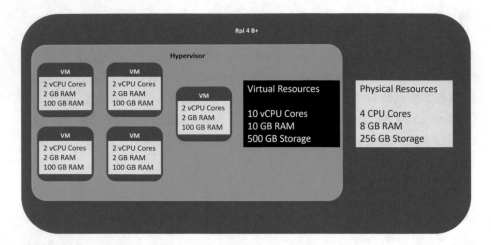

Figure 2-18. *VM Overcommitment*

Storage

The storage for ESXi that is used for and by the VMs on the Pi is limited to being connected via the USB ports or accessed via the network. Both the USB port and onboard NIC are limited by the bus that they run on. I have tested a fair number of storage devices on a Pi, and the best performance I have seen is a transfer rate of 100MBps.

I have also seen issues when copying files between two storage devices connected to the Pi's USB ports. My grossly simplified block diagram of the Pi 4B+ (Figure 2-19) shows that all the USB ports go through the same bus, and I believe this is where the bottleneck lies.

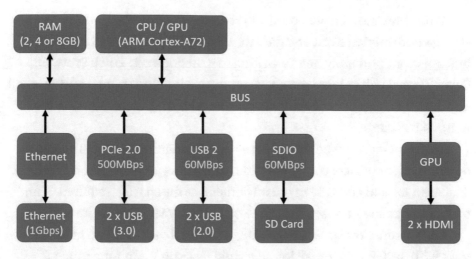

Figure 2-19. *RPi 4B+ Block Diagram*

When adding a new virtual disk for a VM (Figure 2-20), you have three different options: Thick Provision Lazy Zeroed, Thick Provision Eager Zeroed, and Thin Provision.

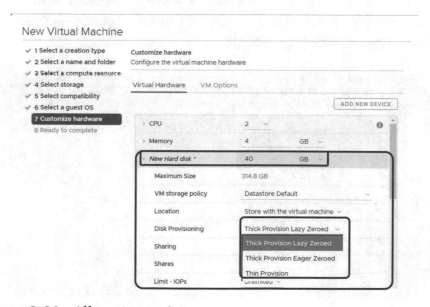

Figure 2-20. *Allocating Disk Space*

Thick Provision Lazy Zeroed will reserve space on the underlying storage and only zero out any data that may have previously resided on that space immediately before writing to it. In contrast, Thick Provision Eager Zeroed will reserve the space on the underlying storage and zero out any data that may have previously resided on that space before the first write to it is made.

Thin Provision can be thought of as overcommitting storage. The VM does not reserve space; you only set the maximum space that it can consume. Space is allocated and zeroed out on demand as the space is required. Thin provisioning allows unused storage to be used by VMs that require it.

Let's assume that you have a 750GB physical disk and you have three VMs with 300GB thin-provisioned virtual disks on them for a total of 900GB of thin-provisioned storage; however, each of these VMs is only actually using 100GB of space on the disk for a total of 300GB of actual-used disk space. You also have another VM that has a 200GB thick-provisioned disk that is only using 50GB of the disk, but (as it is thick-provisioned) the entire 200GB is allocated and unavailable for other usage. In this example, what we have is a total of 1,100GB of provisioned space on a 750GB physical disk (Figure 2-21).

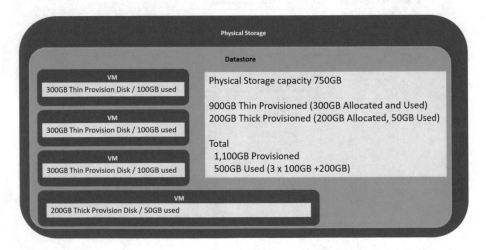

Figure 2-21. *Provisioned Disk Space*

RAM

The Pi supports a maximum of 8GB of RAM, which limits the number of VMs that can efficiently run on it. ESXi is a very lightweight process, and I have observed that it consumes less than 1GB of RAM; however, that only leaves 7GB for the VMs, so you need to be judicious in how much RAM you give the VMs that are running on your hosts.

If you overcommit the memory on your VMs, and the VMs consume all the memory, ESXi will attempt to deal with it in a few ways, including transferring memory from idle to active VMs, using a memory balloon driver, using memory compression, and then finally swapping memory to storage. Swapping memory is the least desirable solution as it uses relatively slow storage devices to replace relatively fast memory.

You can reserve memory for critical VMs, using the vSphere Client (Figure 2-22). This gives those VMs exclusive access to the memory.

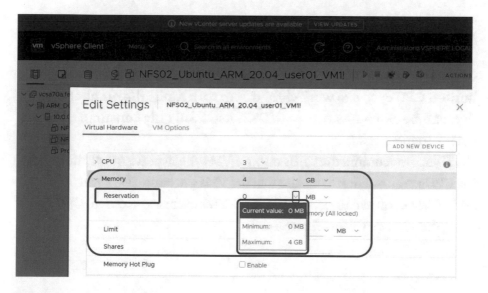

Figure 2-22. *Reserving Memory*

If all the memory on a system has been reserved by VMs, other VMs will not be able to be started (Figure 2-23).

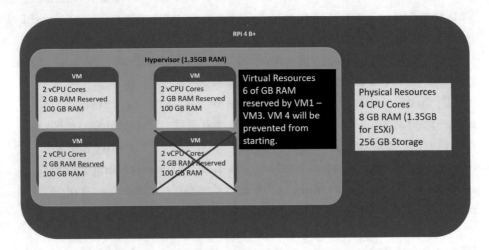

Figure 2-23. *All Memory Reserved*

CPU

Given that the Pi has a limited number of cores and that there are limited CPU cycles to work with, this in turn limits the number of VMs that can be efficiently run on it. ESXi itself will only consume a few cycles in most cases.

If you overcommit the CPUs on your VMs, the hypervisor will time-slice the CPUs in an attempt to ensure that the VMs get some CPU cycles. For critical VMs, you can reserve and give the VMs exclusive access to CPU cycles using the vSphere Client (Figure 2-24).

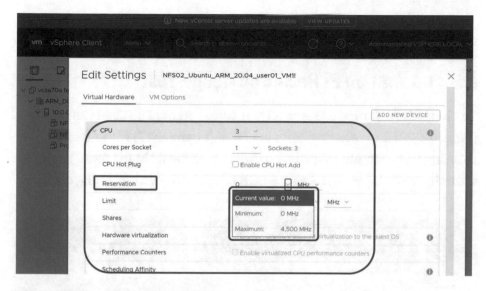

Figure 2-24. *Reserving CPU Cycles*

In the case that all the CPU cycles on a system have been reserved by VMs, other VMs will not be able to be started. An example of this is shown in Figure 2-25 where only three VMs are able to start.

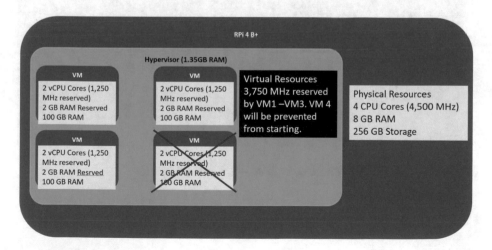

Figure 2-25. *All CPU Cycles Reserved*

In a VDI environment, it is common to have up to five virtual CPUs for every physical CPU.

ESXi on Arm on Pi Resource Usage Test

To check the resource usage of ESXi running on my Pi, I used ControlUp (Figure 2-26) and then the vSphere Client (Figure 2-27) without any running VMs. I found that it was using 18% of the RAM (~1.35GB) and virtually no CPU cycles, leaving 6.6GB RAM for the VMs running on it.

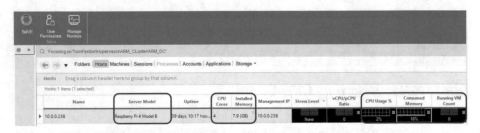

Figure 2-26. *ESXi Resource Usage Test – ControlUp*

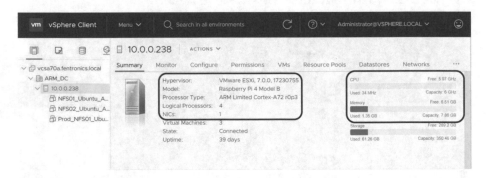

Figure 2-27. *Resource Usage Test – vSphere Client*

Licensing ESXi on Arm

Licensing of ESXi on Arm is as tricky as it is interesting. Most VMware products come with a 60-day fully functional trial license, but ESXi on Arm comes with a 180-day license. When the license expires, you can reinstall ESXi on it to reset the trial license. ESXi on Arm can be licensed using an ESXi host license; however, ESXi licenses are designed for enterprise use and are not inexpensive.

While VMware does support a free version of ESXi and the license can be used on ESXi on Arm, the free ESXi version does come with some limitations – the most important of which is that you will not be able to use vCenter Server and PowerCLI to interact with and manage it. The free license is also limited in terms of how many CPUs and how much RAM the server can have, but these limits are well below what the Pi 4B+ is capable of.

For home lab-ers, VMware does have the VMUG Advantage program that costs $200 per year, but this also includes VMware licenses for various VMware products including ESXi and vCenter Server. For smaller production installations, VMware does have the vSphere Essentials Kit for under $600. It supports three ESXi dual-proc hosts and comes with vCenter Server.

Because VMware is constantly reevaluating its package and licensing, you should always check with them to see what licensing options are currently available.

CHAPTER 3

ESXi on Arm on Pi Use Cases

ESXi on Arm running on a Raspberry Pi is a low-cost entry point into the world of virtualization and VMware, but, as we discussed in the previous chapter, its hardware does limit what this setup can do. This said, it is still able to accomplish some remarkable feats for something so small. In this chapter, we'll take a look at use cases for ESXi on Arm on Pi, some of which are actively being used, while others less so. Some are simple uses that I've seen for this setup but have not actually tried myself.

To unlock many of the functions of a true VMware vSphere environment, you will also need to install vCenter Server. Fortunately, there is a trial version currently available, but it only comes with a 60-day nonrenewable trial. The vCenter Server Appliance (VCSA) comes prepackaged as an OVF file and needs to be installed on a VMware hypervisor, but the hypervisor must be an x64 – not an Arm hypervisor. At first blush, this may be an issue as you may assume that you will also need to set up an x64 ESXi system, but fortunately it can also be used with VMware Player, a free Type 2 x64 hypervisor. We'll walk through this process later in this book.

© Thomas Fenton and Patrick Kennedy 2022
T. Fenton and P. Kennedy, *Running ESXi on a Raspberry Pi*,
https://doi.org/10.1007/978-1-4842-7465-1_3

Learning Environment

Being that ESXi on Arm is a fully functional hypervisor, it serves as an ideal learning environment for those who want to become acquainted with the VMware hypervisor or the features of vSphere. A fully functional vSphere environment can be assembled for less than $100, and a two-node cluster with a network switch to connect them together can be assembled for slightly over $200.

While this book will provide you with basic knowledge of using ESXi on an Arm system, you may want to dive deeper into the topic. Fortunately, there are many resources available to help you along your journey.

VMware has some excellent hands-on training for people wanting to learn about vSphere; they are professional and well done and provide you with an individual sandbox environment in which to work. The instructors are top-notch and can answer any question that you ask them. The classes are usually four days and cost around $3,000 – a cost that is a worthy investment if you are serious about coming quickly up to speed on VMware technology and you, or the company you work for, can afford this cost.

VMware hosts hands-on labs that allow you to work with a specific technology from VMware or their partners. These labs are a good way to become familiar with a VMware or one of their partners' technology without having to set up an environment. But, as they are preconfigured, they can only offer an approximation of an actual environment, and for security reasons portions of the product may be locked down. These labs can be found at `https://hol.vmware.com/`. As a sidenote, I wrote many of the hands-on labs for ControlUp.

VMware has also partnered with higher-education institutions to offer a training program called IT Academy (`www.vmware.com/company/it-academy.html`) whose stated goal is to train students in academic institutions on VMware products to prepare them for VMware certification. Many institutions offer this training at a fraction of the cost of VMware's courses, but these courses are spread out over a semester and are taught by the faculty at the institution rather than full-time dedicated VMware instructors.

LinkedIn, Udemy, and other online education sites also offer free or low-priced training options. Many of the courses that I looked at on these sites, though somewhat outdated, still provide good information. Most do not include a VMware hands-on environment, but many of these lessons can be duplicated on a Pi.

Regardless of the training route you choose in order to learn more about your ESXi server, the Pi is an excellent low-cost platform on which to do so.

Home Labs

Many of us whose day jobs involve working with VMware and other technologies choose to set up home labs in order to get a better understanding of these technologies; we home lab-ers like to push them in ways that our corporate implementations will not allow or to continue to work out problems we have encountered at work from the comfort of our own homes. The Pi serves as an excellent platform for these types of situations when cost is a key driver.

In my home lab, I have a few out-of-date servers and small Intel NUC (Next Unit of Computing) systems, but I find I use the Pi systems as often as these others. x64 servers that are a generation or two back can be procured at a reasonable price considering the hardware that you get. For instance, I found a used dual-proc Dell R720 on eBay with 96GB RAM and eight 3TB HDDs (36TB of raw storage) for under a thousand dollars. On the surface, this may seem like a good deal based on the amount of the resources you would get, but it would overwhelm an ordinary electric circuit and be too noisy to be housed near the person using it. Also, as it has most likely been used in a datacenter, the components have probably been under constant and high usage during its entire life.

Another option people find as an attractive alternative are Intel NUCs. These come in a variety of form factors, with the smallest one capable of running ESXi measuring at just over 4" × 4" × 2" and the largest measuring at 9.4" × 8.5" × 3.8". The smallest one has an Intel quad-core i7 processor with 8GB of RAM, while the larger one has an eight-core Xeon processor with 64MB of RAM and a PCI slot (Figure 3-1).

Figure 3-1. *Intel NUCs*

NUCs solve the issues that a repurposed server has regarding noise and power consumption for home lab use. However, the downside to NUCs is that the ones that are capable of running ESXi can cost just as much as a repurposed server, but lack the resources that the repurposed server would provide since they can only house one or at the most two storage devices and are limited to 64GB of RAM and a single Intel processor.

For the preceding reasons, a Pi system, although somewhat limited in terms of resources, serves as a good home lab system for someone who has a limited budget and space.

Corporate Sandboxes

Closely associated with home lab systems are corporate sandboxes. These systems tend to be used for small-scale proof-of-concept systems to prove out new applications and processes. Some companies use older systems for this purpose; however, their support cost can easily be more than the cost of a couple Pi systems.

Many corporations have licensing agreements with VMware that make the consumption of ESXi licenses within the facility very attractive. Given that a standard vCenter Server allows up to 2,000 hosts, adding a few additional ESXi hosts for a corporate sandbox usually isn't an issue.

Lightweight VDI Hosts

Virtual desktop infrastructure (VDI) is the process where users connect to VMs running a desktop OS on a hypervisor. VDI has been going strong for over a decade now, and many organizations have VDI environments with tens of thousands of virtual desktops. Companies use VDI for security, business continuity, and cost containment reasons.

While you will not be able to run thousands of virtual desktops on a Pi given its limited resources, I have been able to host four virtual desktops on an ESXi Pi server (Figure 3-2). This is an interesting proposition as you can host them all on a device that is slightly larger than a deck of cards. Using these desktops, I was only able to complete ordinary tasks using LibreOffice and light web browsing using a 1920 × 1080 desktop.

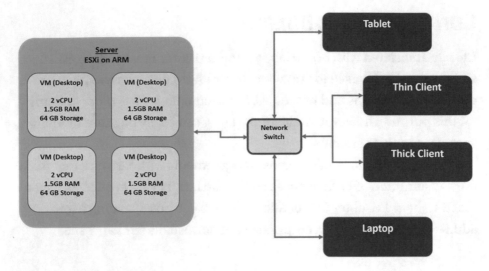

Figure 3-2.   *VDI on Pi*

VMware Horizon and Citrix agents are not supported on Arm, so their connection servers and remote protocol cannot be used. I had the VDI clients use Remote Display Protocol (RDP) and an individual IP address to connect them to their Linux virtual desktop.

Virtual desktops are surprisingly lightweight, and mine only consumed 10 IOPS. Networking traffic is highly dependent on what applications are being used. The following is the network traffic that I saw being consumed by various applications:

- Idle session – 0.5Kbps

- LibreOffice Writer (word processor) – 150Kbps

- LibreOffice Calc (spreadsheet) – 150Kbps

- LibreOffice Impress (presentations) – 4Mbps

- Chrome (web browsing) – 6Mbps

Each desktop was comprised of two vCPUs, 1.5GB RAM, and 64GB storage.

To view the performance and resource usage of the virtual desktops on Pi, I used ControlUp (Figure 3-3), an EUC monitoring tool, which is sold by VMware.

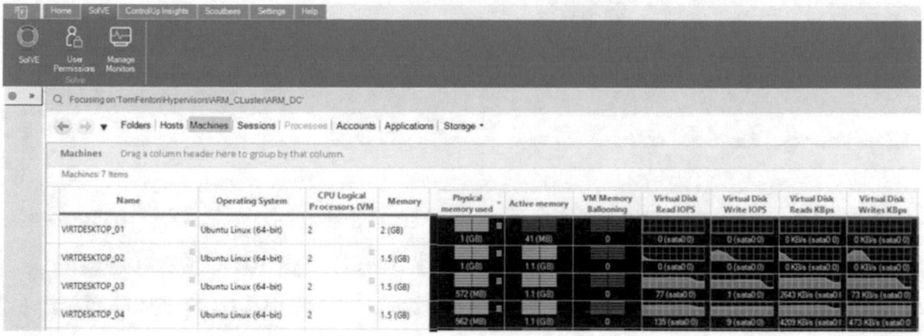

Figure 3-3. *Virtual Desktop Resource Usage*

We'll take a more detailed look at using virtual desktops on the Pi later in this book.

Web Development

One of the more popular deployment modes for websites is using the LAMP software stack (LAMP is an acronym for Linux, Apache, MySQL, and PHP). Although these components can be run on a single instance, to more closely replicate an actual working environment, they should run on separate OS instances.

The back-end functions of the web development of websites are carried out using the instances on VMs running on the Pi, while the developer's desktop is used for content creation and website testing (Figure 3-4).

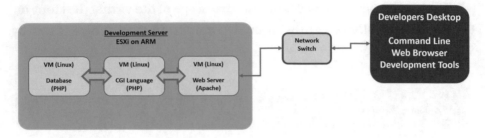

Figure 3-4. *LAMP on ESXi*

Due to resource restrictions, the size and sophistication of the website would have to be limited. Since it is likely that the production servers would be x64-based, vMotioning the entire VM over to the production server is not possible.

Having small, inexpensive web development boxes will free up expensive resources for production deployment and will encourage developers to experiment more with their web development environments.

Edge Server/Data Collection Point

One likely use case of a Pi or other small, low-cost Arm devices is as an edge server or data collection point. In this case, a small inexpensive edge device captures the data and then completes some rudimentary data functions on it before passing it back to a datacenter for further analysis and permanent storage. The edge server also caches the data if the network is unavailable (Figure 3-5).

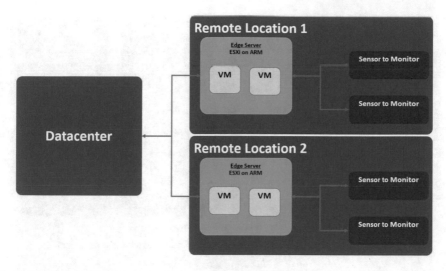

Figure 3-5. *Edge Server*

By using ESXi, you could have multiple instances of an OS running on the device to act on different services and provide some BC and DR services if needed.

vSAN Witness

Perhaps the most mentioned use case for the Pi is as a witness node for VMware's extremely popular SDS product, vSAN (Figure 3-6) to provide resiliency and capacity, vSAN pools together the local storage on multiple ESXi servers that any node in the cluster can access.

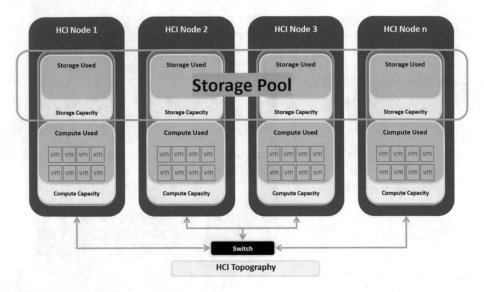

Figure 3-6. *VMware vSAN Cluster*

Smaller deployments, like those in ROBO, may only need the storage capacity and redundancy of two physical servers. One of the issues when clustering together two nodes is what happens when a *split-brain* situation occurs: the nodes are still operational but lose connectivity to each other. If they both continue to deliver storage, the data will be corrupt and need a third or witness node to arbitrate which node should still be active in such a situation (Figure 3-7). The witness node does not need to be powerful or contribute local storage to the storage pool.

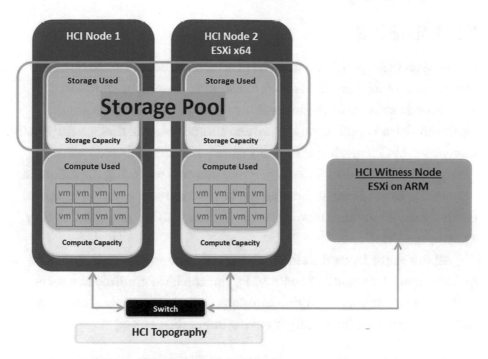

Figure 3-7. *vSAN Witness Node*

For such lightweight use, an inexpensive Pi is an ideal substitution for a low-cost x64 ESXi server that could cost ten times as much.

Automation Environment for PowerCLI

William Lam at virtuallyghetto.com wrote an interesting blog on using an ESXi server for vSphere automation and development on an ESXi on Arm on a Pi. In this blog, he points out that the Pi is an acceptable platform for running PowerShell and PowerCLI, which are two of the most common and useful automation tools in the VM world. For more information, visit his site.

Kubernetes

Kubernetes (K8s) is gaining traction at an astounding speed in terms of enterprise adoption. K8s is an orchestration system for containers, and its orchestration functions include the deployment and scaling of container-based applications. It is open source software that was originally developed by Google, but eventually transferred to the Cloud Native Computing Foundation. There are many nuances regarding the differences between a VM and containers that are beyond the scope of this book, but (with apologies to those who know better) they can be thought of as very lightweight VMs.

All the major Linux distributions support running some form of K8s or containers. By using ESXi with VMs, you can have multiple instances of the K8s and container engine running on the same physical server for redundancy or to mimic a larger environment (Figure 3-8).

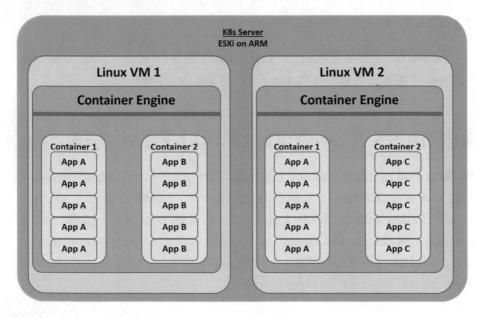

Figure 3-8. *Kubernetes*

Game Server

All the use cases I have highlighted until this point have related to work, but after the day is done, you can use ESXi to server up some games. Many Linux distributions come preconfigured with a few games and allow games to be downloaded and installed using their package management features, or you can compile them locally on your system.

You do need to be aware that the Pi doesn't support a GPU, and its iGPU (Broadcom VideoCore VI) cannot be accessed via the VMs that are running on it. Games with heavy graphic requirements will either run very poorly or not at all. But for those wanting to play a little Tetris, Wolfenstein, Doom, or SuperTuxKart, these games will play fine if you turn off all the other VMs running on the server.

To display the game, you will either need to use the VMware console or use Remote Display Protocol. We'll take a look at how to set these up later in the book.

Summary

The Raspberry Pi offers a unique and inexpensive way to work with the most popular hypervisor in the datacenter, ESXi. You can set up and use your ESXi environments to learn the ins and outs of vSphere. This platform has a diverse set of use cases from being a stand-alone platform for developers to a game server for home use. With that said, the most likely use in the corporate world of small, inexpensive Arm-based systems is as a vSAN witness or data collection point on the edge of the network. It needs to be stressed that ESXi on Arm is a Fling and not an official product. VMware does not guarantee that it will ever become one. Furthermore, the license on it expires after 180 days and will need to be reloaded after that time.

The next chapter will look at some of the other pieces needed to set up a Raspberry Pi, that is, the types of storage you can use with it and some of the cases that can be used to protect and cool it while it is running ESXi.

CHAPTER 4

ESXi on Arm on Pi Build Kits

Before installing ESXi, you will first need to acquire a Pi and a few auxiliary components. While it's certainly possible to put a kit together for as little as $55, a very usable system with a case and power supply will run you closer to $220. All these kits use a CanaKit Raspberry Pi 4 Model B Quad Core 64 for the build. I have found very little price difference between distributors for the Pi.

In this chapter, we will look at the requirements for a Raspberry Pi 4B that is capable of running ESXi and then provide some example build kits.

Requirements

The minimum requirements for ESXi on Arm for Pi, as set out by VMware, are very straightforward. They include

- Raspberry Pi 4B – 4GB or 8GB model (just about everybody I have spoken with is going with the 8GB as it is only $20 more than the 4GB model and doubles the number of VMs that you can run on it).

- 5.5V 3.5A USB-C power supply.

- Micro-SD card (used for Pi firmware).

© Thomas Fenton and Patrick Kennedy 2022
T. Fenton and P. Kennedy, *Running ESXi on a Raspberry Pi*,
https://doi.org/10.1007/978-1-4842-7465-1_4

- 32GB USB thumb drive (used to install ESXi).

- 32GB or larger USB thumb drive (used as a location on which to install ESXi). USB 3.0 is highly recommended:

  - I suggest using two different brands or sizes of thumb drives as it makes it easier to keep track of them.

- Optional micro-HDMI to HDMI adapter (the Pi has two micro-HDMI ports, but if you are going to use a regular HDMI cable to plug into your monitor, you will need an adapter).

The first build I used was the Argon ONE case, and the components of this kit are shown in Figure 4-1. Everything worked as expected, except the 128GB micro-SD; I needed to use a 32GB micro-SD instead.

Figure 4-1. *ESXi on Arm Build Kit*

Notes on the Case

You need to ensure that the Arm processor is properly cooled, either passively using a heat sink or actively using a fan. The Pi has built-in circuitry that, upon detecting a temperature of 60 degrees Centigrade, will slow down the Arm processor to prevent the Pi from overheating. At 80 degrees Centigrade, it may completely stop working.

Notes on Thumb Drives

One option, and one that is highly recommended, is to use another USB 3.0 device to act as storage for the VMs that you want to run on your Pi. You can use a thumb drive or USB-attached storage. I would suggest using a high-quality USB 3.0, 64GB (or larger) thumb drive for the initial installation. You can add another USB storage device later if you desire more VM storage space. In a later chapter, I will discuss the different storage options currently available.

You may be tempted to use a physically small USB thumb drive, like the Samsung FIT Plus or SanDisk Ultra Fit USB thumb drive (see Figure 4-2), as a datastore, but as you will be doing a fair amount of writing to and reading from it, you will be better off using a physically larger drive.

Figure 4-2. *Small USB Thumb Drives*

Physically larger drives, like the Samsung BAR Plus or SanDisk Ultra Flair (Figure 4-3), offer more surface area to keep the drive cooler, and the metal case on these drives may act as a passive heat sink.

Figure 4-3. *Large USB Thumb Drives*

The following are some sample build kits. I didn't include a keyboard or monitor with these builds as you only need to use them during the initial install and then only intermittently afterward.

Low-Cost Naked Build

In my low-cost naked build (Table 4-1), my goal was to compile the cheapest build possible. I used a 4GB Pi, which has the capacity to run one or maybe two VMs. I used a USB drive that I currently had for both the installation and then again for VM storage. To minimize this kit, I did not include a case or any cooling mechanism for the Arm processor. This can lead to the processor running hot, which can in turn cause it to throttle back its speed and decrease its performance.

It has been reported that if you are going to run a Pi without any additional cooling, you should place it with the GPIO header at the bottom and the HDMI ports at the top, as shown in Figure 4-4. By setting it up in this way, you will allow more air to circulate around the board and increase the surface area for cooling of the device.

Figure 4-4. *Pi in Vertical Position for Cooling*

Table 4-1. *Low-Cost Naked Build Price Breakdown*

Item Needed	Part	Cost
Power supply	USB-C power supply 3.5A (repurposed)	$0
Raspberry Pi 4 Model B 4GB	PiShop.us Raspberry Pi 4 Model B (4GB)	$55
1 × micro-SD card	Samsung PRO Endurance 32GB 100MB/s (U1) Micro-SD Memory Card	$9
1 × USB drive for installer ISO/VM storage	USB flash drive 32GB (repurposed)	$0
1 × USB drive for ESXi	32GB USB 3.0 flash drive (repurposed)	$0
Total		**$64**

Cased Builds

The following build kits use a case, power supplies, and new (rather than repurposed) storage devices. While you may be tempted to get a case with a touch screen or other "built-in" features, this would be a waste as ESXi will not support it, and it may even prevent ESXi from installing and/or running correctly.

Cheap Pi Enclosure

For this Pi enclosure build (Table 4-2), I used one of the cheapest cases I could find. This case is made from black plastic and does come with a large 40mm fan and four heat sinks (see Figure 4-5). The micro-SD card is easily accessible. The fan is powered by the GPIO 3.3V pin for low-speed operation or the 5V pin for high-speed operation.

I was pleasantly surprised with this case. It was well made and included decent instructions. When I put the Pi in, it snapped together without any difficulties.

Figure 4-5. *iUniker Pi Case*

Table 4-2. *Cheap Pi Enclosure Cost Breakdown*

Item Needed	Part Found	Cost
Power supply	CanaKit 3.5A Raspberry Pi 4 Power Supply (USB-C)	$10
Raspberry Pi 4 Model B 8GB	CanaKit Raspberry Pi 4 Model B Quad Core 64 Bit WiFi Bluetooth (8GB)	$85
Case and cooling fan combo	iUniker Raspberry Pi 4 Fan ABS Case with Cooling Fan and Heatsinks	$11
1 × micro-SD card for UEFI firmware	Samsung PRO Endurance 32GB 100MB/s (U1) MicroSDXC Memory Card	$9
1 × USB drive for installer ISO	Samsung FIT Plus USB 3.1 Flash Drive 128GB – (MUF-128AB/AM)	$20
1 × USB drive for the actual ESXi installation	PNY Elite-X Fit 128GB USB 3.0 Flash Drive – Read Speeds up to 200MB/sec (P-FDI128EXFIT-GE), Silver	$20
Total		**$155**

Argon ONE Kit M.2

This Argon ONE case is the same one I used for my first build and one of the more popular cases for ESXi on Arm on Pi builds (Table 4-3). The top of the case is made of cast aluminum and comes with a 30mm fan and three heat sinks. It has an expansion board that plugs into the Pi and provides two full-size HDMI connectors (see Figure 4-6). The instruction manual was also very good.

Figure 4-6. *Argon ONE Case*

Table 4-3. *Argon ONE Kit M.2 Cost Breakdown*

Item Needed	Part Found	Cost
Power supply	CanaKit 3.5A Raspberry Pi 4 Power Supply (USB-C)	$10
Raspberry Pi 4 Model B 8GB	CanaKit Raspberry Pi 4 Model B Quad Core 64 Bit WiFi Bluetooth (8GB)	$85
Case and cooling fan combo	Argon ONE Raspberry Pi 4 Case with Cooling Fan and Power Button	$25
1 × micro-SD card for UEFI firmware	Samsung PRO Endurance 32GB 100MB/s (U1) MicroSDXC Memory Card	$9
1 × USB drive for installer ISO	Samsung FIT Plus USB 3.1 Flash Drive 128GB – (MUF-128AB/AM)	$20
1 × USB drive for the actual ESXi installation	PNY Elite-X Fit 128GB USB 3.0 Flash Drive – Read Speeds up to 200MB/sec (P-FDI128EXFIT-GE), Silver	$20
Total		$169

Argon ONE M.2 Case for M.2 SATA Drive

The Argon ONE M.2 case is basically the same case top as the Argon ONE, but the bottom of the case can hold an M.2 SATA SSD device for USB storage (Table 4-4). The SATA drive is connected to the Pi via an external USB connector (see Figure 4-7). This is actually quite useful as you can also use a regular USB device with the case if desired.

You must use an M.2 SATA drive with this case; an NVMe drive will not work. For my build, I used a Kingston 240GB SATA SSD device. Argon also makes an M.2 Expansion Board, which is just the bottom of this case and allows you to use an M.2 SATA drive with a regular Argon ONE case.

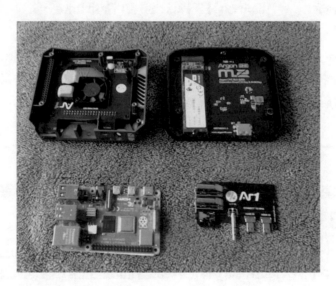

Figure 4-7. *Argon ONE M.2 Case*

Table 4-4. Argon ONE M.2 Case for M.2 SATA Drive Cost Breakdown

Item Needed	Part Found	Cost
Power supply	CanaKit 3.5A Raspberry Pi 4 Power Supply (USB-C)	$10
Raspberry Pi 4 Model B 8GB	CanaKit Raspberry Pi 4 Model B Quad Core 64 Bit WiFi Bluetooth (8GB)	$85
Case and cooling fan combo	Argon ONE Raspberry Pi 4 Case with Cooling Fan and Power Button	$45
1 × micro-SD card for UEFI firmware	Samsung PRO Endurance 32GB 100MB/s (U1) MicroSDXC Memory Card	$9
1 × USB drive for installer ISO	Samsung FIT Plus USB 3.1 Flash Drive 128GB – (MUF-128AB/AM)	$20
1 × USB drive for the actual ESXi installation	PNY Elite-X Fit 128GB USB 3.0 Flash Drive – Read Speeds up to 200MB/sec (P-FDI128EXFIT-GE), Silver	$10
1 × M.2 SATA drive	Kingston Digital 240GB SSDNow M.2 SATA	$45
Total		**$224**

Geekworm Armor Aluminum Alloy Passive Cooling Case

I decided to pick up the Geekworm Armor Aluminum Alloy Passive Cooling Case (see Figure 4-8) as the whole aluminum case acts like a heat sink and only costs $13 (Table 4-5). It comes with three 0.5mm thermal pads that touch the main integrated circuits to the shell body to dissipate heat from them. The top of the case is screwed to the bottom with four hex-head screws. The screws and an Allen wrench, as well as two GPIO extenders, are included with the case.

I ran some heavy workloads on a Pi using this case. The Pi didn't slow down, and the case only warmed up slightly.

Figure 4-8. *Geekworm Armor Aluminum Alloy Passive Cooling Case*

Table 4-5. *Geekworm Armor Aluminum Alloy Passive Cooling Case Kit Cost Breakdown*

Item Needed	Part Found	Cost
Power supply	CanaKit 3.5A Raspberry Pi 4 Power Supply (USB-C)	$10
Raspberry Pi 4 Model B 8GB	CanaKit Raspberry Pi 4 Model B Quad Core 64 Bit WiFi Bluetooth (8GB)	$85
Case with heat sink	Geekworm Armor Aluminum Alloy Passive Cooling Case	$13
1 × micro-SD card for UEFI firmware	Samsung PRO Endurance 32GB 100MB/s (U1) MicroSDXC Memory Card	$9
1 × USB drive for installer ISO	Samsung FIT Plus USB 3.1 Flash Drive 128GB – (MUF-128AB/AM)	$20
1 × USB drive for the actual ESXi installation	PNY Elite-X Fit 128GB USB 3.0 Flash Drive – Read Speeds up to 200MB/sec (P-FDI128EXFIT-GE), Silver	$10
Total		**$147**

3D Printed Cases

If you have access to a 3D printer, it's possible to find CAD drawings for many different cases for the Pi, ranging from basic cases to some pretty cool and futuristic-looking ones.

Summary

There are a plethora of cases for the Pi to meet your environmental or aesthetical desires. It is my recommendation that you look for one with a quality fan or that has a large heat sink. The case that I prefer is the Argon ONE M.2 as it is compatible with the M.2 SATA drive. I also like the fact that it has a built-in micro-HDMI to full-size HDMI adapter.

Do not try to save a few dollars with a cheap power supply – the Pi pulls a fair amount of amps, and you will want a clean source of power for it. I tend to install from, and to, an inexpensive USB device as they don't get read from or written to that often. For VM storage, I use a physically large USB 128GB drive or an M.2 SATA drive if I am using a case that supports it.

You will only be able to run two to four VMs on the Pi at a time, so you can get by with a 64GB drive. If you, like me, tend to have a lot of different VMs for the different Linux distros you work with or if you have a lot of data to store, you will need a larger storage device.

If you don't have a micro-HDMI cable to your monitor, make sure to get an adapter when you get the rest of your components as nothing is more frustrating than getting a new kit and finding out that it will not work with your full-size adapter.

CHAPTER 5

Installing ESXi on a Pi

If you, like many other readers, have been looking forward to getting your hands dirty and starting to work with using ESXi on your Pi, this is the chapter you've been patiently waiting for. You may have even jumped ahead to this chapter if you are really anxious to get started using the hardware. Regardless of which camp you fall into, in this chapter I will walk you through the process of installing ESXi on a Pi.

VMware did a good job documenting the process of installing ESXi on Arm on a Pi, but I found a few parts of their documentation a little bit confusing, and they didn't include many screen captures. To help guide you through this process in an easy-to-understand manner, I will include many screen captures and keep the walk-through as streamlined as possible.

Before outlining the installation process, I am going to take a bit of a flyer and address a question I get asked a lot.

Redirecting the Screen

Before getting started with discussing how to Install ESXi on a Pi, I would like to address one question I get asked a lot: how I get the screenshots I use in my articles, blogs, and books and how can I view with my ESXi host with a laptop or single monitor. This seems like a simple question, as I have found screen captures are essential to the articles that I write as they allow readers to follow along with what I am describing or seeing on my end.

© Thomas Fenton and Patrick Kennedy 2022
T. Fenton and P. Kennedy, *Running ESXi on a Raspberry Pi*,
https://doi.org/10.1007/978-1-4842-7465-1_5

In the past I have tried to take manual photos of screens using everything from USB cameras to cell phones. I have even tried using a high-end digital camera on a tripod, but the results were just not that good. I would get flare and glare or miss time when I took the photos.

About two years ago, inexpensive USB HDMI video capture devices started to come on the market. Figure 5-1 shows how these devices plug in between a computer and its monitor and then that content is streamed to another computer using a USB cable.

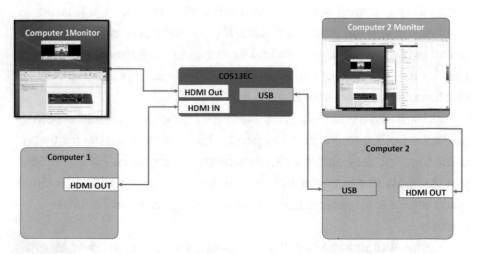

Figure 5-1. *USB Capture Device*

Software is required to display and capture the output that is being streamed. After trying a few different software packages like Windows Camera, VLC, and Camtasia, I found Open Broadcaster Software (OBS) to perform the best. It is a free, widely used open source cross-platform streaming and recording program. It is truly a multiplatform software – there are currently versions of OBS Studio available for Microsoft Windows, macOS, and Linux.

In the past I used a couple low-end, low-cost ($20–$50) USB capture cards and found the output range from fuzzy to pretty good. Occasionally they would fail or stop working, and I would need to disconnect and reconnect them to get them working again.

Then I got a chance to review an Intel NUC 11 Computer Element (CE) AV system (see Figure 5-2). This is a small yet powerful system with an Intel i7 Core processor, 16GB of RAM, and two NICS.

Figure 5-2. *NUC 11 System*

Figure 5-3 shows that on the back it has ports for its built-in video capture device.

Figure 5-3. *Back of NUC 11 CE*

Figure 5-4 shows that it has two HDMI ports labeled **Pass Thru** and **INPUT**. These are used by its internal capture card.

Figure 5-4. *HDMI Capture Card Ports*

To get the screen captures for this book, I plugged the Pi and its monitor into the AV capture ports on the NUC 11 CE (see Figure 5-5).

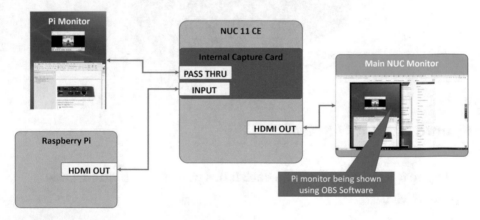

Figure 5-5. *NUC 11 CE and Pi*

I started OBS on the NUC 11 CE and set its input source to the capture card. Figure 5-6 shows that the output from the Pi bootup screen was streamed to it.

Figure 5-6. *OBS*

I have run the capture card on the NUC 11 for hours at a time and captured GBs of streamed video without any issues.

Not only can you use a capture card for documentation, but you can also use it as a Pi's monitor when installing and working with it. You will, of course, need to connect a separate keyboard to the Pi. As a sidenote, I have found more than once that I try to interact with the streamed image using the keyboard attached to the system it is displaying on rather than the keyboard attached to the Pi.

Using an inexpensive USB HDMI capture card is OK for the occasional screen capture, but if you have a lot of content to capture, I highly recommend using a high-end capture card.

Installation Overview

I have said it before, and I will reiterate it here – VMware, at the time of me writing this, clearly and irrevocably states that this product is unsupported and should not be used for production. That said, thousands of users (including myself) have been using it for months and have found it surprisingly solid. The license for it is free, but acquiring one does require you to create a MyVMware account. The license will expire 180 days after installation, at which point you will need to reinstall it. Your VMs, however, will still be viable.

The official documentation of installing ESXi on a Pi isn't found in the most intuitive location; to access it, you need to go to the ESXi on Arm Fling web page: `https://flings.vmware.com/esxi-arm-edition` (see Figure 5-7). From the drop-down menu on the page, select the **ESX-Arm-Fling-Doc.pdf** and the **Fling-on-Rasberry-Pi.pdf** documents. The first document is a general overview of the installation process, and the second deals directly with the nuances of running ESXi on the Pi platform. Both of these documents are good references to have.

Figure 5-7. *ESXi on Arm Fling Web Page*

The installation process can be divided into different sections:

- Verifying the EEPROM running on the Pi and updating it if needed

- Writing the installation ISO to a thumb drive

- Installing ESXi on the Pi

- Setting the Pi to boot off ESXi

- Configuring the ESXi host

To simplify the process, I will be showing just one way to install ESXi on the Pi. There are other, more advanced options to install it, but for the vast majority of users, this is the way that will best suit their needs.

Hardware and Software Preparation

This first step you should take is to make sure that you have the right model of Pi to install ESXi on. This one simple verification may save you countless headaches. To do this, simply look at the markings on your Pi and verify that it's marked as a *Raspberry Pi 4 Model B* as shown in Figure 5-8. This is the only model of Pi that is supported.

Figure 5-8. *Pi Markings*

When I do my initial installation, I leave the Pi outside of the case; heat will not be a problem, and this is just one less variable to consider if something goes wrong when installing it.

Install Pi on a Micro-SD Card

To make sure the Raspberry Pi microcode is up to date, you will need to install Pi OS onto your micro-SD card and then boot it. This is all Pi OS is used for. After checking the microcode, we will use the micro-SD for the EEPROM. The following instructions show how to do it on a Windows system. It can be done on a system running Linux or macOS. However, it is beyond the scope of this book.

To write the image to the card, do the following:

1. Download and install the Raspberry Pi Imager tool for Windows (`www.raspberrypi.org/blog/raspberry-pi-imager-imaging-utility`) to a Windows system. Imager is free, open source, and 20MB in size. If your Windows system does not have a micro-SD slot, you will need to use an adapter to write to it.

2. Run Imager on your Windows system (see Figure 5-9).

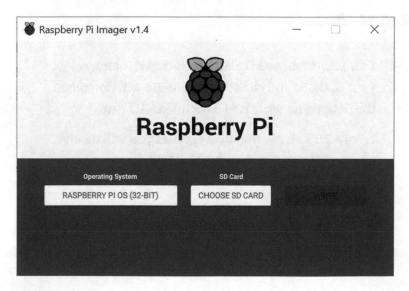

Figure 5-9. *Imager Tool*

3.   From the **Choose OS** drop-down menu (see Figure 5-10), select **Raspberry Pi OS (32-bit)**.

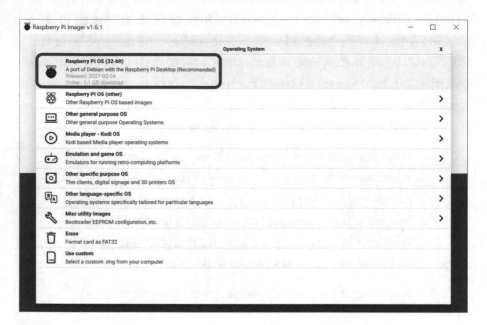

Figure 5-10. *Select OS*

4.   From the **Choose SD Card** drop-down menu, select your SD card and click **Write**. Imager will download the image and write it to your micro-SD card.

5.   Figure 5-11 shows the message that you will receive when the image is written. Click **Continue**, remove the micro-SD card from your Windows system, and close Imager.

Figure 5-11. Imager Finished

Using Pi OS to Check the Pi's EEPROM

You use Pi OS to verify the EEPROM on the Pi and update it if needed.

1. Place the micro-SD card into the Pi. Plug the power supply, a keyboard, your network, and an HDMI monitor into the Pi.

2. Power the Pi on by plugging it in. It will take a minute or two for the system to boot up. You will be greeted with a Raspberry Pi setup screen. Follow the prompts to set up your system.

3. From the top left of the screen, select the terminal icon. Check if your EEPROM is up to date by entering

    sudo rpi-eeprom-update

4. The display will show if the Pi's EEPROM is up to date (see Figure 5-12) or not.

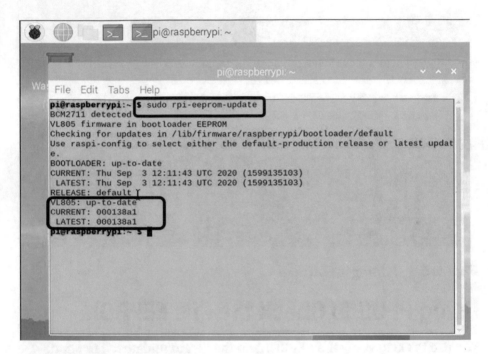

Figure 5-12. *Check EEPROM*

5. If your EEPROM is not up to date by entering

   sudo rpi-eeprom-update -a

   shut down the Pi by entering

   sudo sudo shutdown -t now

6. Once the system has shut down, remove the micro-SD card from it and place it back in the Windows machine.

Prep Micro-SD with UEFI

You will now place the UEFI files on the micro-SD. This allows the Pi to boot ESXi.

1. Download the latest Pi firmware and RPi 4 UEFI firmware from

   https://github.com/raspberrypi/firmware/
   archive/master.zip

   https://github.com/pftf/RPi4/releases/
   download/v1.20/RPi4_UEFI_Firmware_v1.20.zip

2. Extract the contents of the zip files to separate folders: one called master and the other called UEFI.

3. In the master/boot folder, delete all the files that start with kernel (see Figure 5-13).

□ Name	Date modified	Type	Size
☐ fixup4cd.dat	4/21/2021 8:02 AM	DAT File	9 KB
☐ fixup4x.dat	4/21/2021 8:02 AM	DAT File	9 KB
☑ kernel.img	4/21/2021 8:02 AM	Disc Image File	5,859 KB
☑ kernel7.img	4/21/2021 8:02 AM	Disc Image File	6,194 KB
☑ kernel7l.img	4/21/2021 8:02 AM	Disc Image File	6,610 KB
☑ kernel8.img	4/21/2021 8:02 AM	Disc Image File	7,653 KB
☐ LICENCE.broadcom	4/21/2021 8:02 AM	BROADCOM File	2 KB
☐ start.elf	4/21/2021 8:02 AM	ELF File	2,887 KB
☐ start_cd.elf	4/21/2021 8:02 AM	ELF File	778 KB

Figure 5-13. *master/boot Folder*

4. Copy all files within the UEFI directory into the master/boot directory. Allow duplicate files to be overwritten as shown in Figure 5-14.

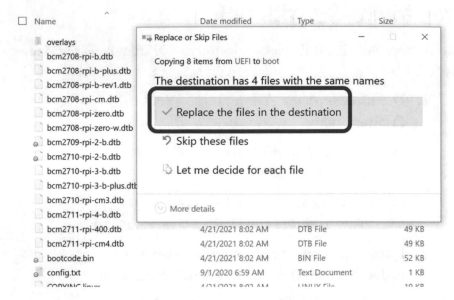

Figure 5-14. *Overwriting Files in the master/boot Folder*

5. Format the micro-SD card with a FAT32 file system (see Figure 5-15).

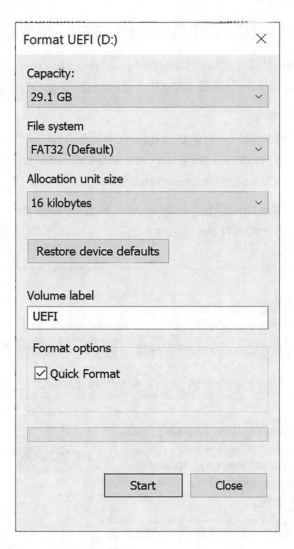

Figure 5-15. *Format Micro-SD*

6. Copy all the files from the master directory to the micro-SD card. This may take a few minutes.

7. Eject the micro-SD card from the Windows system.

Create an ESXi on Arm Install Device

To download the ESXi on Arm Fling, you will need to create a MyVMware account that can be done following the instructions located at `https://my.vmware.com/`.

1. Go to the ESXi on Arm Fling web page `https://flings.vmware.com/esxi-arm-edition` and log in using your MyVMware account.

2. From the Download drop-down menu, select the ESXi-Arm-ISO (see Figure 5-16).

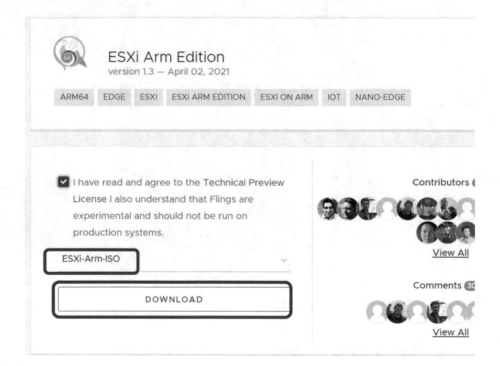

Figure 5-16. *Download ESXI on Arm Fling*

3. This will redirect to the VMware download site (see Figure 5-17). Select **Download Now** for the **ESXi for Arm ISO image (no VMware Tools)**. The ISO will be about 130MB.

Figure 5-17. *ISO Download*

4. Place the thumb drive that you want to use to install ESXi from in your Windows system.

5. Download Rufus from `https://rufus.ie/en_US/` to your Windows system.

6. Launch Rufus.

7. In Rufus select your ESXi on ARM ISO image and the thumb drive and click **Start** (see Figure 5-18).

Figure 5-18. *Rufus*

8.   When it has written the ISO image to the drive, click
     Close and remove the thumb drive.

Installing ESXi on the Pi

1.   Place the micro-SD and the thumb drive in the Pi.

2.   Power on the Pi.

3. Repeatedly press the **Esc** key while the Pi boots up.

4. From the Pi UEFI configuration screen, use the keyboard to select **Device Manager** (see Figure 5-19).

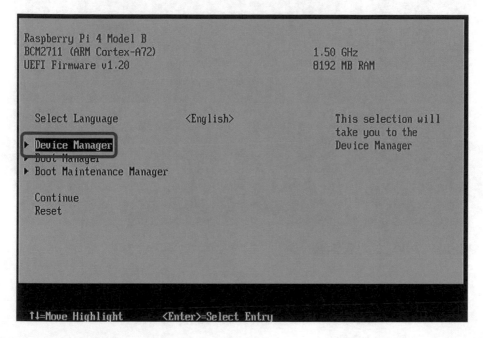

Figure 5-19. *Pi configuration screen*

5. Select **Raspberry Pi Configuration ➤ Advanced Configuration**.

6. Disable **Limit RAM to 3 GB** (see Figure 5-20).

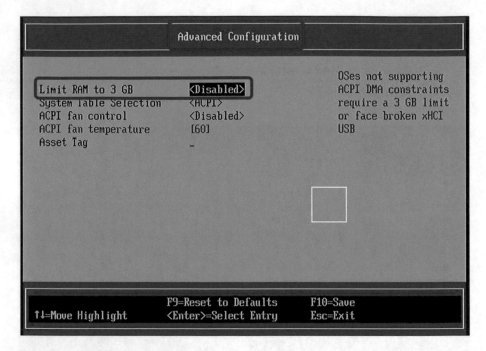

Figure 5-20. *RAM Limit*

7. Press **F10** and confirm your selection.

8. Press **Esc** three times and select **Continue** (see Figure 5-21).

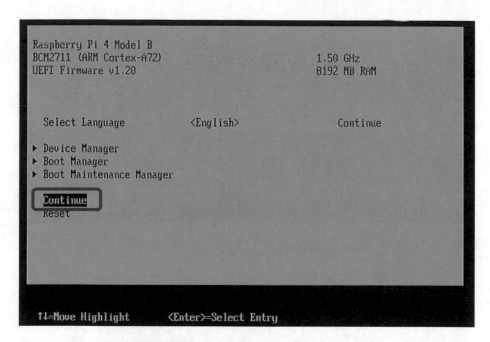

Figure 5-21. *Exit Pi Configurator*

9. This will start ESXi ISO to boot.

Installing ESXi on the Pi RPi

1. While the ESXi installer is booting, you will see a
    yellow screen. It will take a few minutes for ESXi to
    fully boot.

2. At the ESXi install screen (see Figure 5-22),
    press **Enter**.

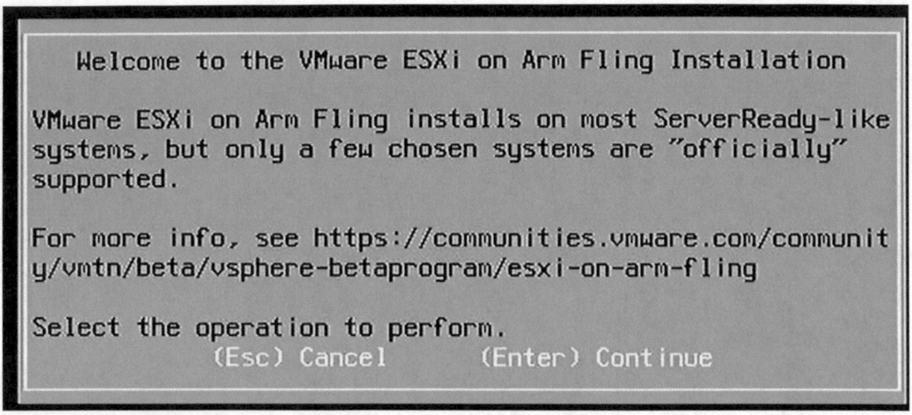

```
   Welcome to the VMware ESXi on Arm Fling Installation

VMware ESXi on Arm Fling installs on most ServerReady-like
systems, but only a few chosen systems are "officially"
supported.

For more info, see https://communities.vmware.com/communit
y/vmtn/beta/vsphere-betaprogram/esxi-on-arm-fling

Select the operation to perform.
            (Esc) Cancel        (Enter) Continue
```

Figure 5-22. *Welcome Screen*

3. Select the drive that you want to install ESXi on (see
    Figure 5-23). I find it easiest to have two different
    brands or sizes of drives so I can tell the install
    thumb drive from the drive I want to install on.

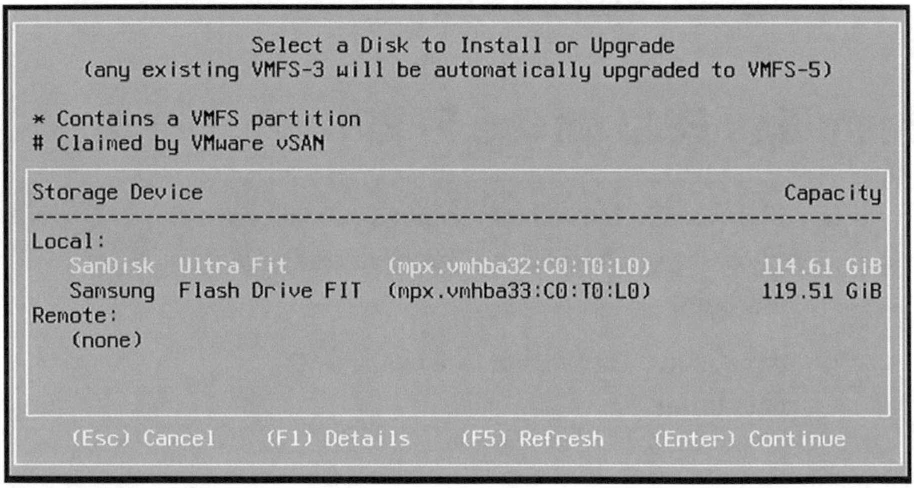

```
                Select a Disk to Install or Upgrade
     (any existing VMFS-3 will be automatically upgraded to VMFS-5)

* Contains a VMFS partition
# Claimed by VMware vSAN

Storage Device                                             Capacity
-------------------------------------------------------------------
Local:
   SanDisk  Ultra Fit       (mpx.vmhba32:C0:T0:L0)        114.61 GiB
   Samsung  Flash Drive FIT (mpx.vmhba33:C0:T0:L0)        119.51 GiB
Remote:
   (none)


   (Esc) Cancel     (F1) Details     (F5) Refresh   (Enter) Continue
```

Figure 5-23. *Selecting Drive to Install On*

4. Accept the installation defaults.

5. When instructed, remove the installation media and press **Enter** to reboot the system.

6. If your system shows Figure 5-24 for more than a few minutes, power the Pi off manually.

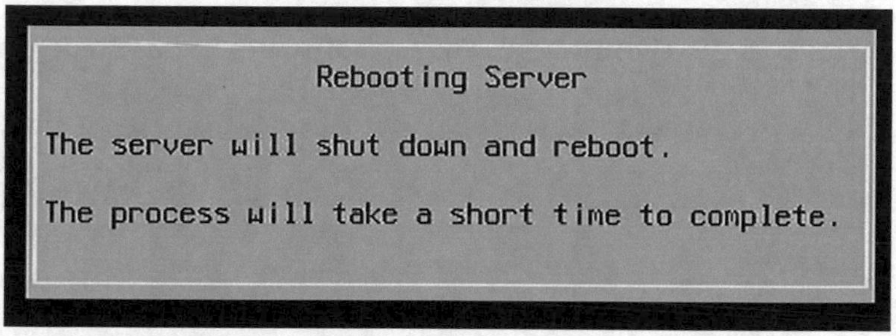

Figure 5-24. *Installation Reboot*

Modify RPi Boot Order

After ESXi is installed, you will specify the boot drive for it.

1. Power on the Pi.

2. Repeatedly press the **Esc** key while the Pi boots up.

3. From the Pi UEFI configuration screen, use the keyboard to select **Boot Maintenance Manager ➤ Boot Options ➤ Change Boot Order** (see Figure 5-25).

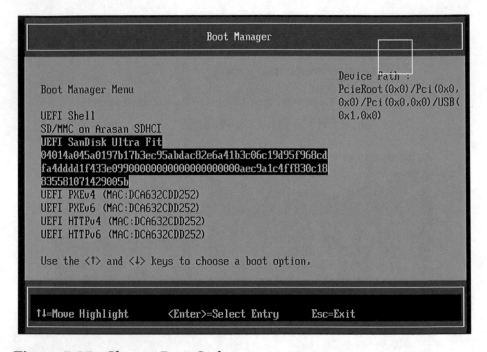

Figure 5-25. *Change Boot Order*

4.   Select the thumb drive that you installed ESXi on as the first boot device.

5.   Press **F10**, confirm your selection, and then press **Esc** three times and then select **Continue**.

Post-installation Configuration: ESXi Console

After ESXi has finished installing, you will need to configure its networking from the ESXi console.

1.   After the system boots, you will see the ESXI screen.

2. Press **F2**, enter *root* in the **Login Name** text box
    and the password that you set when you installed
    ESXi in the **Password** text box, and press **Enter** (see
    Figure 5-26).

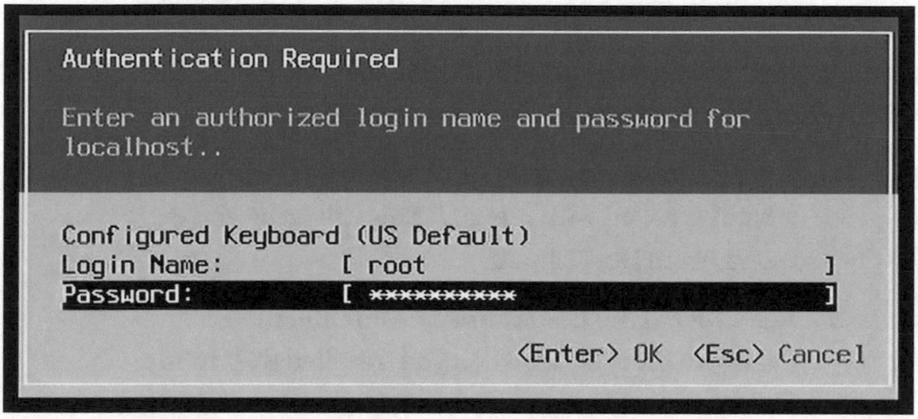

Figure 5-26. *ESXi Log-On*

3. Select **Configure Management Network**.

4. Set your hostname and change your networking if
    needed.

5. Press **Esc**. Select yes to **Apply changes and restart
    management network**.

6. Select **Troubleshooting Options**.

7. Enable ESXi shell and SSH.

8. Press **Esc**. Select yes to **Apply changes and restart
    management network**.

9. Press **Esc** to log out of the ESXi console.

Post-installation Configuration: VMware Host Console

Having accurate time on your ESXi is critical.

You use the web-based VMware Host Client to configure the time on the ESXi host. As I have found that the time on the Pi is usually months or even years from the actual time, I first manually set it and then turn on the NTP service to keep the time accurate on the Pi.

1. In a web browser, enter the IP address of your ESXi system prefixed with https://. This will bring you to the VMware Host Client.

2. Enter *root* in the **User name** text box and the password that you set when you installed ESXi in the **Password** text box and click **Log in** (see Figure 5-27).

Figure 5-27. *Log In to the VMware Host Console*

3. On the home screen, verify that you are running the
ESXi on ARM Fling on a Raspberry Pi (see Figure 5-28).

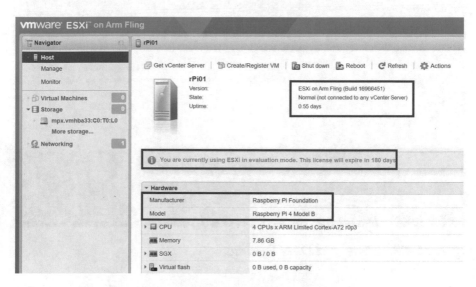

Figure 5-28. *VMware Host Console Home Page*

4. From the Navigator pane, select **Manage**, select the
System tab, and select **Time & date** (see Figure 5-29).

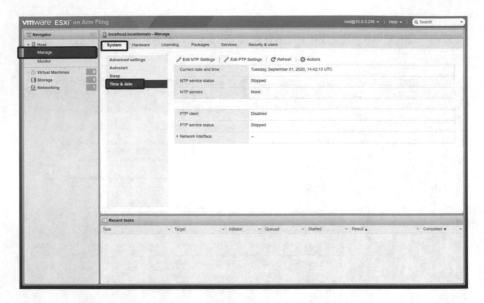

Figure 5-29. *Time and Date Settings*

5.   Click **Edit NTP Settings**.

6.   Select **Manually configure the date and time on
     this host**, set the date to the current UTC time, and
     click **Save** (see Figure 5-30).

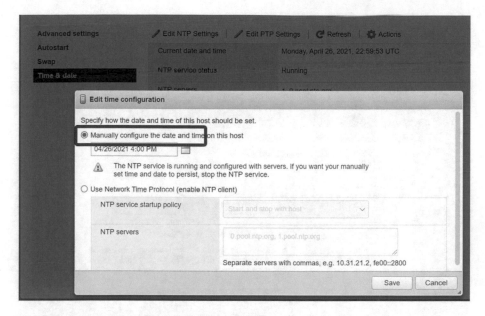

Figure 5-30. *Manual Time Settings*

7. Click **Edit NTP Settings**.

8. Select **Use Network Time Protocol**, select **Start and stop with host**, enter 0.pool.ntp.org, 1.pool.ntp.org, and click **Save** (see Figure 5-31).

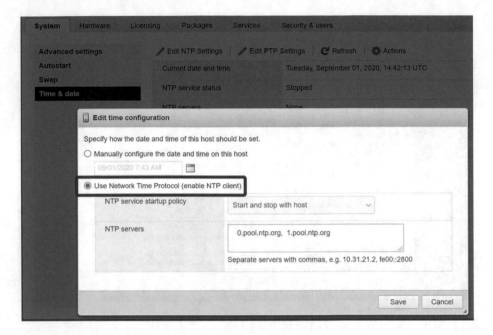

Figure 5-31. *NTP Server Settings*

9. Select the **Services** tab, right-click **ntpd**, and select **Start**.

10. Click **Refresh** and verify that the NTP daemon is running (see Figure 5-32).

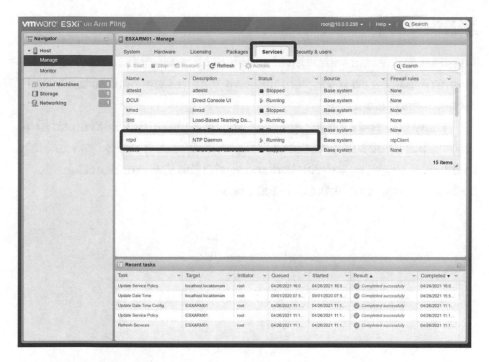

Figure 5-32. *Services*

11. From the user drop-down menu, select **Log out**
     (see Figure 5-33).

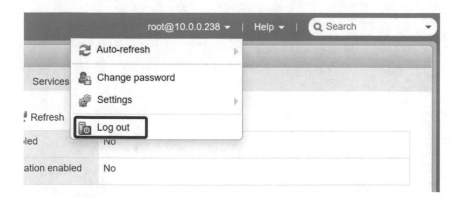

Figure 5-33. *Log Out*

Summary

There are many more steps involved when installing ESXi on an Arm platform than on an x64 system that only requires you boot off the install medium and install it.

It may take you an hour or so the first time you install ESXi on an Arm system, but if you follow the preceding instructions, it should go smoothly. In the next chapters, we will work more with the VMware Host Console and add storage and VMs to the ESXi host.

CHAPTER 6

VMware Host Client

In the previous chapter, you were introduced to the VMware Host Client. In this chapter, we will take a deeper look at it. This chapter is short but important as much of the work that you will be doing with your ESXi host from now on will involve using either the VMware Host Client or the vSphere Client. The purpose of this chapter is to give you a high-level overview of what the client is capable of and not to do actual tasks as we will cover in subsequent chapters.

Overview of the Client

The VMware Host Client was originally released as a VMware Fling known as *ESXi Embedded Host Client.* When vSphere 6.5 U2 was released, the VMware Host Client was incorporated into ESXi. The client allows an HTML5 web browser to be used to view and manage an individual ESXi host. If you want or need to manage multiple ESXi hosts, you will need to use vCenter Server and the vSphere Client.

As the VMware Host Client is web-based, it can be used on almost any OS: Windows, OS X, Android, or any other that supports an HTML5 browser. The ESXi host has an embedded web server on it, so all that is required is to point a web browser to the IP address of the ESXi host and then log in to it (see Figure 6-1). To access the host, enter *root* for the username and the password that you set when you installed ESXi.

© Thomas Fenton and Patrick Kennedy 2022
T. Fenton and P. Kennedy, *Running ESXi on a Raspberry Pi,*
https://doi.org/10.1007/978-1-4842-7465-1_6

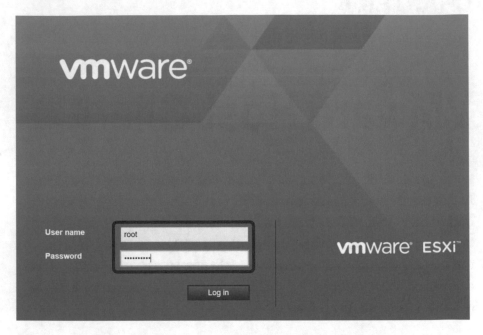

Figure 6-1. *VMware Host Client Login*

Managing ESXi Using the Host Client

After logging in, you will be presented with a dashboard divided into different sections. The Navigator at the left of the screen allows you to customize what is shown on the main dashboard. The Recent tasks pane is at the bottom of the main dashboard. The main dashboard itself provides a summary of the system. If you click **Actions,** you will see a list of actions you can perform on the ESXi host, such as rebooting it and creating/ registering VMs.

Managing ESXi and VMs

Basic management functions can be accomplished using the client. To see what management functions are available, click **Manage** within the Navigator pane.

Changing Default Timeout

By default, the timeout for the client is 900 seconds (15 minutes). As my client resides in a secure environment, I set the timeout to the maximum duration allowed (120 minutes). If you would like to do this, select the **System** tab and then **Advanced settings**. Enter *SessionTimeout* in the search box, and select **UserVars.HostClient.SessionTimeout**. Select **Edit option** and enter *7200* (i.e., 120 minutes) and then click **Save** (see Figure 6-2).

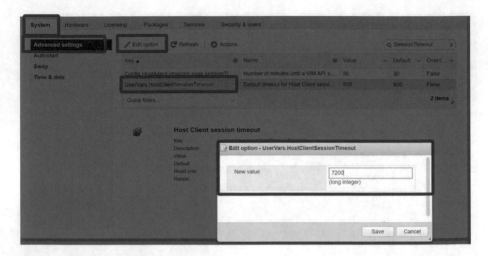

Figure 6-2. *Session Timeout*

There are many other values under the Advanced settings tab, but it is best not to change these unless you are implicitly instructed to do so as serious and unexpected results may occur.

Starting VMs Automatically

One of the settings that I have found useful is to have VMs start up automatically when the ESXi server starts. This comes in handy when the ESXi goes down due to a power outage or other unexpected events, especially for VMs that host your critical applications like your active directory (AD) services.

To have a VM automatically start, select the **System** tab, and click **Autostart**. Figure 6-3 will look different than what you will see on your system at this point as you haven't created any VMs yet, but this screenshot shows how you can enable autostart for a VM and then specify a delay in the startup and shutdown times for it. These times are useful when you want one VM that is dependent on another to start before or after the other. A prime example of this is having a VM with a database start before a VM that hosts an application that depends on the database.

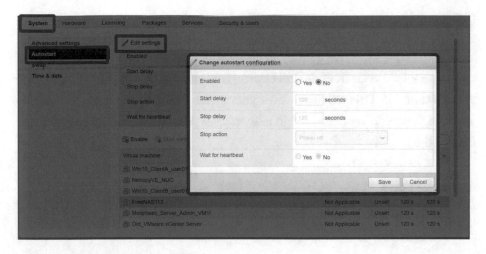

Figure 6-3. Autostart

ESXi Host Hardware

The **Hardware** tab is currently empty as Arm is not yet fully supported. Figure 6-4 shows the PCI devices on an x64 ESXi server.

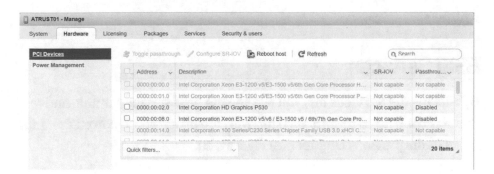

Figure 6-4. x64 Hardware

ESXi License Status

By clicking the **Licensing** tab, you can verify that your key is all zeroes and examine when your license will expire; this should be 180 days from when you installed it. This will also show you which features are licensed for your ESXi server. You can assign a license to your system here as well (see Figure 6-5).

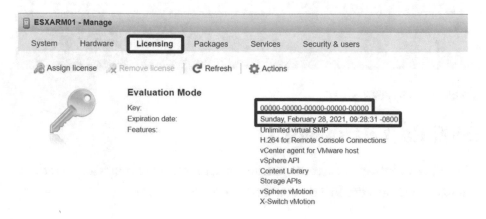

Figure 6-5. *Licenses*

ESXi Services

By clicking the **Services** tab, you will see the *ntpd* service running and that it is configured to start and stop with the host if you followed the steps listed in the previous chapter (see Figure 6-6).

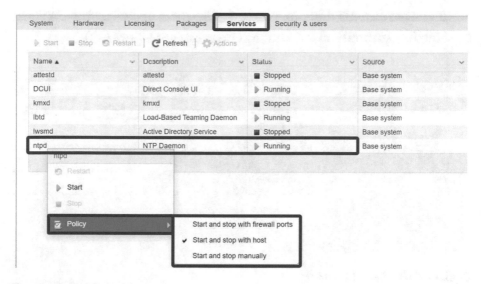

Figure 6-6. *Services*

ESXi Users

You can add additional local users and allow active directory (AD) users to access the client. To do this, click the **Security & users** tab and then click **Users** (Figure 6-7).

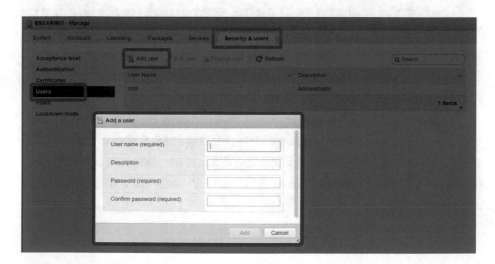

Figure 6-7. *Local Users*

If you have an AD domain, you can allow them access to the ESXi host by selecting **Authentication** and **Join domain** (see Figure 6-8).

Figure 6-8. *Join Domain*

Monitoring ESXi Using the Host Client

The host client monitoring features are rudimentary when compared to the vSphere Client and some third-party tools; however, these tools will give you some insight to what is happening on your host.

The host client allows you to see the resource usage of the host and the VMs that reside on it. The performance information is only stored for an hour. To find this information, click **Monitor** in the **Navigator** pane, and then select the **Performance** tab. From the drop-down menu, select **CPU**, **Memory**, **Network**, and then **Disk**.

These values will be low or nonexistent as only ESXi is running, and we have yet to add any storage or VMs to it. Figure 6-9 shows that ESXi only uses about 1.3GB of RAM, leaving the rest for VMs. On a Pi with 8GB of RAM, this leaves 6.6GB of RAM; on a Pi with 4GB, this only leaves 2.6GB of RAM.

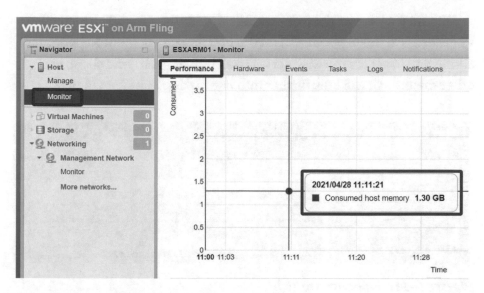

Figure 6-9. *Performance Monitoring*

Select the **Hardware**, **Events**, **Tasks**, **Logs**, and **Notification** tabs, and view the information displayed.

The **Virtual Machines** and **Storage** tabs in the **Navigator** pane show a value of zero (see Figure 6-10) as we haven't added any storage or VMs yet.

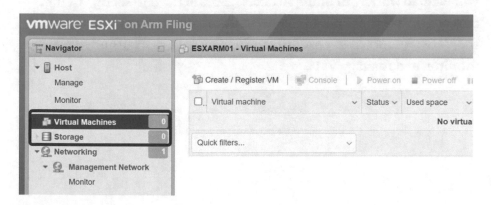

Figure 6-10. *Virtual Machines Tab*

Figure 6-11 shows the Networking tab and VM Network, which allows VMs access to the physical NIC on the Pi. The Management Network allows you to access the ESXi server itself by using SSH, the client, and other means. We will look further into networking in a later chapter.

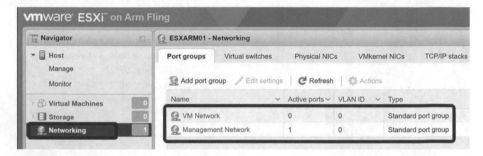

Figure 6-11. *Networking Tab*

Summary

In this chapter, we touched on a few of the features in the VMware Host Client. The key points to remember about the VMware Host Client are that it is used to manage, monitor, and maintain a single ESXi host; if you want to work with multiple hosts, you will need to set up vCenter Server and use the vSphere Client. In forthcoming chapters, we will use the VMware Host Client extensively to work with storage and to create, monitor, and manage VMs.

CHAPTER 7

Local Storage for ESXi

When VMware first started to support enterprise servers with their hypervisors, they realized that they needed a different type of storage object to store them on. This storage object needed to store not only the files that create a virtual machine (VM) but also the ISO images that are used to install VMs. It also needed to be accessed from multiple ESXi hosts. The term that VMware came up with was *datastore*. In this chapter, we will create a datastore on the Raspberry Pi that can be used by a single ESXi host.

Different Types of Datastores

ESXi supports different types of datastores, including

- Virtual Machine File System (VMFS) – Examples of VMFS include block storage devices like local SSDs, HDDs, and NVME devices. VMFS also supports Internet Small Computer Systems Interface (iSCSI) for network-attached storage and Fibre Channel storage.

- Network File System (NFS) – An ESXi host can use an NFS 3 or NFS 4.1 share as a datastore.

© Thomas Fenton and Patrick Kennedy 2022
T. Fenton and P. Kennedy, *Running ESXi on a Raspberry Pi*,
https://doi.org/10.1007/978-1-4842-7465-1_7

- Virtual Volumes (vVols) – These were created by VMware and require a storage array to support them. They are an additional layer of abstraction that allows VMs to have their own storage attributes like redundancy and performance.

- Virtual Storage Area Network (vSAN) – This was created by VMware and is used to create a virtual SAN that uses the local storage of the ESXi hosts to create a pool of storage for the hosts in a vSAN cluster. vSANs are used by VMware to create a hyperconverged infrastructure and are extremely popular.

In this chapter, we will use a USB device as a VMFS datastore.

Setting Up a Datastore on a USB Device

As the Pi does not have the ability to connect to a SATA or NVMe device directly, we must use the USB port on it as the conduit to our datastore. This is not a great idea for production systems, but for our Pi it is an option.

VMware has supported mounting USB drives to ESXi since vSphere 5.0. Currently, the biggest use case for them is moving VMs from one system to another when the network is too slow or network connectivity is not available between two ESXi hosts. Many people who are migrating from an on-premise to cloud infrastructure use large USB drives to transfer the data as it is quicker than doing a network transfer.

Make sure you use the USB 3 rather than the USB 2 port with your thumb drive. If you look at the USB ports, the blue one is the USB 3 port. It has been reported that 8GB and smaller USB devices will not work as datastores. In this example, I will be using a 256GB Samsung USB 3.1 thumb drive for my datastore.

The easiest way I have found to add a USB drive is using the ESXi shell. I use an SSH connection to the shell so I can cut and paste commands into it. If you didn't enable SSH as shown in a previous chapter, you may wish to do so now. If you are using a Windows 10 machine, you can use its built-in SSH client from the command line. Other OSs also have SSH clients.

From the command prompt, enter *ssh root@<IP address of your ESXi server>* and then enter your password (see Figure 7-1).

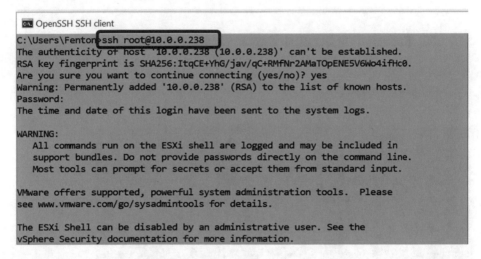

Figure 7-1. SSH to ESXi

The following are the steps to manually add a USB datastore. In the next section, I will show you how to download and run a script that does these steps for you:

1. Stop the USB arbitrator service. This will prevent USB devices from being used as pass-through devices by entering

    /etc/init.d/usbarbitrator stop
    chkconfig usbarbitrator off

```
OpenSSH SSH client
[root@ESXARM01:~] /etc/init.d/usbarbitrator stop
watchdog-usbarbitrator: Terminating watchdog process with PID 132342
stopping usbarbitrator...
usbarbitrator stopped
[root@ESXARM01:~] chkconfig usbarbitrator off
[root@ESXARM01:~]
```

2. See what disks are already known to the system
    by entering

    ls /dev/disks.

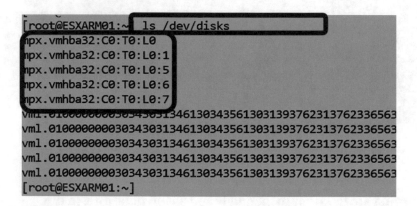

```
[root@ESXARM01:~] ls /dev/disks
npx.vmhba32:C0:T0:L0
npx.vmhba32:C0:T0:L0:1
npx.vmhba32:C0:T0:L0:5
npx.vmhba32:C0:T0:L0:6
npx.vmhba32:C0:T0:L0:7
vml.010000000030343031346130343561303139376231376233d6563
vml.010000000030343031346130343561303139376231376233d6563
vml.010000000030343031346130343561303139376231376233d6563
vml.010000000030343031346130343561303139376231376233d6563
vml.010000000030343031346130343561303139376231376233d6563
[root@ESXARM01:~]
```

3. Plug your USB device into your Pi and reenter *ls /
    dev/disks*. A new device with the prefix *vmhba* will
    be shown. Make a note of the new device as you will
    need it for the next commands.

```
[root@ESXARM01:~  ls /dev/disks
mpx.vmhba32:C0:T0:L0
mpx.vmhba32:C0:T0:L0:1
mpx.vmhba32:C0:T0:L0:5
mpx.vmhba32:C0:T0:L0:6
mpx.vmhba32:C0:T0:L0:7
mpx.vmhba34:C0:T0:L0
mpx.vmhba34:C0:T0:L0:1
vml.0100000000030333732323232303037303036323239384 66c6173
vml.0100000000030333732323232303037303036323239384 66c6173
vml.0100000000030343031346130343356130313937623137623365
vml.0100000000030343031346130343356130313937623137623365
vml.0100000000030343031346130343356130313937623137623365
vml.0100000000030343031346130343356130313937623137623365
vml.0100000000030343031346130343356130313937623137623365
[root@ESXARM01:~] _
```

My device was **vmhba34:C0:T0:L0**, and I will use it in the rest of this example, but yours may be different.

4. Write a GPT label to the device by entering

    *partedUtil mklabel /dev/disks/mpx.**vmhba34:C0:T0:L0** gpt*

```
[root@ESXARM01:~] partedUtil mklabel /dev/disks/mpx.vmhba34:C0:T0:L0:1 gpt
[root@ESXARM01:~] _
```

5. Obtain information on the sectors of the device by entering

    *partedUtil getptbl /dev/disks/mpx.**vmhba34:C0:T0:L0***

```
[root@ESXARM01:~] partedUtil getptbl /dev/disks/mpx.vmhba34:C0:T0:L0:1
gpt
31200 255 63 501242017
[root@ESXARM01:~] _
```

6. Calculate the end sector using the first field output from the previous command. The calculated number will be needed in the next step:

    31200 * 255 * 63 – 1 = *501227999*

7. Create a partition table on the device by entering

    *partedUtil setptbl /dev/disks/mpx.**vmhba34:** **C0:T0:L0** gpt "1 2048 **501227999** AA31E02A400F11DB 9590000C2911D1B8 0"*

```
[root@ESXARM01:~]
[root@ESXARM01:~] partedUtil setptbl /dev/disks/mpx.vmhba34:C0:T0:L0 gpt "1 2048 501227999
AA31E02A400F11DB9590000C2911D1B8 0"
gpt
0 0 0 0
1 2048 501227999 AA31E02A400F11DB9590000C2911D1B8 0
[root@ESXARM01:~] _
```

8. Create a VMFS on the device by entering

    *vmkfstools -C vmfs6 -S rPi-USB-Datastore-01 / dev/disks/**mpx.vmhba34:C0:T0:L0:1***

```
[root@ESXARM01:~] vmkfstools -C vmfs6 -S rPi-USB-Datastore-01 /dev/disks/mpx.vmhba34:C0:T0:L0:1
create fs deviceName:'/dev/disks/mpx.vmhba34:C0:T0:L0:1', fsShortName:'vmfs6', fsName:'rPi-USB-Da
tastore-01'
deviceFullPath:/dev/disks/mpx.vmhba34:C0:T0:L0:1 deviceFile:mpx.vmhba34:C0:T0:L0:1
ATS on device /dev/disks/mpx.vmhba34:C0:T0:L0:1: not supported
.
Checking if remote hosts are using this device as a valid file system. This may take a few second
s...
Creating vmfs6 file system on "mpx.vmhba34:C0:T0:L0:1" with blockSize 1048576, unmapGranularity 1
048576, unmapPriority default and volume label "rPi-USB-Datastore-01".
Successfully created new volume: 608a0c81-ae4cbd81-4337-dca632cdd252
[root@ESXARM01:~] _
```

9. See more information about the file system
    by entering

    esxcli storage vmfs extent list

```
[root@ESXARM01:~] esxcli storage vmfs extent list
Volume Name                                    VMFS UUID
                                               -------------------
rPi-USB-Datastore-01                           608a0c81-ae4cbd81-4337-d
OSDATA-5f4e57d3-0b46cfa9-5986-dca632cdd252     5f4e57d3-0b46cfa9-5386-d
[root@ESXARM01:~]
```

The ESXi host now has a device named
vmhba34:C0:T0:L0:1 that has a volume named
rPi-USB-Datastore-01. This datastore can be used to
store VMs and ISO images.

Directories are held in a tree structure that is
accessible from the console.

10. Change to the directory and list the datastores
     by entering

     cd /dev/
     ls

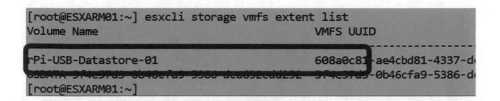

```
[root@ESXARM01:~] cd /vmfs/volumes
[root@ESXARM01:/vmfs/volumes] ls -l
total 2560
drwxr-xr-t  1 root    root        77824 Sep  1 14:13 5f4e57d3-0b46cfa9-5386-dca632cdd252
drwxr-xr-t  1 root    root        73728 Sep  1 14:26 5f4e5a0e-38bfb8ec-7563-dca632cdd252
drwxr-xr-x  1 root    root            8 Jan  1 1970 71f875e6-58464d9c-d6a8-520a3b1574e9
lrwxr-xr-x  1 root    root           35 Sep  1 14:29 BOOTBANK1 -> 71f875e6-58464d9c-d6a8-5
lrwxr-xr-x  1 root    root           35 Sep  1 14:29 BOOTBANK2 -> c407cb4d-974d25b8-df8b-0
lrwxr-xr-x  1 root    root           35 Sep  1 14:29 OSDATA-5f4e57d3-0b46cfa9-5386-dca632c
drwxr-xr-x  1 root    root            8 Jan  1 1970 c407cb4d-974d25b8-df8b-0d120c510e18
lrwxr-xr-x  1 root    root           35 Sep  1 14:29 rPi-USB-Datastore-01 -> 5f4e5a0e-38bf
```

rPi-USB-Datastore-01 is a link to the actual
file system.

11. See how much space in human-readable format (-h)
     is on the file system by entering

     df -h

```
[root@ESXARM01:/vmfs/volumes/5f4e5a0e-38bfb8ec-7563-dca632cdd252] df -h
Filesystem    Size    Used Available Use% Mounted on
VMFS-6        238.8G   1.4G   237.3G   1% /vmfs/volumes/rPi-USB-Datastore-01
VMFS-L        106.2G   2.6G   103.6G   2% /vmfs/volumes/OSDATA-5f4e57d5-6b46cfa9-5:
vfat            4.0G 117.9M    3.9G   3% /vmfs/volumes/BOOTBANK1
vfat            4.0G  64.0K    4.0G   0% /vmfs/volumes/BOOTBANK2
[root@ESXARM01:/vmfs/volumes/5f4e5a0e-38bfb8ec-7563-dca632cdd252]
```

Examining the Datastore from the Host Client

Now that you have a datastore on your Pi, you can examine it using the
ESXi Host Client.

1. From your ESXi Host Client, in the **Navigator** pane
    select **Storage**. This will show you the
    new datastore.

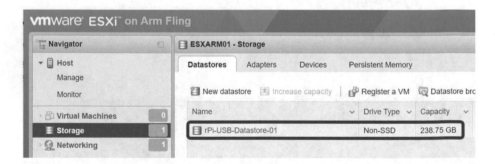

2. To get more detailed information about the
    datastore, click the datastore. The information
    displayed includes how much space is free and how
    much is being used.

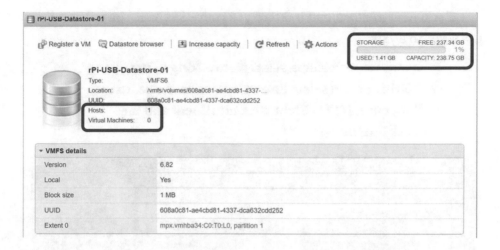

Script to Automate Creating a USB Storage Device

There are many steps involved in creating a datastore on a USB device, and if you make a typo at any point, the process will fail. To prevent this from happening, I created a script to automate the process. This script is accessible via GitHub.

Caution!   This is a very bare-bones script, and it doesn't do a lot of error checking. I have used it dozens of times without any issues, but it is supplied as is, and you should examine the code very carefully before executing it, and you should never use it on a production system.

The script is located at `https://github.com/FentonTom/AutoMountUSB`. You can download it directly from GitHub and then transfer it to your host using SCP, or you can download it directly to the ESXi host using the wget command.

If you wish to download it directly to your ESXi host, the following are the steps to do so:

1. From the host client, select **Networking** in the Navigator and select **Firewall rules**. In the search box, enter *HTTP*. Right-click **httpClient** and then click **Enable**.

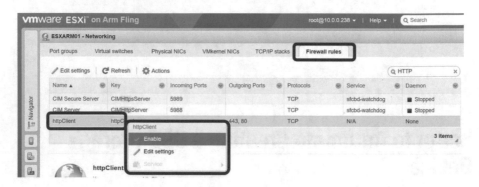

2. Use SSH to connect to your ESXi host.

3. Download the script to the /tmp directory and make it executable by entering

   cd /tmp
   wget https://raw.githubusercontent.com/FentonTom/
   AutoMountUSB/main/AutoMountUSB.bash
   chmod 755 ./AutoMoutUSB.bash

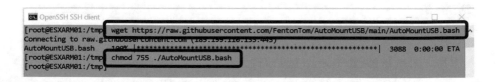

You start the execution of the script and then insert the USB device that will be used as a datastore. When you execute the script, the devices that are already mounted will be shown, and then you will be prompted to insert the USB device and press **Enter**.

4. Start the script by entering

   ./AutoMoutUSB.bash

OpenSSH SSH client

```
usbarbitrator is not running
n list of USB devices currently on system
Bus 001 Device 001: ID 0e0f:8003 VMware, Inc. Root Hub
Bus 001 Device 002: ID 2109:3431 VIA Labs, Inc. Hub
Bus 001 Device 003: ID 0781:5583 SanDisk Corp. Ultra Fit
Bus 001 Device 004: ID 0781:5583 SanDisk Corp. Ultra Fit
Bus 001 Device 005: ID 152d:0562 JMicron Technology Corp. / JMicron USA Te
Bus 001 Device 006: ID 090c:1000 Silicon Motion, Inc. - Taiwan (formerly F
Bus 002 Device 001: ID 0000:0000
n list of disks devices currently on system
mpx.vmhba32:C0:T0:L0
mpx.vmhba32:C0:T0:L0:1
mpx.vmhba32:C0:T0:L0:5
mpx.vmhba32:C0:T0:L0:6
mpx.vmhba32:C0:T0:L0:7
mpx.vmhba33:C0:T0:L0
mpx.vmhba33:C0:T0:L0:1
mpx.vmhba34:C0:T0:L0
mpx.vmhba34:C0:T0:L0:1
mpx.vmhba35:C0:T0:L0
mpx.vmhba35:C0:T0:L0:1
Insert the new storage device and Press [Enter] key to continue
```

5. When prompted, insert your USB device and press **Enter**.

   If a new device is not found, you can try again by entering **Y**; or, if you want to exit the program, enter **Q**.

6. When a new USB device is found, enter a name for the datastore.

7. The script will then mount, format, and name the datastore.

8. Return to the host client and verify that you can see the datastore.

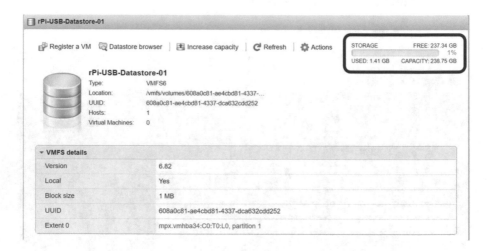

Summary

In this chapter, I showed you how to use a USB device to create a datastore. The datastore can be used for storage for VMs and ISO images. You can add the storage using the commands presented previously or by running my script. If you do use the script, please use caution as I have not had a chance to extensively test it; as such, it should not be used on production systems. In the next chapter, we will create VMs!

CHAPTER 8

Virtual Machines on ESXi

While many readers may be looking forward to finding out how to create virtual machines (VMs) – which we will cover in this chapter – this may be the most unexciting chapter in this book, but for good reason: VMware has spent considerable time and effort to make creating VMs as easy as installing an OS on a physical machine. Yes, there are few nuances that you need to be aware of, and you will need to make sure that you get the correct ISOs for Arm processors, but in general the process of creating a VM on ESXi is straightforward.

In this chapter, I will provide you with step-by-step instructions for how to create a VM from a few different Linux ISO distributions. I will also discuss why Windows will not work with your system, how to make copies of your VMs, and what a snapshot is. Finally, I will give an overview of VMware Tools: what it is, why it is important, and how to install it on your Linux systems.

Note   The ESXi-Arm-Fling-Doc states that Ubuntu, CentOS, openSUSE, Photon, Debian, and Fedora Linux distributions are known to be compatible; however, you need to make sure you get Arm versions of these distributions.

© Thomas Fenton and Patrick Kennedy 2022
T. Fenton and P. Kennedy, *Running ESXi on a Raspberry Pi*,
https://doi.org/10.1007/978-1-4842-7465-1_8

Windows Will Not Work

Because the Pi has an Arm processor, software compiled for x64 systems will not run on it. Fortunately, however, all the major Linux distributions have Arm versions readily available, and they run quite well as VMs (even with a limited amount of memory and CPU cycles).

Microsoft has had an Arm version of Windows since 2011, and their first Surface device, the Surface RT, was powered by an NVIDIA Arm processor. More recently, Microsoft announced a version of Windows 10 for the Arm, and their recently announced Surface Pro X runs it as well.

It is unlikely, however, that you can get it to run on a generic Arm system like the Pi due to driver compatibility issues. Furthermore, Microsoft has announced that they do have an Arm-based server running Windows in its cloud, but they also stated that it is doubtful that we will see this version made available to the public in the near future.

VMware Tools

VMware Tools is a set of utilities that increases the performance of a VM and gives the ESXi Host Client and vSphere Client visibility into the VM. VMware Tools also allows the quiescing of disk when snapshots are taking place, allowing a consistent state of the disk to be saved. Most Intel-based VMs have precompiled VMware Tools that can be installed using the client, but Arm systems do not, and as such it will need to be compiled on your machines. Your VMs will function without VMware Tools, but the enhancements that the included tools add make it worthwhile to install.

As there are many commands involved in compiling and installing VMware Tools on your system, I created scripts to do this. These scripts are available and can be downloaded from GitHub. Please examine the code carefully before running.

Types of Virtual Disks

When creating a VM, you can choose to thin- or thick-provision it. By default, a thick disk will be used. To see the option to change the disk, you need to expand the hard disk and select it (see Figure 8-1).

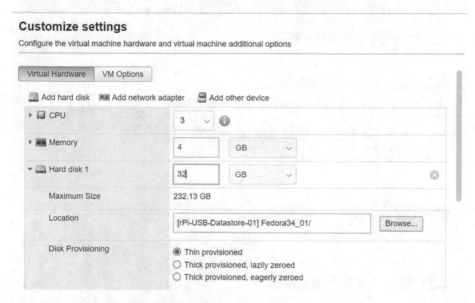

Figure 8-1. *Disk Provisioning*

We covered the different disk types in an early chapter, and you may wish to review the section to see them. I tend to use thin-provisioned disks.

Installing Ubuntu

Ubuntu is one of the most popular Linux distributions and comes in a desktop and server version. The desktop version includes a graphical interface, and this is the version that I will be installing. I will be installing Ubuntu 20.04 as it is a long-term support (LTS) distribution and will be supported with general patches for 5 years and security patches for 10 years.

The download site for the Arm Ubuntu images is `https://ubuntu.com/download/server/arm`.

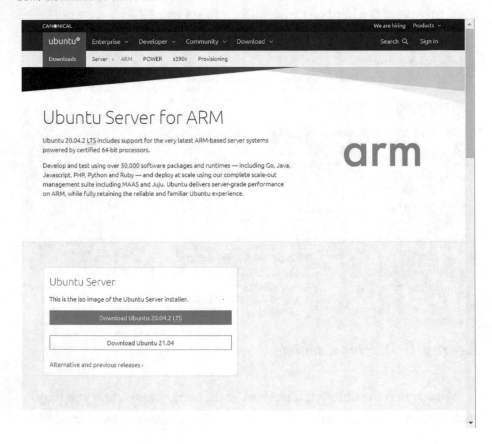

The following are the steps to install it on your Pi.

Download Ubuntu 20.04 ISO

We will be downloading the installation ISO directly to the ESXi datastore. Later we will use the ISO to install the system.

1. SSH into the ESXi host.

2. Gain root user privileges by entering

    sudo bash

3. Change to the directory where you want to store the ISO by entering

    cd /vmfs/volumes/rPi-USB-Datastore-01

4. Open the firewall to allow the HTTP connections by entering

    esxcli network firewall ruleset set --enabled=true --ruleset-id=httpClient

5. Download the Ubuntu 20.04 server image by entering

    wget https://cdimage.ubuntu.com/ releases/20.04/release/ubuntu-20.04.2-live-server-arm64.iso

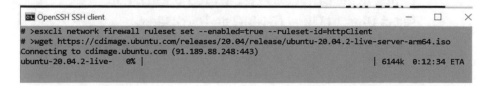

It will take a few minutes for the ISO to be downloaded.

You can also download the ISO to your desktop system and copy it over to your ESXi host using SCP.

Create an Ubuntu VM

1. Log in to the ESXi Host Client.

2. In the Navigator select **Virtual Machines** and then click **Create / Register VM**.

3. In the New virtual machine wizard, select **Create a new virtual machine**, and click **Next**.

4. In the **Name** text box, enter *Ubuntu2004_A*. From the **Guest OS family** drop-down menu, select **Linux**. In the **Guest OS version** drop-down menu, select **Ubuntu Linux (64-bit)** and click **Next**.

5. Verify that rPi-USB-Datastore-01 is the datastore, and click **Next**.

6. Set the virtual hardware to three CPUs and 4GB of memory.

7. Expand **CD/DVD Drive 1**, select **Datastore ISO file**, and select your Ubuntu ISO image. Verify that **Connect at power on** is selected. Click **Next**.

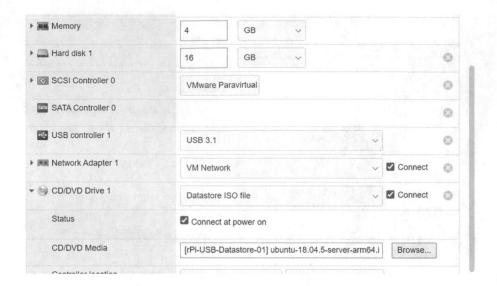

8. Verify your settings and click **Finish**.

Install Ubuntu 20.04 on the VM

Installing an OS on a VM is just like installing an OS on a physical machine.

When accessing a virtual machine from the host client, you have the option to use the web browser or VM Remote Console (VMRC). The VMRC runs as a stand-alone application that works on Windows, macOS, and Linux OSs and allows you to not only view the VM console but also perform functions on it that the web browser does not including installing an operating system, configuring the operating system settings, running applications, monitoring performance, etc.

In this chapter I will be using VMRC.

1. Right-click the Ubuntu virtual machine and select **Download VMRC**.

2. This will take you to a VMware download page for VMRC. Download it and install it on your system.

3. Right-click the virtual machine and select **Launch remote console**.

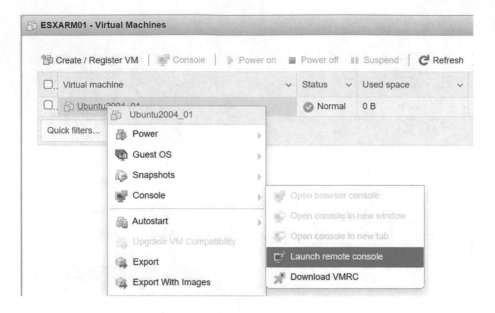

4. At the top of the VMRC, click the **Power On** icon.

5. In the display, select **Install Ubuntu Server**.

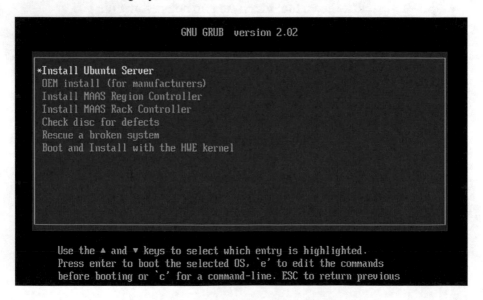

6. Follow the prompts to install Ubuntu. When asked
    to install OpenSSH server, select yes and accept
    all other defaults or modify them to suit your
    environment.

7. It takes a few minutes to install the OS. I find it
    useful to monitor the ESXi system resource usage
    using the ESXi Host Client to verify that the install is
    taking place.

8. When the install has completed, select **Reboot Now**.

```
        configuring target system bootloader
        installing grub to target devices
    finalizing installation
        running 'curtin hook' -
final system configuration
  configuring cloud-init
  installing openssh-server
  restoring apt configuration
downloading and installing security updates
subiquity/Late/run
```

```
                            [ View full log ]
                            [ Reboot Now     ]
```

9. It will take a few minutes to reboot. If it seems
    to hang, go to the host client, click the VM in the
    Navigator, and select **Monitor**.

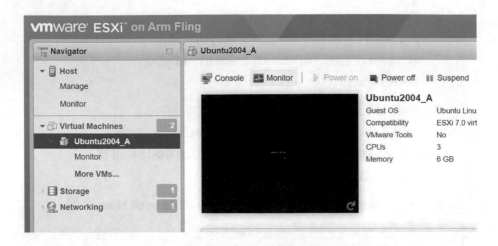

10.   From the drop-down menu, select **CPU**. If you don't
       see any activity in the graph for a few minutes, select
       Reset in the **Actions** drop-down menu.

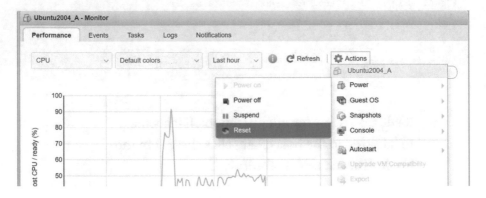

11.   It may not be apparent when the system finishes
       bootup as the bootup process continues to writhe to
       the screen, but pressing the Enter key will bring up a
       login prompt.

Installing VMware Tools on Ubuntu

VMware Tools should be installed on Ubuntu. It will take 10–15 minutes to compile and install it, and I would recommend that you keep your VM configured with three vCPUs and 6GB of RAM while installing it.

The steps to compile VMware Tools are rather long and detailed, so I created a script to do this. Please read the script carefully and do not use it on production systems. I have only used Ubuntu 20.04, but it may work on other versions of Ubuntu.

1. Log in to the VMRC.

2. Enter *ip add* and get the IP address of your system.

```
root@ubuntu2004-a:/tmp# ip add
1: lo: <LOOPBACK,UP,LOWER_UP> mtu 65536 qdisc noqueue state UNKNOWN group default qlen 1000
    link/loopback 00:00:00:00:00:00 brd 00:00:00:00:00:00
    inet 127.0.0.1/8 scope host lo
       valid_lft forever preferred_lft forever
    inet6 ::1/128 scope host
       valid_lft forever preferred_lft forever
2: ens192: <BROADCAST,MULTICAST,UP,LOWER_UP> mtu 1500 qdisc fq_codel state UP group default qlen 1000
    link/ether 00:0c:29:34:37:d9 brd ff:ff:ff:ff:ff:ff
    inet 10.0.0.236/24 brd 10.0.0.255 scope global dynamic ens192
       valid_lft 85416sec preferred_lft 85416sec
    inet6 fe80::20c:29ff:fe34:37d9/64 scope link
       valid_lft forever preferred_lft forever
root@ubuntu2004-a:/tmp# _
```

3. I find it easier to use an SSH session to work in. If you want to use the VMRC, skip the next step.

4. Open an SSH connection to the server.

5. Gain root privileges by entering

   sudo su

6. Change to the *tmp* directory by entering

   cd /tmp

7. Install the tools needed to compile VMware Tools
    by entering

    apt update
    apt install build-essential -y

8. Download the VMware Tools build script, make it
    executable, and execute it by entering

    wget https://raw.githubusercontent.com/
    FentonTom/VMware_Tools_Ubuntu/main/
    Ubuntu2004
    chmod 755 Ubuntu2004
    . /Ubuntu2004

9. When VMware Tools is compiled and installed, you
    will get a message that the service has started.

```
● vmtoolsd.service - Service for virtual machines hosted on VMware
     Loaded: loaded (/etc/systemd/system/vmtoolsd.service; enabled; vendor preset: enabled)
     Active: active (running) since Sat 2021-05-01 19:07:40 UTC; 40ms ago
       Docs: http://github.com/vmware/open-vm-tools
   Main PID: 71222 (vmtoolsd)
      Tasks: 1 (limit: 6971)
     Memory: 620.0K
     CGroup: /system.slice/vmtoolsd.service
             └─71222 /usr/local/bin/vmtoolsd

May 01 19:07:40 ubuntu2004-a systemd[1]: Started Service for virtual machines hosted on VMware.
root@ubuntu2004-a:/home/user01#
```

10. Return to your ESXi Host Client and select the
    Ubuntu VM. It will show that VMware Tools is
    installed and running on it. You may need to refresh
    the screen.

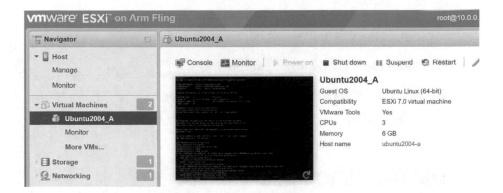

Post-configuration of the Ubuntu VM

Unless you only plan on running a single VM on your ESXi host, you will want to reduce the resources that your VM is using.

1. Power down the VM. This can be done from the VM, the VMRC, or the host client.

2. From the ESXi Host Client, right-click the VM and select **Edit settings**.

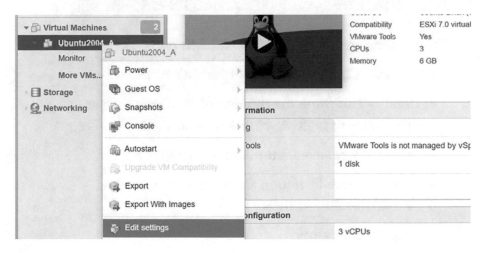

3. Change the vCPU count to 1 and the RAM to 2GB, delete the CD/DVD, and click **Save**.

4. From the VMRC, power on the VM.

5. Verify that the system booted up and then power it off.

Virtual Machine Files

A virtual machine is a collection of files. The files shown in the following contain data and have information that the hypervisor needs to run the VM.

```
[root@ESXARM01:/vmfs/volumes/5f4e5cd6-2dc632aa-9320-dca632cdd252/Fedora34_01_Argon] ls -
total 33561728
-rw-r--r--    1 root     root        159206 Sep 13  2020 vmware.log
-rw-r--r--    1 root     root         91597 Sep 13  2020 vmware-4.log
-rw-r--r--    1 root     root        105961 Sep 13  2020 vmware-3.log
-rw-r--r--    1 root     root         87922 Sep 13  2020 vmware-2.log
-rw-r--r--    1 root     root         86790 Sep 13  2020 vmware-1.log
-rwxr-xr-x    1 root     root          3217 Sep 13  2020 Fresh_Fedora34_NFS.vmx
-rw-r--r--    1 root     root             0 Sep 13  2020 Fresh_Fedora34_NFS.vmsd
-rw-------    1 root     root           479 Sep 13  2020 Fresh_Fedora34_NFS.vmdk
-rw-------    1 root     root        270840 Sep 13  2020 Fresh_Fedora34_NFS.nvram
-rw-------    1 root     root   34359738368 Sep 13  2020 Fresh_Fedora34_NFS-flat.vmdk
```

The following are a few of the files and their purpose:

- nvram – Contains the state of the VM's BIOS.

- vmdk – This stores the contents of a VM's virtual disk. You can have multiple virtual disks on a VM.

- vmsd – Stores metadata about snapshots of a VM.

- vmx – The configuration file for a VM. It stores the virtual machine settings.

- log – Contains logs.

These files can be seen by examining them using the host client.

1. From the host client, expand the **Storage** object and select rPi-USB-Datastore-01.

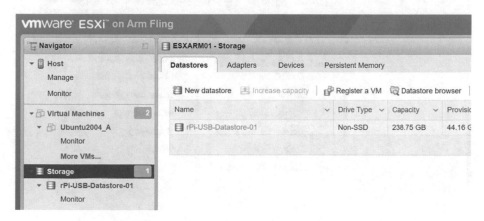

2. Select **Datastore browser**.

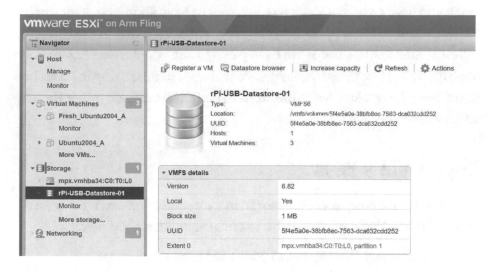

3. Select the VM. The files will be displayed on the right.

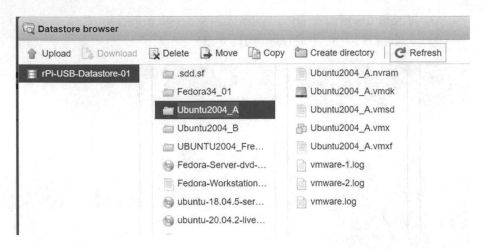

Creating a Copy of a VM

Once you have created a VM, you may want to have another instance of it. VMware makes it easy to create a copy of a VM using a GUI in the vSphere Client's clone feature, but as we have yet to install vCenter Server and only have the ESXi Host Client available, we will need to do it using it. It can be done, but it does take a few more steps to copy a VM using it rather than by using vCenter Server.

Copy a VM's Files

The files that make up a VM are stored in a directory that can be accessed from ESXi. You can copy these files to create a duplicate VM of it.

1. From an SSH session to your ESXi host, change to a directory that contains your VMs:

    ```
    cd /volumes/rPi-USB-Datastore-01
    ```

2. Copy the directory that makes up your VM
    recursively to include all the files in the directory.
    As I wanted to see how much time it took to copy
    the files, I prefixed the command with the *time*
    command:

```
cp -rv Ubuntu2004_A/ Fresh_Ubuntu2004
```

3. It took me 26 minutes to copy the VM. While it was
    being copied, I monitored the disk activity using
    the host client. I refreshed the graph every couple
    minutes.

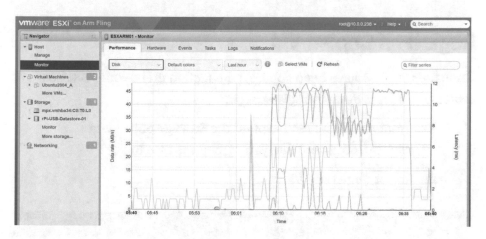

4. Once the copy process had finished, I had a new directory with the VM's files in it.

```
OpenSSH SSH client                                                             −
[root@ESXARM01:/vmfs/volumes/5f4e5a0e-38bfb8ec-7563-dca632cdd252] time cp -r Ubuntu2004_A/ Fresh_Ubuntu2004
real    28m 9.21s
user    7m 40.00s
sys     0m 0.00s
[root@ESXARM01:/vmfs/volumes/5f4e5a0e-38bfb8ec-7563-dca632cdd252] ls -l Fresh_Ubuntu2004/
total 33559552
-rw-------  1 root  root  34359738368 Sep  3 06:09 Ubuntu2004_A-flat.vmdk
-rw-------  1 root  root       270840 Sep  3 06:09 Ubuntu2004_A.nvram
-rw-------  1 root  root          506 Sep  3 06:09 Ubuntu2004_A.vmdk
-rw-r--r--  1 root  root            0 Sep  3 06:09 Ubuntu2004_A.vmsd
-rwxr-xr-x  1 root  root         3277 Sep  3 05:41 Ubuntu2004_A.vmx
-rw-------  1 root  root           47 Sep  3 06:09 Ubuntu2004_A.vmxf
-rw-r--r--  1 root  root       164778 Sep  3 06:09 vmware-1.log
-rw-r--r--  1 root  root        94309 Sep  3 06:09 vmware-2.log
-rw-r--r--  1 root  root       115590 Sep  3 06:09 vmware-3.log
-rw-r--r--  1 root  root       107189 Sep  3 06:09 vmware.log
[root@ESXARM01:/vmfs/volumes/5f4e5a0e-38bfb8ec-7563-dca632cdd252]
```

Register a Copied VM

Once files of a VM have been copied, you need to make your ESXi host aware of it. This is done by registering it.

1. From the host client, expand the **Storage** object and click the datastore that you copied the files to.

2. Select **Register a VM**.

3. Select the **Fresh_Ubuntu2004** directory, right-click the .vmx file, and select **Register VM**.

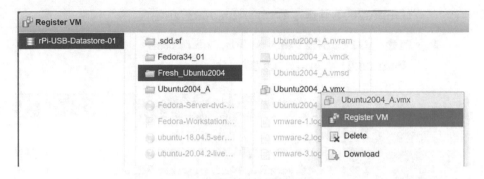

4. Close the datastore browser.

5. Select **Virtual Machines** in the Navigator. Right-click the bottom VM named Ubuntu2004_A, and select **Edit settings**.

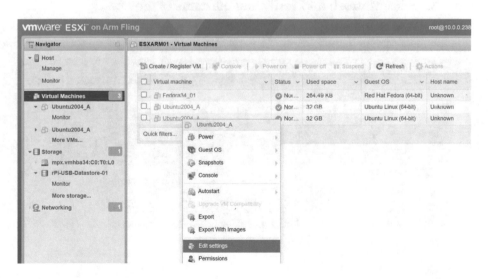

6. Select **VM Options**.

7. Verify that its directory shows that it is Fresh_
    Ubuntu2004; if not, choose the other VM.

8. In the **VM Config File** text box, enter Fresh_
    Ubunu2004_A and click **Save**.

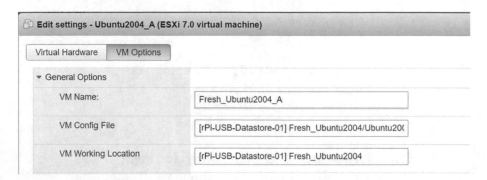

9. Click **Refresh** and verify that the name of the new
    VM is shown.

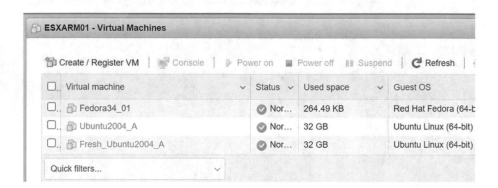

Starting the OS

1. Open a VMRC console to the new VM and power it on.

2. In the pop-up window, select **I Copied It**, and click **Answer**.

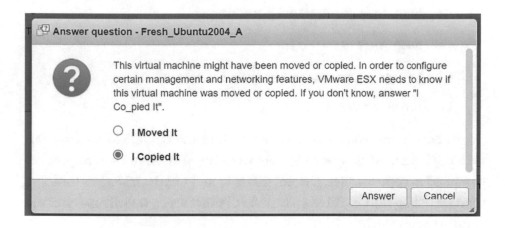

3. Log in to the Ubuntu system.

4. Gain root permissions by entering

    sudo bash

5. Verify that it has a different IP address than the VM that you copied it from by entering

    ip add

6. Verify that it has the same name as the VM that it was copied from by entering

    hostname

7.   Change the hostname by entering

    sudo *hostnamectl set-hostname fresh_Ubuntu2004.*

8.   Verify that the system has the new hostname
     by entering

    hostname

9.   Shut down the system by entering

    sudo init 0

10.   Verify that the system has been shut down.

11.   Close the VMRC.

Although the process to create a VM from an existing VM on a system
with the benefit of using the vSphere web console takes a lot of time as
you need to copy the files, it is not difficult, and I find it takes less time
than installing the OS. After we install vCenter Server, we will use its clone
feature to copy a VM.

There are various third-party tools that can be used to create copies
of VMs, and if you are going to be creating a lot of copies of VMs, I would
suggest investigating them. I like to keep a newly installed or "fresh" VM
and work from a copy from it. I use snapshots as needed but delete them as
soon as possible.

Fedora

Fedora is a popular Linux distribution whose primary sponsor is Red Hat.
Much of Fedora code ends up in Red Hat Enterprise Linux (RHEL) and
RHEL's free community-supported cousin CentOS. Fedora comes in many
editions, but only the Server edition is available for Arm processors. The
process to install Fedora is like installing Ubuntu and many other Linux
distributions.

I will be installing Fedora 34, but many other releases are known to work with ESXi on Arm.

The process of creating a Fedora VM is very similar to installing Ubuntu and many other Linux distributions.

The download site for the Arm Fedora images is `https://getfedora.org/en/server/download/`.

I will download *Fedora 34: Standard ISO image for aarch64* directly from this website to an ESXi datastore.

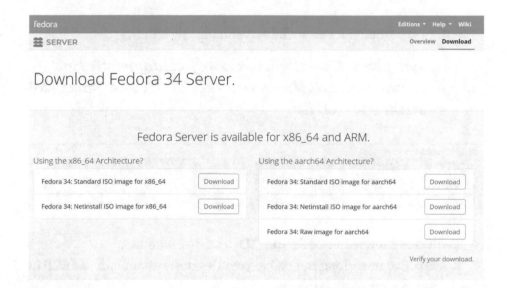

Download the Fedora 34 ISO

I will download the installation ISO directly to an ESXi datastore.

1. SSH into the ESXi system.

2. Gain root user privileges by entering

    sudo bash

3. Change to the directory where you want to store the ISO by entering

   `cd /vmfs/volumes/rPi-USB-Datastore-01`

4. Open the firewall to allow the HTTP connections by entering

   `esxcli network firewall ruleset set --enabled=true --ruleset-id=httpClient`

5. Download the Fedora 34 server image by entering

   `wget https://download.fedoraproject.org/pub/fedora/ linux/releases/34/Server/aarch64/iso/Fedora-Server-dvd- aarch64-34-1.2.iso`

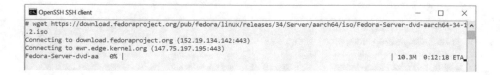

It will take a few minutes for the ISO to be downloaded.

You can also download the ISO to your desktop system and use SCP to copy it over to your ESXi datastore.

Create a Fedora VM

1. Log in to the ESXi Host Client.

2. In the Navigator select **Virtual Machines** and then click **Create / Register VM**.

3. In the New virtual machine wizard, select **Create a new virtual machine**, and click **Next**.

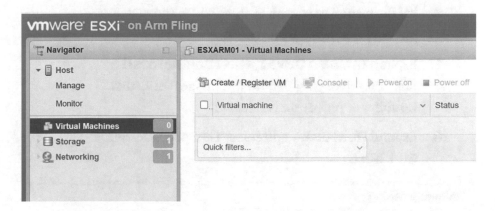

4. In the **Name** text box, enter *Fedora34_01*. From the **Guest OS family** drop-down menu, select **Linux**. In the **Guest OS version** drop-down menu, select **Red Hat Fedora (64-bit)** and click **Next**.

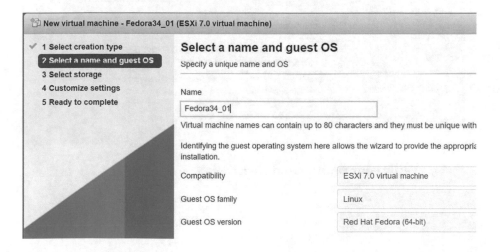

5. Verify that rPi-USB-Datastore-01 is the datastore, and click **Next**.

6. Set the virtual hardware to three CPUs and 4GB of memory and a 32GB hard disk.

7. Expand **CD/DVD Drive 1**, select **Datastore ISO file**, and select your Fedora ISO image. Verify that **Connect at power on** is selected.

8. Expand **Hard disk 1** and select **Thin provisioned**. Click **Next**.

Customize settings

Configure the virtual machine hardware and virtual machine additional options

Virtual Hardware	VM Options

   Add hard disk   Add network adapter   Add other device

▶ ☐ CPU	3 ⌄ ⓘ		
▶ ▦ Memory	4	GB ⌄	
▼ 💾 Hard disk 1	32	GB ⌄	⊗
Maximum Size	232.13 GB		
Location	[rPi-USB-Datastore-01] Fedora34_01/		Browse...
Disk Provisioning	◉ Thin provisioned ○ Thick provisioned, lazily zeroed ○ Thick provisioned, eagerly zeroed		

9. Verify your settings and click **Finish**.

Install Fedora 34 on the VM

Installing an OS on a VM is just like installing it on a physical machine.

I will be using VMRC, which was previously installed, to create the Fedora VM.

1. Right-click the Fedora virtual machine and select
    Launch remote console.

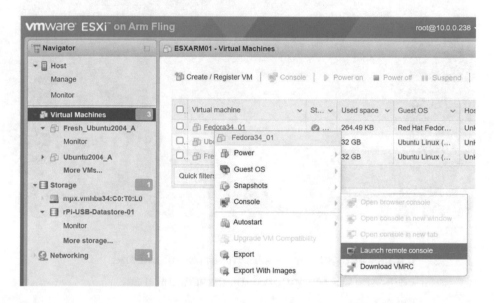

2. At the top of the VMRC, click the **Power On** icon.

3. In the display, select **Install Fedora 34**.

4. Follow the prompts to install Fedora. Set the root password and create a user when prompted.

5. It took about 30 minutes for me to download and install the OS. I monitored the installation from the console.

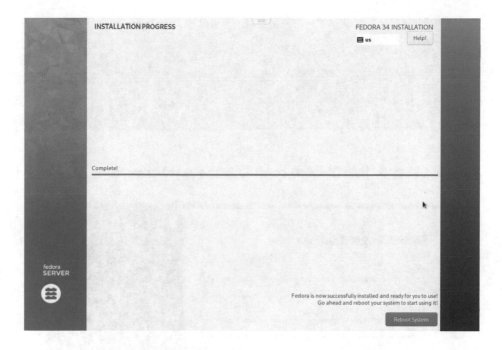

6. When the install has completed, select **Reboot Now**.

Configuring Fedora 34

Once the OS has been installed, you will want to do some post-installation configuration.

1. The system will reboot to the login prompt.

2. Although I could log on the system from the command prompt, I used the web portal to interact with the system. The IP address of the web console was displayed in the VMRC.

```
Fedora 34 (Server Edition)
Kernel 5.11.12-300.fc34.aarch64 on an aarch64 (tty1)

Web console: https://fedora:9090/ or https://10.0.0.234:9090/

fedora login:
```

3.   I logged into the web console as the user I created.

4.   After login into the web console, I was able to set the
     hostname by entering it in the Real **host name** text box.

5. In the logs, I noticed that SELinux was enabled.

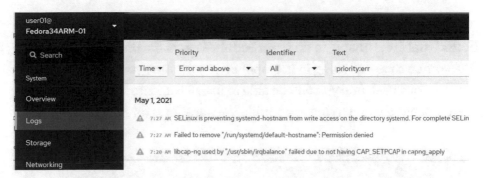

6. SELinux is a powerful security tool, but I have
    seen it to be overly restrictive. As I have a fairly
    secure environment, I opted to remove it. In the
    Applications tab, I selected it and clicked **Removed**.

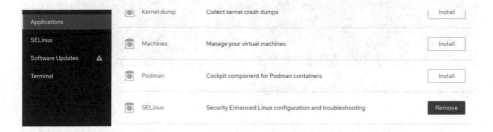

7. In the upper right, I selected Shutdown from the
    drop-down menu. In the host client, I used Edit
    settings to change the VM to have one CPU and 2GB
    RAM. This is needed as I plan on running multiple
    VMs on the ESXi server.

Installing VMware Tools on Fedora

VMware Tools should be installed on all guest OSs if possible. However, I found that I was unable to do so on Fedora 34 as at the time that I wrote this the source code had a bug in it. Hopefully, by the time you read this, the bug will be corrected, and you will be able to install it. Figure 8-2 shows the error that I received when trying to compile VMware Tools on Fedora 34.

```
/usr/include/glib-2.0/glib/gatomic.h:117:5: error: argument 2 of '_atomic_load' discards 'volatile' qualifier [-Werror=
incompatible-pointer-types]
  117 |     __atomic_load (gapg_temp_atomic, &gapg_temp_newval, __ATOMIC_SEQ_CST); \
      |     ^~~~~~~~~~~~~
/usr/include/glib-2.0/glib/gthread.h:260:7: note: in expansion of macro 'g_atomic_pointer_get'
  260 |     (!g_atomic_pointer_get (location) &&                          \
      |      ^~~~~~~~~~~~~~~~~~~~
pollGtk.c:1488:8: note: in expansion of macro 'g_once_init_enter'
 1488 |     if (g_once_init_enter(&inited)) {
      |        ^~~~~~~~~~~~~~~~~
cc1: all warnings being treated as errors
make[2]: *** [Makefile:509: pollGtk.lo] Error 1
make[2]: Leaving directory '/tmp/open-vm-tools/open-vm-tools/lib/pollGtk'
make[1]: *** [Makefile:500: install-recursive] Error 1
make[1]: Leaving directory '/tmp/open-vm-tools/open-vm-tools/lib'
make: *** [Makefile:544: install-recursive] Error 1
● vmtoolsd.service - Service for virtual machines hosted on VMware
     Loaded: loaded (/etc/systemd/system/vmtoolsd.service; enabled; vendor preset: enabled)
     Active: activating (auto-restart) (Result: exit-code) since Sat 2021-05-01 09:42:27 PDT; 46ms ago
       Docs: http://github.com/vmware/open-vm-tools
    Process: 11679 ExecStart=/usr/local/bin/vmtoolsd (code=exited, status=203/EXEC)
   Main PID: 11679 (code=exited, status=203/EXEC)
        CPU: 5ms

May 01 09:42:27 fedora34arm-01 systemd[1]: vmtoolsd.service: Failed with result 'exit-code'.
[root@fedora34arm-01 tmp]#
```

Figure 8-2. *VMware Tools Build Error*

Creating a Fedora 34 VM was straightforward. Although I was unable to install VMware Tools, it still performed well.

Photon OS

Photon OS is not an extremely popular OS, but it is an important OS for ESXi as it is primarily maintained by VMware. It is an extremely lightweight OS that has been highly optimized to run on ESXi and only includes the drivers necessary to run on a VMware hypervisor (ESXi, Workstation, and

Fusion) or on one of the supported public clouds. It's freely available, is easy to install on vSphere, and can be used as a base OS for your project. It is a little bit different to install and use than other Linux distributions.

There is a Raspberry Pi and full ISO Arm64 image. The Pi image is meant to run natively on a Pi you will want to install the full Arm64 Photon OS 4.0 GA release.

The download site for the Arm images is `https://github.com/vmware/photon/wiki/Downloading-Photon-OS`

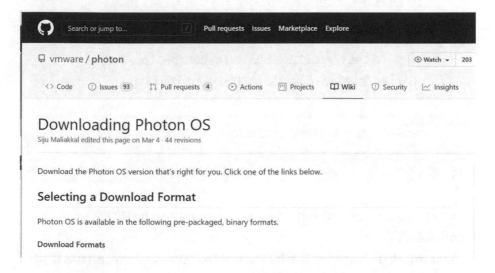

The following are the steps to install Photon OS on your Pi.

Download Photon OS

We will be downloading the installation ISO directly to the ESXi datastore. Later we will use the ISO to install the system.

1. SSH into the ESXi system.

2. Gain root user privileges by entering

   sudo bash

3. Change to the directory where you want to store the ISO by entering

    `cd /vmfs/volumes/rPi-USB-Datastore-01`

4. Open the firewall to allow the HTTP connections by entering

    `esxcli network firewall ruleset set --enabled=true`
    `--ruleset-id=httpClient`

5. Download the Arm image by entering

    wget `https://packages.vmware.com/photon/4.0/`
    `GA/iso/photon-4.0-1526e30ba-aarch64.iso`

It is 2.9GB in size and will take a few minutes for the ISO to be downloaded.

You can also download the ISO to your desktop system and use SCP to copy it over to your ESXi host.

Create a Photon VM

1. Log in to the ESXi Host Client.

2. In the Navigator select **Virtual Machines** and then click **Create / Register VM**.

3. In the New virtual machine wizard, select **Create a new virtual machine**, and click **Next**.

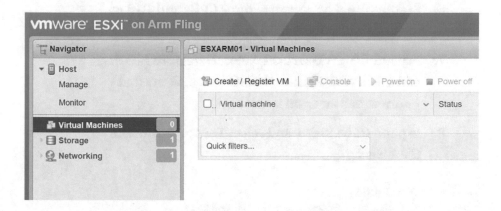

4. In the **Name** text box, enter *PhotonOS40*. From the **Guest OS family** drop-down menu, select **Linux**. In the **Guest OS version** drop-down menu, select **VMware Photon OS (64-bit)** and click **Next**.

5. Verify that rPi-USB-Datastore-01 is the datastore, and click **Next**.

6. Set the virtual hardware to three CPUs and 4GB of memory and a 32GB hard disk.

7. Expand **CD/DVD Drive 1**, select **Datastore ISO file**, and select your Photon OS ISO image. Verify that **Connect at power on** is selected.

8. Expand **Hard disk 1** and select **Thin provisioned**. Click **Next**.

Customize settings

Configure the virtual machine hardware and virtual machine additional options

Virtual Hardware	VM Options

🖴 Add hard disk   ▦ Add network adapter   🖴 Add other device

▸ 🖴 CPU	3 ⌄ ℹ️
▸ ▦ Memory	4 | GB ⌄
▾ 🖴 Hard disk 1	32 | GB ⌄

Maximum Size	126.6 GB
Location	[rPi-USB-Datastore-01] PhotonOS40/ Browse...
Disk Provisioning	⦿ Thin provisioned
	○ Thick provisioned, lazily zeroed
	○ Thick provisioned, eagerly zeroed

9. Verify your settings and click **Finish**.

Install Photon on the VM

I will be using VMRC, which was previously installed, to install the OS.

1. Right-click the Photon OS virtual machine and select **Launch remote console**.

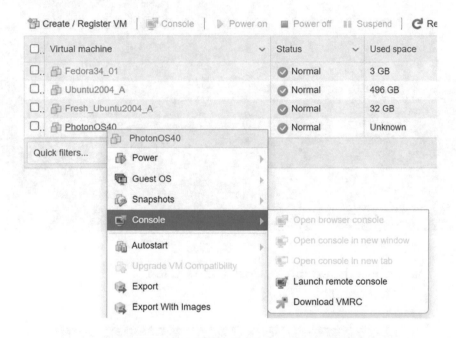

2. At the top of the VMRC, click the **Power On** icon.

3. Accept the EULA.

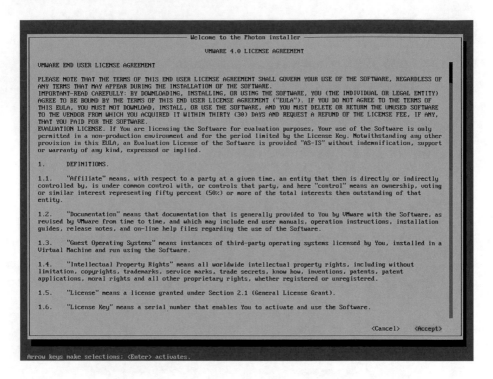

4. Follow the prompts to install the Photon Minimal OS.

5. Accept all the defaults.

6. It takes a few minutes to install the OS. It displays an elapsed timer during the install. It took me 96 seconds to install it.

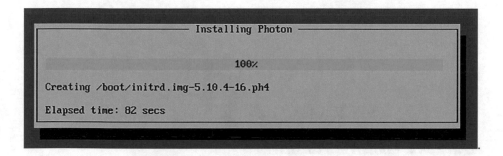

7. When the install has completed, press any key to boot it.

Configuring Photon

Once the OS has been installed, you will want to do some post-installation configuration.

1. The system will reboot with a splash screen. The OS does some configuration during this time, and so you will see the splash screen while it does the configuration (see Figure 8-3).

Figure 8-3. *Photon Splash Screen*

2. It took a few minutes, but I was finally presented with a login prompt.

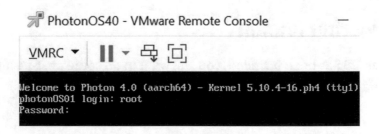

3. Verify the IP address by entering

   Ip addr

4. I ran the following sed command to allow SSH root login:

   sed -i 's/PermitRootLogin no/PermitRootLogin yes/g' /etc/ssh/sshd_config

5. Restart the SSH service by entering

    systemctl restart sshd

6. Verify that the root user can log in using SSH:

    ssh root@localhost

7. Log out of the SSH session by entering

    exit

8. Shut down the VM by entering

    Init 0

9. Edit the settings to change it to one CPU and 2GB
    RAM if you plan on running multiple instances of
    Photon on it. You can even use 1GB of RAM.

Installing VMware Tools on Photon

VMware Tools should be installed on all guest OSs if possible. Fortunately,
you can install open-vm-tools as a package rather than having to build it.

1. Power on the VM and log in to it as root from VMRC
    or SSH.

2. Install the open-vm-tools package by entering

    tdnf -y install open-vm-tools

3. Enable and start VMware Tools by entering

    systemctl enable vmtoolsd.service
    systemctl start vmtoolsd.service

4. Verify what services are started by entering

    systemctl status

5. In the output verify that vmtoolsd.service is shown.

Select OpenSSH SSH client

```
root@photonOS01 [ ~ ]# systemctl enable vmtoolsd.service
root@photonOS01 [ ~ ]# systemctl start vmtoolsd.service
root@photonOS01 [ ~ ]# systemctl status
● photonOS01
    State: running
     Jobs: 0 queued
   Failed: 0 units
    Since: Tue 2020-09-01 15:24:58 UTC; 8 months 1 days ago
   CGroup: /
           ├─user.slice
           │ └─user-0.slice
           │   ├─session-c1.scope
           │   │ ├─501 sshd: root@pts/0
           │   │ ├─555 -bash
           │   │ ├─674 systemctl status
           │   │ └─675 less
           │   └─user@0.service …
           │     └─init.scope
           │       ├─540 /usr/lib/systemd/systemd --user
           │       └─541 (sd-pam)
           ├─init.scope
           │ └─1 /usr/lib/systemd/systemd --switched-root --system --deserialize 16
           └─system.slice
             ├─systemd-networkd.service
             │ └─511 /usr/lib/systemd/systemd-networkd
             ├─systemd-udevd.service
             │ └─446 /usr/lib/systemd/systemd-udevd
             ├─vgauthd.service
             │ └─630 /usr/bin/VGAuthService -s
             ├─systemd-journald.service
             │ └─425 /usr/lib/systemd/systemd-journald
             ├─systemd-userdbd.service
             │ ├─522 /usr/lib/systemd/systemd-userdbd
             │ ├─523 systemd-userwork
             │ ├─524 systemd-userwork
             │ └─525 systemd-userwork
             ├─vmtoolsd.service
             │ └─631 /usr/bin/vmtoolsd
             ├─systemd-resolved.service
             │ └─513 /usr/lib/systemd/systemd-resolved
             ├─dbus.service
             │ └─485 /usr/bin/dbus-daemon --system --address=systemd: --nofork --nopidf
             ├─systemd-timesyncd.service
             │ └─474 /usr/lib/systemd/systemd-timesyncd
             ├─system-getty.slice
             │ └─getty@tty1.service
             │   └─534 /sbin/agetty -o -p -- \u --noclear tty1 linux
             └─systemd-logind.service
               └─486 /usr/lib/systemd/systemd-logind
root@photonOS01 [ ~ ]# 
```

6. In the host client verify that VMware Tools
    is running.

Photon OS is an extremely lightweight OS. After I rebooted my VM,
it only used 0.5GB of RAM. It was nice that it had a package for the
installation of VMware Tools. It is a little bit different to administer than
other Linux distributions, but there are user and admin guides on the
Photon OS website.

Fun fact: The package manager tdnf is an acronym for Tiny
Dandified Yum!

Snapshots

ESXi has the ability to take snapshots of VMs. This is a powerful technology
as it allows you to preserve the state and data of a machine at a particular
point of time. I find it useful to take a snapshot before doing a big change
to a VM like updating it or installing an application on it. If the update
completes successfully, I commit the snapshot into the VM.

I have also found this feature useful when teaching classes. After
walking my students through a process, I can revert the machine back to its
original state and have the next class do the same exercise without having
to reinstall the OS.

A VM can have multiple snapshots, and you can take snapshots regardless if a VM is powered on or off. If a snapshot is taken of an active VM, it will capture the current state of its RAM as well as its disks. Due to the resources required when taking a live snapshot, I take snapshots of VMs that have been powered down. There are many nuances with snapshots that we will not be covering here, but VMware has many excellent documents available to assist and answer questions on the topic.

Working with Snapshots

Snapshots can be initiated from the ESXi Host Client.

1. Log on the ESXi Host Client.

2. In the Navigator double-click **Virtual Machines**.

3. Verify that the Fedora machine is powered off.

4. Right-click the Fedora VM and from the **Snapshots** drop-down menu select **Take snapshot**.

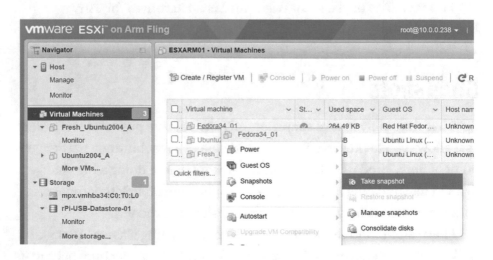

5. In the **Name** text box, enter *First Snapshot,* and click
   Take snapshot.

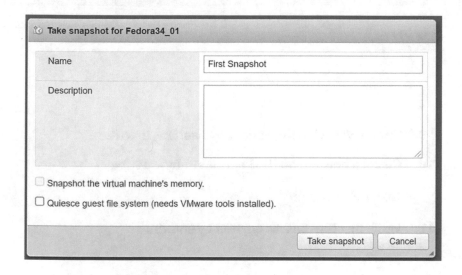

6. Taking a snapshot of a powered-off machine is
   very quick.

7. Right-click the Fedora VM and from the **Snapshots**
   drop-down menu select **Manage snapshots**.

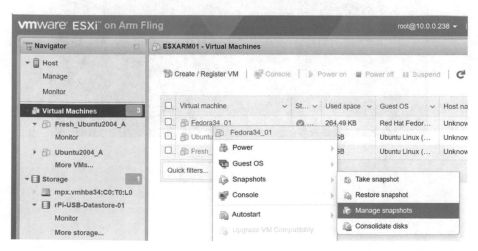

8.   Verify that **First Snapshot** is shown, and click **Close**.

9.   Open a VMRC to the Fedora VM and log in to it.

10.   Create a new file on the Fedora VM by entering

Touch MyNewFile

11.   Verify that the file was created by entering

ls -lart

12.   Shut down the VM using the VMRC.

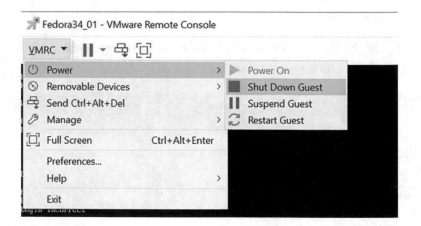

13. Right-click the Fedora VM and from the **Snapshots**
     drop-down menu select **Manage snapshots**.

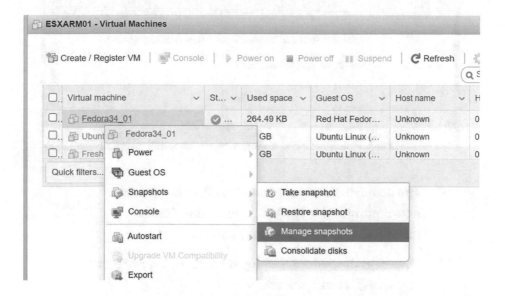

14. Click **First Snapshot** and click **Delete snapshot**.

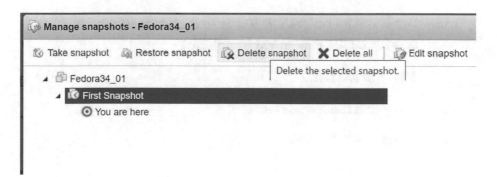

15.   Click **Remove**.

16.   The snapshot is removed, and all the changes are
      now committed to the VM, and all the changes
      made to the VM are now permanent.

17.   Power on the Fedora VM, log on to it, and verify that
      MyNewFile is still present.

18.   Power down the Fedora VM. Take a snapshot of it
      called *Second Snapshot*.

19.   Power on the Fedora VM, log on to it, and create a
      new file on the Fedora VM by entering

      touch NewFile002

20.   Verify that the file was created.

21.   Power down the VM.

22.   In the snapshot manager select **Second Snapshot**
and click **Restore snapshot**, and click **Restore.**

23.   Power on the Fedora VM and verify that *NewFile002*
is no longer present.

24.   Power down the VM.

Summary

In this chapter, we created Fedora, Ubuntu, and Photon OS VMs and
copied the files that compose a VM to create another VM from them. We
also talked about VMware Tools, the types of virtual disks that can be used
with VMs, and how to take snapshots.

We used USB devices to store our VMs on. These are less than ideal,
but they are usable. I monitored the USB that I was using for storage and
noticed that when copying the files to create a new VM, it reached 121
degrees Fahrenheit (50 degrees Celsius); this can have an adverse effect on
the performance and life of the device. In the next chapters, we will look at
a few other storage options that are more appropriate.

CHAPTER 9

Network Storage Options for ESXi

Network storage is a huge game changer for vSphere – it both frees ESXi hosts from the physical limits of how much storage a host can support and allows the VMs stored on it to run on any host with access.

In this chapter, I will be going over and explaining how to set up two different network storage methods: Network File System (NFS) and Internet Small Computer Systems Interface (iSCSI). I will demonstrate how to provide network storage using a Windows and Linux system and will use a Type 2 hypervisor to run the Linux system as a VM on a laptop.

Note A key difference between NFS and iSCSI to remember as you work through this chapter is that NFS shares files over the network, whereas iSCSI shares a block device over it; NFS is for files, and iSCSI is for blocks.

So far, we have only used local storage to create and store VMs. While this setup is acceptable for limited use cases, the real power of virtualization lies within the layers of abstraction that it provides. These layers allow a VM to be started on any server that has access to those files. Figure 9-1 shows that a VM on shared storage can run on any connected ESXi host, thereby greatly increasing business continuity.

© Thomas Fenton and Patrick Kennedy 2022
T. Fenton and P. Kennedy, *Running ESXi on a Raspberry Pi*,
https://doi.org/10.1007/978-1-4842-7465-1_9

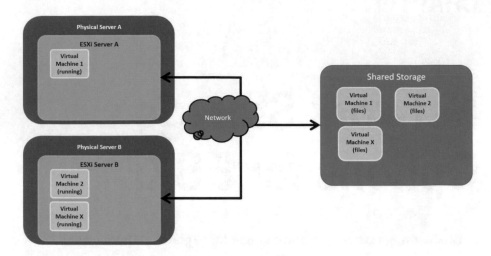

Figure 9-1. *Shared Storage and ESXi*

If an ESXi host goes down, you can restart the VMs on a host that is still operational (see Figure 9-2).

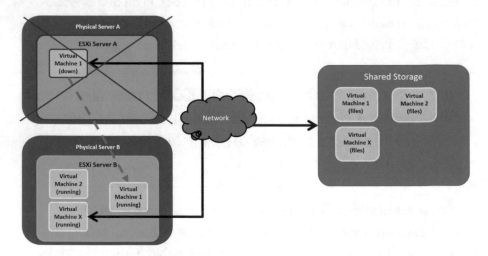

Figure 9-2. *Failed System*

You can also place VMs on the host with the most resources (e.g., CPU, RAM, etc.) to balance the workload for performance reasons (see Figure 9-3).

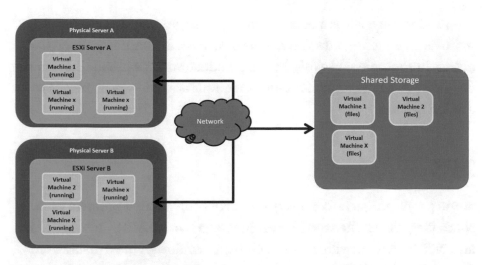

Figure 9-3. *Balanced Workload*

Figure 9-4 shows how you can use NFS and iSCSI on multiple ESXi hosts.

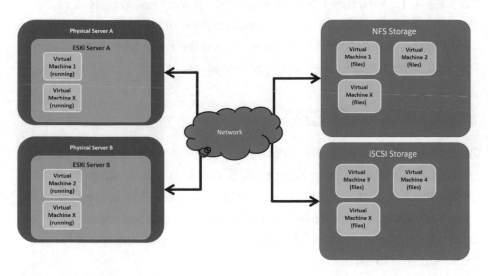

Figure 9-4. *iSCSI and NFS on ESXi Hosts*

Production environments use storage arrays or appliances connected to hosts via a high-bandwidth network. As it is unlikely that you will have access to equipment like this, in this demonstration I will show how to use Windows and Linux machines for the storage and delivery of the VMs over a 1GbE network.

NFS

Some people might be confused about NFS and another protocol used to share files over the network, Server Message Block (SMB). Although SMB and NFS both work with various OSs (e.g., Windows, Linux, macOS, etc.), the reality is that SMB is most often used by Windows and macOS systems, while NFS is more often used by Linux and Unix systems. **ESXi does not support SMB**.

Initially, ESXi only supported NFS v3, but it later gained support for NFS v4.1. The major difference between these versions is that v4.1 supports having multiple network connections, or multipathing. This setup allows multiple IP addresses to access the same NFS share, thereby increasing both redundancy and performance.

Using NFS with ESXi

In the early days of ESXi, NFS was by far the most popular shared storage method. This was not surprising as NFS has been around since the 1990s and has proven to be an extremely robust, reliable, and efficient mechanism to deliver files between different systems. All modern operating systems support NFS, and it is supported by a range of systems, from Android to mainframes.

Figure 9-5 shows the architecture of NFS. It uses an *NFS Server* to store and share the files and an *NFS Client* to access the files that are being shared. In the examples shown, the NFS Client will run on the ESXi host, and we will set up another system to act as an NFS Server. Clients *mount* the folder that is being shared by the NFS Server, while the NFS Server holds the file system with directory and files being shared.

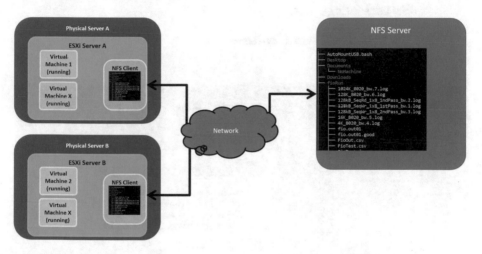

Figure 9-5. *NFS Architecture*

Both Linux and Windows Server can be used as NFS Servers. If you do not have an extra physical system to run Windows or Linux on, you can run a Type 2 hypervisor, such as VMware Player, on an existing Windows or Linux system. In a later section, I will walk you through using Player to set up a Linux VM to act as an iSCSI target, but you can run Windows Server on it as well.

Setting Up an NFS Server on Windows

Windows Server has long supported acting as an NFS Server. The following instructions were done using Windows 2016 Server, but other versions of Windows Server will work as well.

1. In the Run command window, enter *ServerManager.exe*.

2. Click **Add roles and features**.

3. In the Add Roles and Features Wizard, click **Next**.

4. Selected **Role-based or feature-based installation**, and click **Next**.

5. Click **Next**.

6. Expand **File and Storage Services**, and expand **File and iSCSI Services**.

7. Click the **Server for NFS** checkbox. When the *Add features that are required for Server for NFS?* dialog box appears, click **Add features**, and then click **Next**.

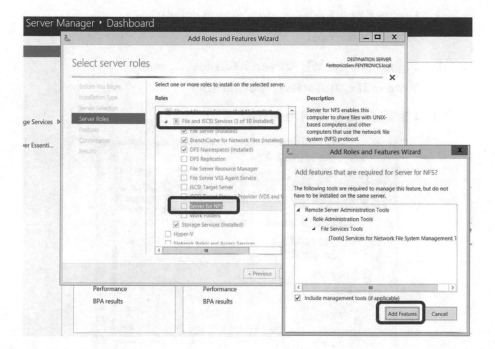

8. Click **Next** and then **Install**.

9. Click **Close**.

10. Restart your system and log back into it.

Share a Windows Server Directory via NFS

Once NFS has been installed, you can share a folder on your Windows system via NFS.

1. Create a new folder on the desktop called WinServerNFS01.

2. Right-click the **WinServerNFS01** folder, select **Properties**, and select **NFS Sharing**.

3. Click **Manage NFS Sharing**.

4. Click **Share this folder**, click the **Permissions** button, and click **Allow root access**.

5. From the **Type of access** drop-down menu, select **Read-Write**.

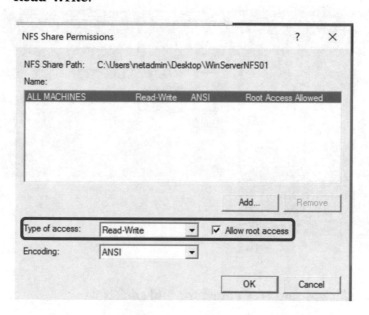

6. Click **OK**, click **Apply**, and click **OK**.

7. Click **Close**.

Connecting an ESXi Host to an NFS Server

As a disclaimer, VMware does not endorse, recommend, or support using Windows Server as an NFS datastore on ESXi, and it is not on their Hardware Compatibility List (HCL). The following instructions are to show that it can be done, not that it should be done. That said, I mounted the NFS on my ESXi host and have used it without any problems.

1. From the VMware Host Client Navigator, click **Storage**.

2. Click **New datastore**.

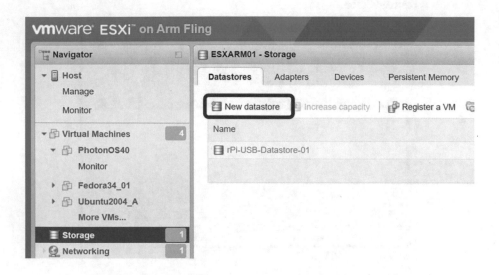

3. Click **Mount NFS datastore**, and click **Next**.

4. Give the NFS share a name and enter the IP address of your NFS Server (the Windows Server). Select **NFS 3** and click **Next**.

5. Click **Finish**.

6. In the Navigator select **Storage** and verify that the NFS share is shown.

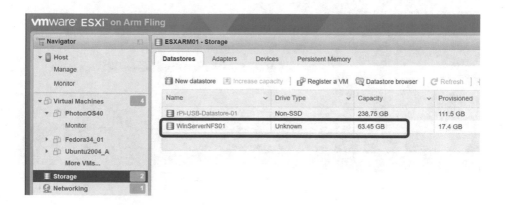

Creating a VM Using NFS Storage

VMs can be stored on an NFS share just like any other datastore.

1. In the Navigator right-click **Virtual Machines** and select **Create/Register VM**.

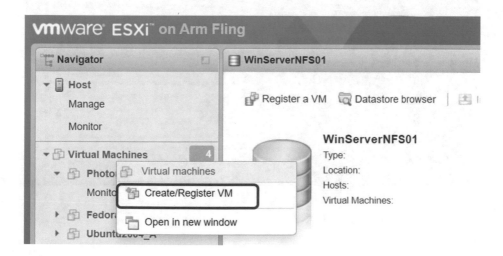

2. Create a VM as you would with any other VM but select an NFS share for its storage.

3. Verify that the VM will be using NFS storage.

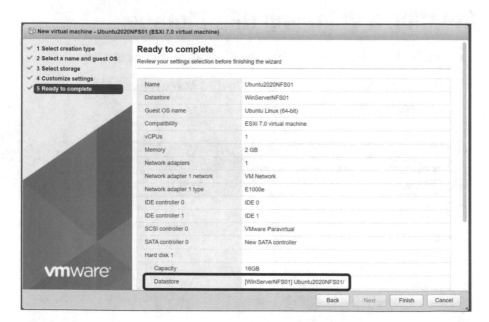

4. You can use the **Datastore browser** to see the files
    that make up the VM are stored on the NFS Server.

Copying a VM Stored on a Local Datastore to an NFS Share

NFS shares are shown under /vmfs/volumes like the local datastores we
created. In the following, I will show you how to copy an existing VM from
a local datastore to NFS from the ESXi host command line.

1. Log on to your ESXi host from the host console or
    using SSH.

2. Change to the datastore directory by entering

    cd /vmfs/volumes

3. Create a new directory and copy an existing VM to it.
    I used the *time* command to see how long the copy
    took by entering

    mkdir WinServerNFS01/Ubuntu_NFS01
    time cp -r rPi-USB-Datastore-01/Fresh_Ubuntu2004/*
    WinServerNFS01/Ubuntu_NFS01

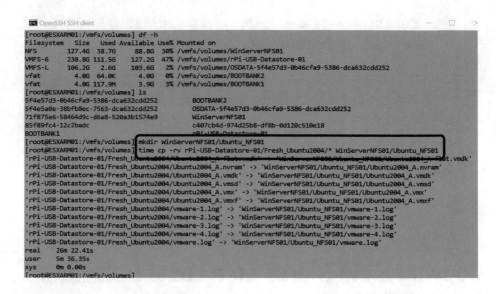

4.   You may want to monitor the network and disk
     activity using the VMware Host Client while the copy
     takes place. It took me 26 minutes to copy the VM
     from my USB backed local storage to my NFS share.

5.   Once the files have been copied, use the Datastore
     browser in the VMware Host Client to register the VM.

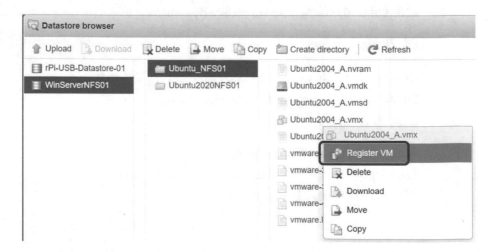

6. The VM can now be started like any other VM.

Connecting an NFS Share to a Linux System

You can connect a Linux system to an NFS share. Although it is best practice to have an NFS share dedicated to an ESXi host, in the past I have found it useful to connect an NFS share to a Linux host while troubleshooting issues. We will connect the Windows NFS share to the Ubuntu system that we had previously installed on our ESXi host (Figure 9-6).

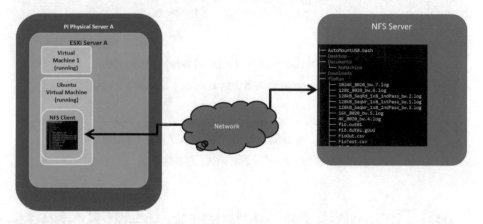

Figure 9-6. *NFS to Linux System*

1. Power on the Ubuntu system.

2. Log in to the system using SSH or from its terminal.

3. Switch to root user by entering

    sudo su

4. Install the NFS Client by entering

    apt install nfs-common

5. Create a mount point, mount the NFS on the mount point, and list the NFS by entering

```
mkdir /mnt/NFS01
mount.nfs 10.0.0.209:/WinServerNFS01 /mnt/NFS01
mount
```

```
root@ubuntu2004-a:/home/user01# apt install nfs-common
Reading package lists... Done
Building dependency tree
Reading state information... Done
nfs-common is already the newest version (1:1.3.4-2.5ubuntu3.3).
0 upgraded, 0 newly installed, 0 to remove and 62 not upgraded.
root@ubuntu2004-a:/home/user01# mkdir /mnt/NFS01
root@ubuntu2004-a:/home/user01# mount.nfs 10.0.0.209:/WinServerNFS01 /mnt/NFS01
```

6. If you would like the NFS mounted every time the system boots up, you can add an entry in /etc/fstab by entering

```
echo '10.0.0.209:WinServerNFS01 /mnt/NFS01
NFS    defaults 0 0' >> /etc/fstab
```

Final Thoughts on Setting Up an NFS Share

In total, it took me less than 15 minutes to create an NFS Server on my Windows Server and mount it to my ESXi host.

VMware Player

VMware has three Type 2 hypervisors: Workstation, Fusion, and Player. These products are used by developers, students, and home users who want to run different OSs on their desktops and laptops. Workstation runs on Windows and Linux x64 systems and is VMware's first and oldest product. Workstation is reasonably priced and has a loyal following of users.

Fusion runs on macOS and is used by people who want to run Windows and Linux systems on their macOS. Player runs on Windows and Linux x64 systems and can be thought of as a stripped-down or limited version of Workstation. Player has a free unsupported version as well as a supported version that is not free.

In this section, I will show how I installed the free version of Player. In a later section, I will show how to use Player to create a Linux VM that will act as an iSCSI target. Figure 9-7 shows how Player runs just as any other Windows or Linux application.

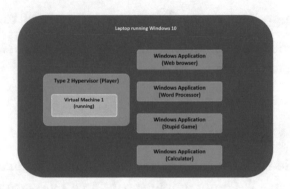

Figure 9-7. *VMware Player*

VMware Player Requirements

The free version of Player is limited to managing a single VM at a time, cannot take snapshots of the VMs, and has limited networking options and other limitations.

The requirements for Player are quite modest:

- 1GHz or faster 64-bit processor (2GHz recommended)

- 2GB RAM minimum (4GB RAM recommended):

  - The RAM required for each guest operating system and for applications on the host and guest is not included in the 2GB requirement (and thus 4GB is recommended).

- 215MB of disk space to download Player

- 150MB of disk space to install Player

- Enough disk space for the VM that you will be creating

- A supported version of Windows or Linux it will run

See Player documentation for the full requirements at `www.vmware.com/support/pubs/player_pubs.html`.

Installing VMware Player

Player is installed in the manner as any other application and is very lightweight when a VM is not running on it. Once a VM is running, it will consume the resources needed for the VM.

The following instructions show you how to install Player on a Windows 10 system.

1. From your Windows system, use a web browser to go to `www.vmware.com/products/workstation-player.html` and download VMware Workstation Player. The ISO image is ~215MB in size and should download quickly.

2. Double-click the downloaded file and accept the
   prompts to install it.

3. At the end of the install, you will be asked if you
   want to license it or not. Click **Finish** to run the
   unlicensed version.

4. In your Windows search box, enter *player* and
   launch Player.

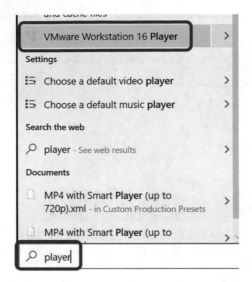

5.   Follow the prompts to start Player.

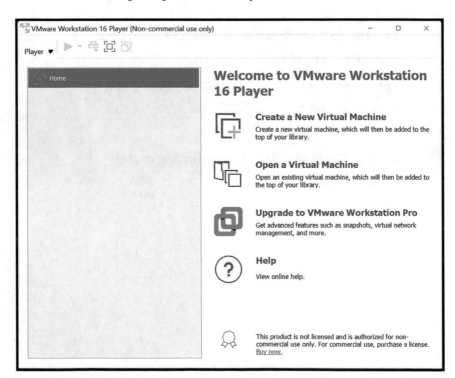

Installing Ubuntu on Player

You will be installing Ubuntu-20.04 desktop on Player. You will not be able to use the ISO that you previously used to create VMs on the Pi as you need an x64-compatible installation ISO.

You will initially create a VM with a 32GB virtual disk and then add a second 100GB virtual disk to it to act as an iSCSI target.

1. From your Windows system, use a web browser to go to `https://releases.ubuntu.com/20.04/` and download Ubuntu 20.04 server. The ISO image is ~1.1GB in size and will take a while to download.

ubuntu® releases

Ubuntu 20.04.2.0 LTS (Focal Fossa)

Select an image

Ubuntu is distributed on four types of images described below.

Desktop image

The desktop image allows you to try Ubuntu without changing your computer at all, and at your option to install it permanently later. This type of image is what most people will want to use. You will need at least 1024MiB of RAM to install from this image.

64-bit PC (AMD64) desktop image

Choose this if you have a computer based on the AMD64 or EM64T architecture (e.g., Athlon64, Opteron, EM64T Xeon, Core 2). Choose this if you are at all unsure.

Server install image

The server install image allows you to install Ubuntu permanently on a computer for use as a server. It will not install a graphical user interface.

64-bit PC (AMD64) server install image

Choose this if you have a computer based on the AMD64 or EM64T architecture (e.g., Athlon64, Opteron, EM64T Xeon, Core 2). Choose this if you are at all unsure.

199

2. In Player select **Create a New Virtual Machine**.

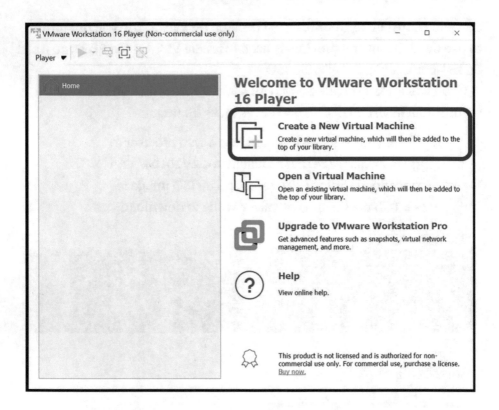

3. Select **Installer disc image file**, browse to and select the Ubuntu ISO image, and click **Next**.

4. In the **Full name** text box, enter *Ubuntu2004 iSCSI Server*, enter a username and password, and click **Next**.

5. In the **Virtual Machine name** text box, enter *Ubuntu2004 iSCSI Server*, **and** click **Next**.

6. In the **Maximum disk size** text box, enter *32*, and click **Next**.

7. Click **Finish**.

8. Player will mount the ISO and start the VM.

9. Allow the system to download and install VMware Tools.

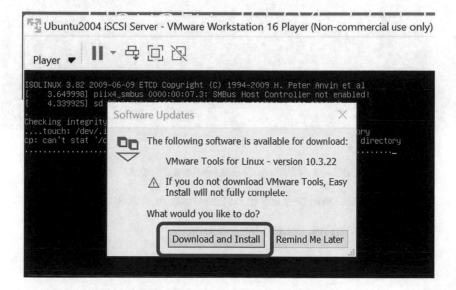

10. Accept the defaults. When asked for the machine name, enter *ubuntuiscsiI01*.

11. When asked to install an OpenSSH server, say yes.

12. Allow the system to install.

13. Watch the upper left of Player to indicate that the install has completed.

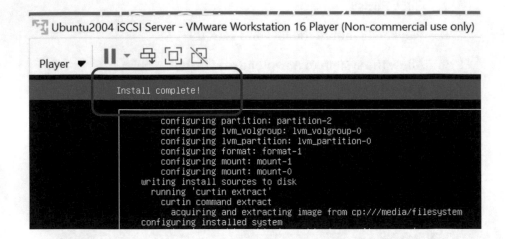

14. At the bottom of Player, select **Reboot Now**.

15. Verify that you can log in to the Ubuntu system.

16. Shut down the system by entering

    sudo init 0

Add a Second Hard Drive to a Player VM

Once the VM has been installed, you will add a second 100GB virtual hard drive to the VM. This VM will be used as an iSCSI target. If you lack the disk space, you can create a 36GB virtual hard drive.

1. Launch Player.

2. Right-click the Ubuntu VM. Select **Settings**.

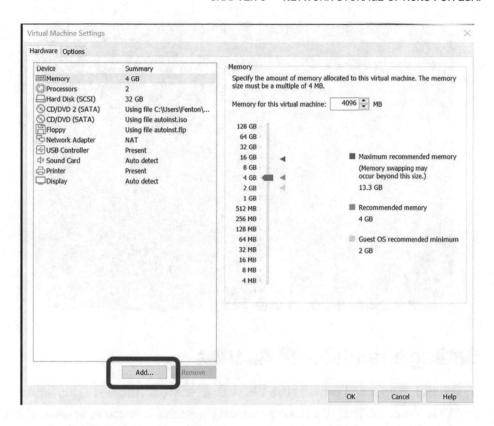

3. Click **Add**, select **Hard Disk**, and click **Next**.

4. Verify that **SCSI** is selected, and click **Next**.

5. Select **Create a new virtual disk**, and click **Next**.

6. Set the size to 100GB, and click **Next**.

7. In the **File Name** text box, enter *iSCSI Target*, and click **Finish**.

8. Click **OK** to close the Settings dialog box.

9. The VM will now have two virtual disks associated with it. Linux presents these disks as sda and sdb.

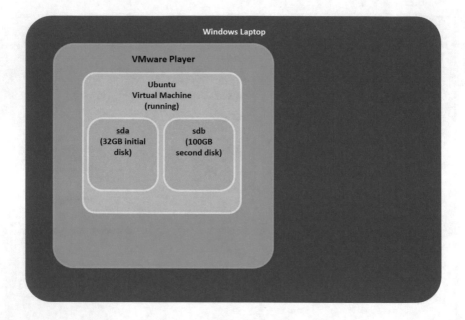

Getting a Routable IP Address

By default, Player will provide the VM with a Network Address Translation (NAT) IP address. This IP can be accessed through the same address as the laptop. We will want bridged networking for the address for iSCSI as it will get its own IP address from your physical network rather from the system Player is running on.

Figure 9-8 shows the difference between a VM with a NAT and a bridged IP address.

Figure 9-8. *NAT IP Address vs. Bridged*

1. Right-click the Ubuntu VM and select **Power On**.

2. Log on to the system.

3. In the terminal, enter *ip add*.

   The IP address will be a Network Address
   Translation (NAT) IP address, which is provided by
   Player. We will change it to a bridged IP address.

4. From the **Player** drop-down menu, select **Manage
   ➤ Virtual Machine Settings**.

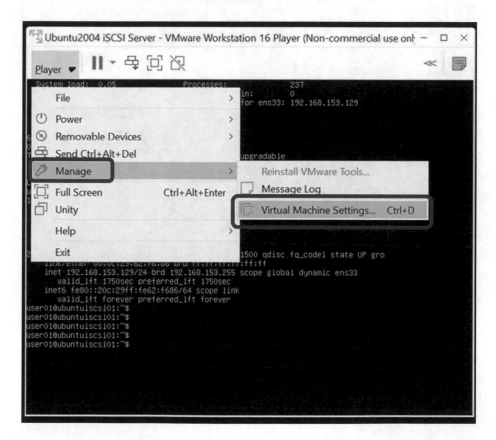

5. Select **Network Adapter**, select **Bridged**, and click **Configure Adapters**.

6. If you have multiple adapters, deselect all the network adapters except the one that has connectivity to your network. Click **OK**.

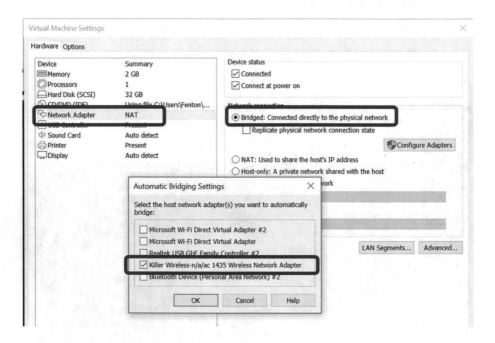

7. Click **OK** to close the Settings dialog box.

8. In the terminal enter **ip add** and verify that you have a bridged IP address.

iSCSI

As noted earlier, NFS shares files, and iSCSI shares block devices. This means that a VMFS will need to be put on the iSCSI target after it has been shared with an ESXi system. There are different reasons why people choose to use either NFS or iSCSI for storage, and it would take a rather long time to discuss the advantages of one over the other. As a matter of principle, however, vSphere can use either NFS or iSCSI, and many systems use both simultaneously.

Before diving in, here are some quick definitions of some key iSCSI concepts shown in Figure 9-9. An *iSCSI target* is the block device to be shared, an *iSCSI initiator* is the client that attaches to the target, and the *iSCSI Qualified Name (IQN)* is the name that's used to identify both targets and initiators.

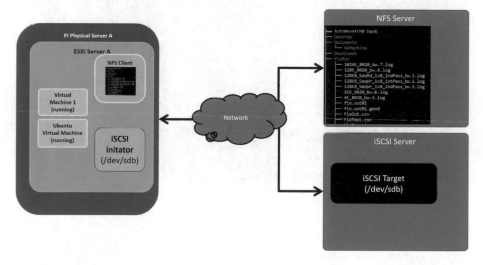

Figure 9-9. *iSCSI Topography*

In this section, you will learn how to create an iSCSI target on the Ubuntu 20.04 system running on Player.

Installing and Configuring iSCSI on Ubuntu

As iSCSI shares a block device rather than files, you will use the second hard disk for the iSCSI target, rather than a directory like you did with NFS.

1. Log in to your Ubuntu system and switch to root user by entering

   sudo su

2. Show the block devices on the system by entering

   lsblk

3. Verify that the new block device is identified as */dev/sdb*.

```
root@ubuntuiscsi01:/home/user01# lsblk
NAME                       MAJ:MIN RM   SIZE RO TYPE MOUNTPOINT
fd0                            2:0  1   1.4M  0 disk
loop0                          7:0  0  31.1M  1 loop /snap/snapd/10707
loop1                          7:1  0  55.4M  1 loop /snap/core18/1944
loop2                          7:2  0  69.9M  1 loop /snap/lxd/19188
sda                            8:0  0    32G  0 disk
├─sda1                         8:1  0     1M  0 part
├─sda2                         8:2  0     1G  0 part /boot
└─sda3                         8:3  0    31G  0 part
  └─ubuntu--vg-ubuntu--lv    253:0  0    20G  0 lvm  /
sdb                           8:16  0   100G  0 disk
sr0                           11:0  1  93.2M  0 rom
sr1                           11:1  1   1.1G  0 rom
root@ubuntuiscsi01:/home/user01#
```

4. Create a new Linux primary partition on */dev/sdb*
    using *fdisk*. Allow it to consume all the space on the
    drive by entering

    ```
    fdisk /dev/sdb
    n
    p
    1
    Enter
    Enter
    w
    ```

```
root@ubuntuiscsi01:/home/user01# fdisk /dev/sdb

Welcome to fdisk (util-linux 2.34).
Changes will remain in memory only, until you decide to write them.
Be careful before using the write command.

Device does not contain a recognized partition table.
Created a new DOS disklabel with disk identifier 0xfc0d3db3.

Command (m for help): n
Partition type
   p   primary (0 primary, 0 extended, 4 free)
   e   extended (container for logical partitions)
Select (default p): p
Partition number (1-4, default 1): 1
First sector (2048-209715199, default 2048):
Last sector, +/-sectors or +/-size{K,M,G,T,P} (2048-209715199, default 209715199):

Created a new partition 1 of type 'Linux' and of size 100 GiB.

Command (m for help): w
The partition table has been altered.
Calling ioctl() to re-read partition table.
Syncing disks.

root@ubuntuiscsi01:/home/user01#
```

5. Show the block devices on the system and verify that
    the new partition on the device is identified as *sdb1*
    by entering

    lsblk

```
root@ubuntuiscsi01:/home/user01# lsblk
NAME                      MAJ:MIN RM   SIZE RO TYPE MOUNTPOINT
fd0                           2:0  1  1.4M  0 disk
loop0                         7:0  0 31.1M  1 loop /snap/snapd/10707
loop1                         7:1  0 55.4M  1 loop /snap/core18/1944
loop2                         7:2  0 69.9M  1 loop /snap/lxd/19188
sda                           8:0  0   32G  0 disk
├─sda1                        8:1  0    1M  0 part
├─sda2                        8:2  0    1G  0 part /boot
└─sda3                        8:3  0   31G  0 part
  └─ubuntu--vg-ubuntu--lv 253:0  0   20G  0 lvm  /
sdb                          8:16  0  100G  0 disk
└─sdb1                       8:17  0  100G  0 part
sr0                          11:0  1 93.2M  0 rom
sr1                          11:1  1  1.1G  0 rom
root@ubuntuiscsi01:/home/user01#
```

6. Install the iSCSI target framework tgt by entering

    apt install tgt -y

7. Verify that iSCSI has been started by entering

    systemctl status tgt

```
root@ubuntuiscsi01:/home/user01# systemctl status tgt
● tgt.service - (i)SCSI target daemon
     Loaded: loaded (/lib/systemd/system/tgt.service; enabled; vendor preset: enabled)
     Active: active (running) since Sun 2021-05-16 16:10:42 UTC; 2min 33s ago
       Docs: man:tgtd(8)
   Main PID: 4085 (tgtd)
     Status: "Starting event loop..."
      Tasks: 1
     Memory: 1.3M
     CGroup: /system.slice/tgt.service
             └─4085 /usr/sbin/tgtd -f

May 16 16:10:42 ubuntuiscsi01 systemd[1]: Starting (i)SCSI target daemon...
May 16 16:10:42 ubuntuiscsi01 tgtd[4085]: tgtd: iser_ib_init(3431) Failed to initialize RDMA; load kernel modules?
May 16 16:10:42 ubuntuiscsi01 tgtd[4085]: tgtd: work_timer_start(146) use timer_fd based scheduler
May 16 16:10:42 ubuntuiscsi01 tgtd[4085]: tgtd: bs_init(387) use signalfd notification
May 16 16:10:42 ubuntuiscsi01 systemd[1]: Started (i)SCSI target daemon.
root@ubuntuiscsi01:/home/user01#
```

8. tgt allows you to configure a device as an iSCSI
    target by using a configuration file. Create a file
    called */etc/tgt/conf.d/target01.conf* with the
    following information:

```
<target iqn.2021-05.iscsiexample.local:lun1>
     # The device that will be used as an iSCSI target
     backing-store /dev/sdb1
</target>
```

9. I recommend reading the tgt documentation at
    `http://stgt.sourceforge.net/` to verify the
    parameters for the tgt configuration file.

10. Restart the iSCSI service and display the iSCSI target
    being shared by entering

```
systemctl restart tgt
tgtadm --mode target --op show
```

```
root@ubuntuiscsi01:/home/user01# tgtadm --mode target --op show
Target 1: iqn.2021-05.iscsiexample.local:lun1
    System information:
        Driver: iscsi
        State: ready
    I_T nexus information:
    LUN information:
        LUN: 0
            Type: controller
            SCSI ID: IET      00010000
            SCSI SN: beaf10
            Size: 0 MB, Block size: 1
            Online: Yes
            Removable media: No
            Prevent removal: No
            Readonly: No
            SWP: No
            Thin-provisioning: No
            Backing store type: null
            Backing store path: None
            Backing store flags:
        LUN: 1
            Type: disk
            SCSI ID: IET      00010001
            SCSI SN: beaf11
            Size: 107373 MB, Block size: 512
            Online: Yes
            Removable media: No
            Prevent removal: No
            Readonly: No
            SWP: No
            Thin-provisioning: No
            Backing store type: rdwr
            Backing store path: /dev/sdb1
            Backing store flags:
    Account information:
    ACL information:
        ALL
root@ubuntuiscsi01:/home/user01#
```

Adding an iSCSI Target to an ESXi Host

You will add the iSCSI target to your ESXi host. It can be used as the backing for a VMFS datastore.

1. Log in to your VMware Host Client.

2. In the Navigator select **Storage**.

3. Select **Adapters, and** click **Software iSCSI**.

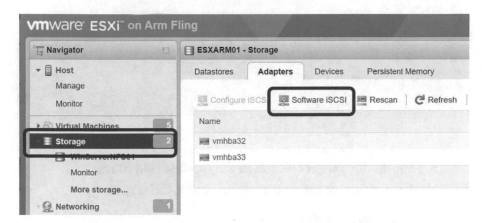

4. Select **Enabled**, and click **Add dynamic target**.

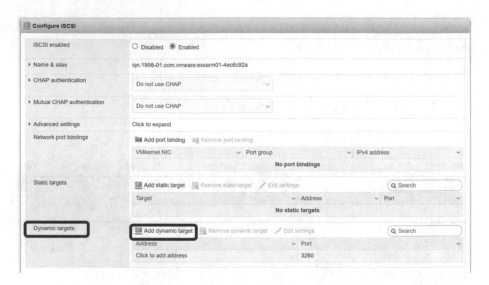

5. Under the **Target** column in the **Click to add name** text box, enter the IP address of your iSCSI target.

6. Click **Save configuration**.

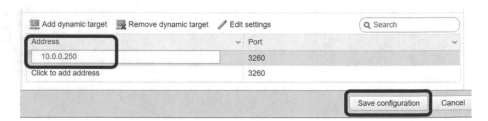

7. Select the **Devices** tab and click **Rescan**.

8. Verify that the iSCSI disk is being shown. As there is only one path to the iSCSI target, it is shown as degraded.

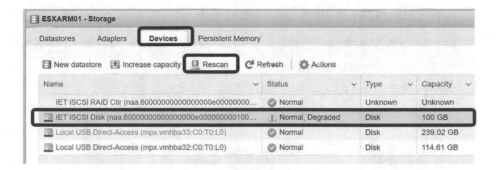

9. In the Navigator right-click **Storage** and select **New datastore**.

10. Verify that **Create new VMFS datastore** is selected and click **Next**.

11. Enter *iSCSI01* in the **Name** text box, select the iSCSI disk, and click **Next**.

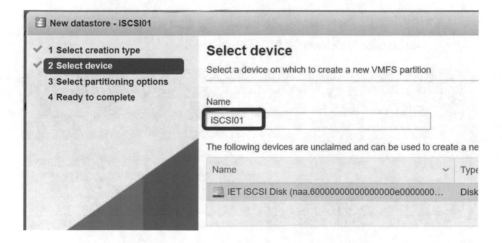

12. Verify that the entire partition will be used, and click **Next**.

13.   Verify your settings and click **Finish**.

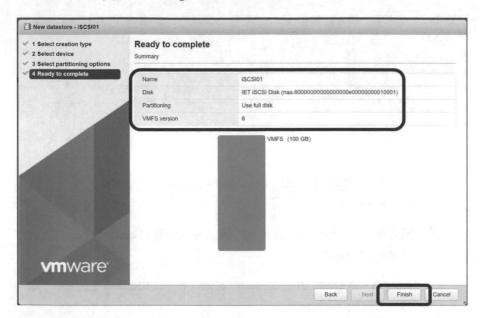

14.   Select the **Datastores** tab and verify that the iSCSI01
      datastore is shown.

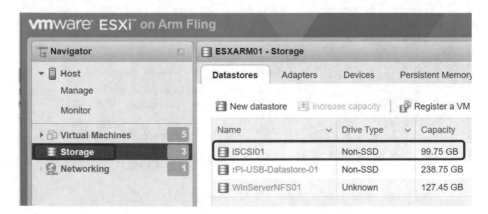

15.   The iSCSI datastore can be used just as any other
      datastore.

iSCSI Final Thoughts

As with NFS, setting an iSCSI target on Linux is relatively easy and straightforward, as is attaching an ESXi host to the iSCSI target and using it as a datastore.

Note   Using Player to host a Linux system supplying an iSCSI target is not something that I would advise doing without extensive testing. I would not completely trust the performance, reliability, or robustness of this configuration to that of a dedicated iSCSI appliance; however, for ad hoc testing and home lab use, it should be fine. The system on which Player is running will see a performance hit, and the busier the host is, the less performance your iSCSI will have.

Case Study: Using a VM as an iSCSI Server for the ESXi Host

Early on in my career, I needed to create a training platform for vSphere. I didn't have access to a storage array yet, and I needed to show my students how to access shared storage in order to demonstrate advanced features such as vMotion. Figure 9-10 shows how I got around this limitation by setting up a Linux VM on the ESXi host to serve iSCSI to the ESXi host on which it resided.

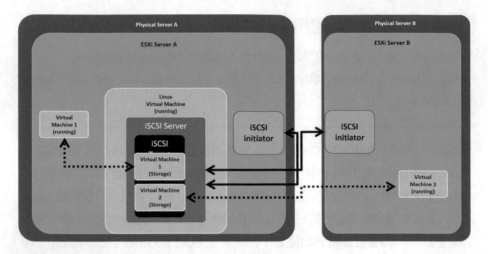

Figure 9-10. *ESXi Hosting an iSCSI Share*

It surprised me how well this worked, but this is an inefficient setup for a production environment; for the purposes of learning, however, it works fine. It might be possible to perform a setup like this using a Pi, but due to its limited resources (especially around I/O and storage), the performance would be dismal.

Summary

As mentioned at the start of this chapter, NFS is used to share the files that make up a VM, while iSCSI shares a block device (such as a disk over the network). When used with an ESXi host, NFS has slightly less overhead as all the overhead associated with a file system is done by the NFS Server, but with iSCSI (as the file system is being managed by the ESXi host) it may have features that are unavailable on an NFS share.

In production environments, ESXi is almost always used with shared storage. Very seldom will you see a production ESXi host with just local storage. Setting up a Windows or Linux server to act as an iSCSI host is very simple, and it allows you to store considerably more VMs than the local storage and allows them to run on any of the ESXi hosts attached to it.

The performance of the underlying storage has a direct impact on the performance of the VM. In the next chapter, I will measure the performance of many different storage devices.

CHAPTER 10

Testing Storage Performance

So far in this book, we have used both local and network storage with ESXi. At this point, you may be asking yourself what to use for storage – and it should come as no surprise that there are far too many variables for me to give a blanket or definitive answer.

For instance, you may have a slow USB drive that you are using for your local storage, or you may have a congested or unreliable network that is causing issues with your NFS storage. On the other hand, you may have a stand-alone system acting as an iSCSI server or an M.2 drive in an enclosure attached to your Raspberry Pi.

In this chapter, I will provide an overview of the results from testing I did on both local and network storage, as well as highlights of the tool that I used to perform these tests. I conducted my testing in an extremely casual manner with the sole intent of demonstrating the range of available storage options and to provide a very rough approximation of what you can likely expect from the performance of these devices.

© Thomas Fenton and Patrick Kennedy 2022
T. Fenton and P. Kennedy, *Running ESXi on a Raspberry Pi*,
https://doi.org/10.1007/978-1-4842-7465-1_10

Testing Configuration

To conduct my tests, I used an 8GB Pi housed in an Argon M.2 case. I tested the performance of different storage devices by attaching them to the Pi and then performing my tests for each one.

I tested my locally attached storage using the Pi's USB 3.0 port. The machine that I used to run the test was an Ubuntu 20.04 instance residing on a SanDisk 256GB Ultra Fit USB 3.1 Flash Drive (SDCZ430-256G-G46) plugged into a USB 2.0 port. The Ubuntu VM had three CPU cores and 6GB of RAM to ensure that the Pi's resources would not hamper its performance. For network storage, I connected it to the storage over a 1Gbe network with only a single switch between the Pi and the storage. My testing configuration is shown in Figure 10-1.

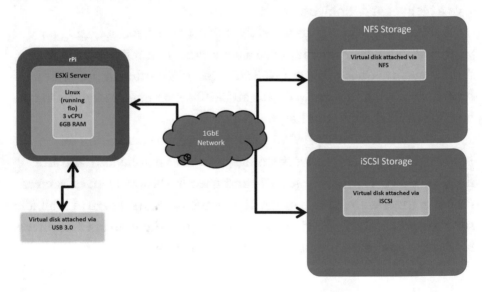

Figure 10-1. *Testing Configuration*

Initial USB Storage Performance Testing

I conducted my initial testing on two different devices: a 256GB thumb drive and a 500GB Western Digital Blue SATA SSD (WDS500G2B0B) in the M.2 case (see Figure 10-2).

Figure 10-2. *Top of Argon M.2 Case*

As mentioned in an earlier chapter, the M.2 Argon case has a SATA SSD housed within the case and connects to the Pi via a U-shaped USB connector (see Figure 10-3).

Figure 10-3. *SATA SSD Drive in M.2 Case*

The case is quite flexible as it supports a SATA M.2 NGFF Key B or B+M SSD. The M.2 device can be any of the commonly used M.2 form factors: 2280, 2260, 2242, or 2230. The case uses an ASMedia Technologies ASM1153E chipset to support the SATA M.2 drive for USB transfer.

As heat can hamper performance, both the top and bottom surfaces of the case have ventilation slots, with the top housing a fan for cooling. There are seven connection ports on the back of the case: two HDMI, one USB-C (power only), two USB 2.0, and two USB 3.0 (one of which is used to connect to the M.2 device in the lower part of the case). Also on the back of the case are an RJ45 1GB Ethernet port and the power button.

I performed my first test on the SATA SSD device in the case. I accessed my ESXi host using SSH and mounted and created a VMFS datastore on it using my AutoMountUSB script (see Figure 10-4).

```
 list vmfs
Volume Name                                       VMFS UUID                               Extent Number
----------------------------------------          ----------------------------------      -------------
Arm02-USB-SanUltraFit-01                          5f4f7a06-18798bc8-ae16-dca632cdd252                 0
Arm02-USB-02                                      5f4ea933-f7a25d79-b8e5-dca632cdd252                 0
OSDATA-5f4e570c-8c6974da-ade8-dca632cdd252        5f4e570c-8c6974da-ade8-dca632cdd252                 0

 Storage Script Finished

[root@localhost:~]
```

Figure 10-4. *M.2 Datastore*

To test the device, I added a 55GB virtual disk backed by the SATA SSD storage to the Ubuntu VM (see Figure 10-5).

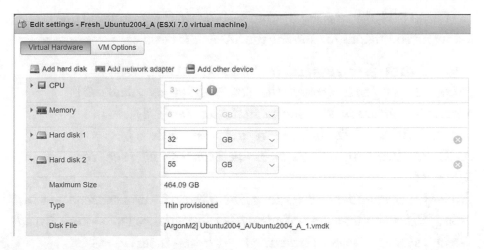

Figure 10-5. *55GB Virtual Disk*

From experience, I know that different commands can report different types of information pertaining to the drive. The following are some of the commands that I ran on the second virtual disk:

- *lshw* – To list information about the hardware on a system; "-*C disk*" will list the disk and storage controllers.

- *fdisk* – To configure and report on the partitions on a device; "-*l*" will list the partitions on a drive.

- *hdparm* – To obtain and set the device's parameters on a SATA/IDE device.

- *dd* – To convert and copy a file (I use this to time how long it takes to copy a file).

- *fio* – A flexible I/O tester used to measure the performance of I/O devices including storage.

I used SSH to access my Ubuntu instance and then entered the following commands to examine the SATA SSD device:

```
lshw -C disk [see results in Table 1]
fdisk -l  ## [this showed the 50GiB drive as /dev/sdb]
hdparm -I /dev/sdb ## [see results in Table 1]
hdparm -Tt /dev/sdb ## [see results in Table 1]
dd if=/dev/zero of=/dev/sdb bs=4k count=5M ## [see results in
Table 1]
fio --filename=/dev/sdb --ioengine=libaio --rw=randread --bs=4k
--numjobs=1 --size=50g --iodepth=32 --runtime=120 --time_based
--end_fsync=1 --name=4krandread --status-interval=15
```

I then ran the same test on a Samsung 128GB thumb drive using the USB 3 and USB 2 ports. The results of these test are seen in Table 10-1.

Table 10-1. *Initial Performance Test*

	Kingston SATA SSD USB 3	Samsung Thumb Drive USB 3	Samsung Thumb Drive USB 2
hdparm -Tt (Cached Read)	835MBs	835MBs	833MBs
hdparm -Tt (Buffered Read)	99MBs	60MBs	**314MBs**
Dd	**54MBs**	28MBs	Failed
fio 4K (Random Read)	**32MiBs/8121 IOPS**	25MiBs/6075 IOPS	11MiBs/3004 IOPS

Observations on My Initial Tests

fio showed that the SATA SSD was 28% and 290% more performant than the thumb drive when it was plugged into USB 3 and USB 2 ports.

The *hdparm* test, which only ran for a few seconds, gave the same results for all the devices and showed far better performance than the *dd* and *fio* tests, leading me to believe that there was some caching or buffering taking place. The *dd* command showed that the SATA SSD drive was 50% more performant than the thumb drive when plugged into the USB 3 port; this command failed when the thumb drive was plugged into the USB 2 port.

As this was just ad hoc testing, I was not surprised to find that the performance of the SSD did not come close to matching the theoretical performance of the USB 3.0 bus (625MB) or even the M.2 device (560MB). There are many reasons why this could have been the case, such as the USB and Ethernet ports sharing the same bus. Also, I was running a Fling from VMware that probably hadn't been entirely fleshed out for performance, and the Ubuntu instance that I was running the test from was a VM. These (or other factors) can cause bottlenecks.

Despite these issues, however, my basic testing still showed that the SATA SSD drive was clearly preferable to a thumb drive with regard to performance. I was a little bit worried about the SATA SSD and the *first write* effect where the first write of a flash-based device is considerably faster than subsequent reads; however, seeing how the SATA SSD didn't even come close to the performance of which I know it is capable, I believe the limitation in this scenario is the I/O subsystem on the Pi – not the device itself.

For the rest of my testing, I only used fio as I felt it gave the most complete and accurate results. I rebooted the Ubuntu guest between the tests.

Fio

Flexible I/O tester (fio) was initially written by Jens Axboe to test the Linux I/O subsystem and schedulers. It has since been ported to Solaris, Windows, and other OSs. It has become the *de facto* tool for testing storage due to its flexibility. Although it is very powerful and configurable, it is also very easy to use and understand.

To install fio on my Ubuntu instance, I entered *apt install fio -y*. To test the throughput of a device with sequential reads, I entered

```
fio --filename=/dev/sdb --ioengine=libaio --rw=randread --bs=4k
--numjobs=1 --size=50g --iodepth=32 --runtime=120 --time_based
--end_fsync=1 --name=4krandread --status-interval=120
```

The official fio documentation (`https://fio.readthedocs.io/en/latest/`) does a very good job outlining what each parameter does. The following is a quick synopsis of the parameters used in the preceding example:

- *filename* – To specify the device or file to write to. For the majority of my testing, I wrote to a device; the second drive (*/dev/sdb*) I attached to my Linux instance. For NFS, I specified a filename on the NFS share.

- *ioengine* – To indicate how the I/O is to be issued to the file, and there are two dozen ways that you can use this. For instance, *libaio* uses native Linux asynchronous I/O; this can be used with non-buffered I/O or buffered I/O by using *direct=1* or *buffered=0*.

- *rw* – To confirm the type of I/O; these can be sequential or random reads or writes.

- *bs* – To define the block size to read and write.

- *numjobs* – To specify the number of clones of the job.

- *iodepth* – To set the number of I/O units to keep queued up against the file.

- *runtime* – To indicate the maximum time the job will run. The default time unit is seconds, but you can postfix the number with *m* for minutes or *h* for hours.

- *time_based* – To make a job continue to loop and run even if the device or file has been completely written to.

- *end_fsync* – To sync the file when the job ends.

- *name* – To signal the name of a new job.

- *status-interval* – To specify how often to show the status of the job.

For more complex testing, a *job file* can be created; this runs various tests in an organized manner but beyond the scope of what I needed to do.

Random and Sequential Test Script

The following is the script I used to run the fio tests:

```
echo
echo "### fio to run a random read 4k test ###"
echo

fio --filename=/dev/sdb --ioengine=libaio --rw=randread --bs=4k
--numjobs=1 --size=50g --iodepth=32 --runtime=120 --time_based
--end_fsync=1 --name=4krandread --status-interval=120
echo
echo "### fio to run a random write 4k test ###"
echo
```

```
fio --filename=/dev/sdb --ioengine=libaio --rw=randwrite
--bs=4k --numjobs=1 --size=50g --iodepth=32 --runtime=120
--time_based --end_fsync=1 --name=4krandwrite --status-
interval=120

echo
echo "### fio to run a sequential read 4k test ###"
echo

fio --filename=/dev/sdb --ioengine=libaio --rw=read --bs=4k
--numjobs=1 --size=50g --iodepth=32 --runtime=120 --time_based
--end_fsync=1 --name=4kSeqRead --status-interval=120

echo
echo " ### fio to run a sequential write 4k test ###"
echo

fio --filename=/dev/sdb --ioengine=libaio --rw=write --bs=4k
--numjobs=1 --size=50g --iodepth=32 --runtime=120 --time_based
--end_fsync=1 --name=4kSeqWrite --status-interval=120
```

Testing Network Storage

With a baseline on the performance of local storage devices, I was
interested to determine how well network storage would perform.
Following the same procedure that I used for testing local storage, I tested
NFS and iSCSI storage devices.

iSCSI on Player

The first network storage I tested was the iSCSI target that I set up on
Ubuntu running on Player that I set up in a previous chapter.

Figure 10-6 shows the connection between the ESXi host and the iSCSI target.

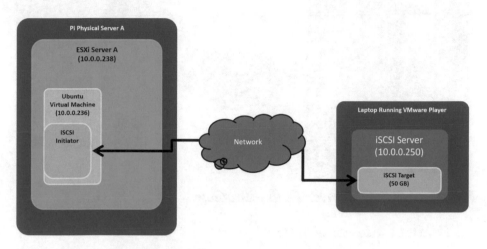

Figure 10-6. *iSCSI Testing Topology*

Here are the results of the test:

	Fio 4K – RAND Read	Fio 4K – RAND Write	Fio 4K – SEQ Read	Fio 4K – SEQ Write
iSCSI on Player	bw=5.2MiB/s	bw=1.2MiB/s	bw=76.9MiB/s	bw=101MiB/s

NFS on Windows

I tested the NFS share that was setup in a previous section.

Figure 10-7 shows the connection between the ESXi host and the NFS Server.

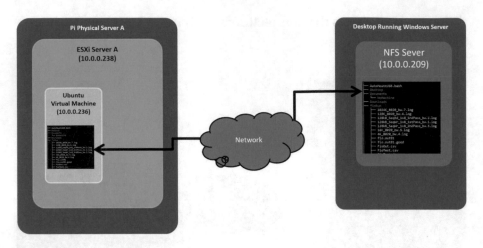

Figure 10-7. *NFS Player Testing Topology*

Here are the results of the test:

	Fio 4K – RAND Read	Fio 4K – RAND Write	Fio 4K – SEQ Read	Fio 4K – SEQ Write
NFS on Windows Server	bw=6.1MiB/s	bw=5.3MiB/s	bw=94.2MiB/s	bw=67.6MiB/s

NFS on QNAP TS-431K Storage Appliance

I have a QNAP TS-431K that I use for media streaming and backups and as an NFS Server. It is a relatively inexpensive and lightweight server. It is powered by an Alpine AL214, a four-core, 1.7GHz (32-bit Arm) processor, 1GB of RAM, and a 1GbE adapter.

For back-end storage, I had a 2TB Seagate ST2000LX001-1RG174 HDD with a SanDisk SSD Plus – 240GB SSD that was used as a read/write cache.

Figure 10-8 shows the connection between the ESXi host and the NFS Server.

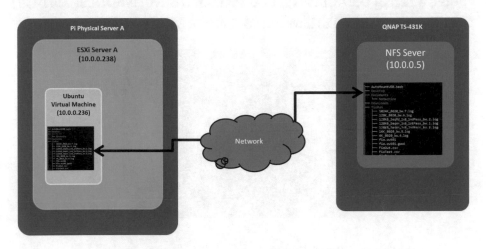

Figure 10-8. *QNAP Testing Topology*

	Fio 4K – RAND Read	Fio 4K – RAND Write	Fio 4K – SEQ Read	Fio 4K – SEQ Write
TS-431KSSD cache	bw=9.2MiB/s	bw=9.2MiB/s	bw=82.2MiB/s	bw=21.5MiB/s

Testing Thumb Drives

I have seen many people use thumb drives on Pi devices for VM and ISO storage. In my testing, I used some thumb drives that I have had for years and purchased others. If the manufacturer had any performance numbers for the drives, I included them.

PNY Elite-X Fit

I tested a 128GB USB 3.1 PNY Elite-X Fit thumb drive (P-FDI128EXFIT-GE). The drive is advertised to have a read speed of 200MB/s.

Here are the results of the test:

	Fio 4K – RAND Read	Fio 4K – RAND Write	Fio 4K – SEQ Read	Fio 4K – SEQ Write
PNY Elite-X Fit	**Failed**	**Failed**	**bw=89.8MiB/s**	**bw=7.1MiB/s**

Samsung BAR Plus 256GB

I tested a 256GB USB 3.1 Samsung BAR Plus drive (MUF-256BE3/AM). The drive is advertised to have a read speed of 300MB/s.

Here are the results of the test.

	Fio 4K – RAND Read	Fio 4K – RAND Write	Fio 4K – SEQ Read	Fio 4K – SEQ Write
Samsung BAR Plus 256GB	bw=7.5MiB/s	bw=12.9MiB/s	bw=57.2MiB/s	bw=63.7MiB/s

Samsung BAR Plus 128GB

I tested a 128GB USB 3.1 Samsung BAR Plus drive (MUF-256BE4/AM). The drive is advertised to have a read speed of 300MB/s.

Here are the results of the test:

	Fio 4K – RAND Read	Fio 4K – RAND Write	Fio 4K – SEQ Read	Fio 4K – SEQ Write
Samsung BAR Plus 128GB	bw=6.9MiB/s	bw=16.5MiB/s	bw=77.8MiB/s	bw=69.1MiB/s

SanDisk Ultra Flair

I tested a 64GB USB 3.1 SanDisk Ultra Flair thumb drive (SDCZ73-064G-A46). The drive is advertised to have a read speed of 150MB/s.

When I ran the test, I received the error message shown in the following:

```
root@freshubuntu2004:/home/user01# fio --filename=/dev/sdb --ioengine=libaio --rw=write --bs=4k --numjobs=1 --size=50g
-iodepth=32 --runtime=120 --time_based --end_fsync=1 --name=4kSeqWrite --status-interval=120
4kSeqWrite: (g=0): rw=write, bs=(R) 4096B-4096B, (W) 4096B-4096B, (T) 4096B-4096B, ioengine=libaio, iodepth=32
fio-3.16
Starting 1 process
fio: job '4krandwrite' (state=5) hasn't exited in 300 seconds, it appears to be stuck. Doing forceful exit of this job.
```

Here are the results of the test:

	Fio 4K – RAND Read	Fio 4K – RAND Write	Fio 4K – SEQ Read	Fio 4K – SEQ Write
SanDisk Ultra Flair	bw=35.2MiB/s	Failed	Failed	Failed

Stress Testing a Thumb Drive

Thumb drives are not designed to have a continual load placed on them; they are designed for occasional loads and to be written to intermittently. To see how well the drive would hold up, I completely wrote to the Samsung BAR Plus 256GB drive 100 times using the following script:

```
for ((i=1;i<=100;i++));
do
    echo " Start of loop  $i"
    time fio --filename=/dev/sdb --ioengine=libaio --rw=write
    --bs=128k --numjobs=1 --size=100% --iodepth=32 --end_
    fsync=1 --name=4kSeqWrite --status-interval=600
done
```

The drive reached 43°C and 119°F during the run. Figure 10-9 shows the drive's performance using the stress test when compared to the 4K tests conducted previously. Initially, the performance of the drive was sporadic.

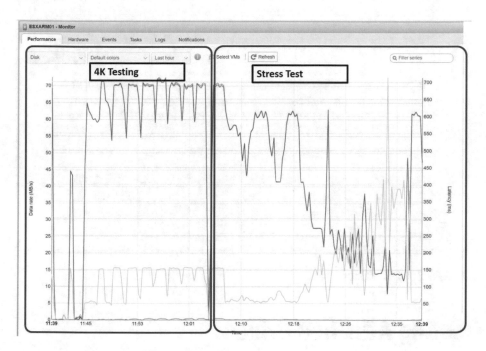

Figure 10-9. *Initial Stress Test Run*

Figure 10-10 shows how the device eventually reached a steady state of about bw=69.4MiB/s at a temperature of 121 degrees.

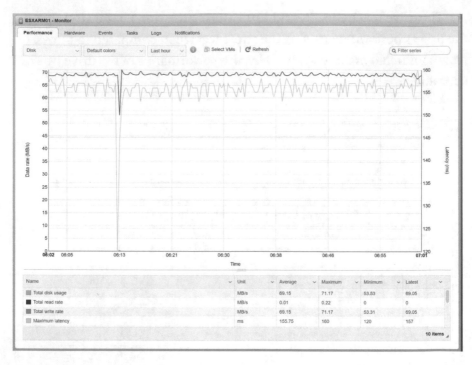

Figure 10-10. *Stress Test*

Testing Attached Drives

Thumb drives were designed for a far different workload than HDD, SSD, or NVMe drives. However, the Pi only has a USB connector, not an NVMe or SATA connector. However, these devices can be placed in an enclosure and attached to the Pi via the USB port. By doing this, you will be using a device that was designed for this type of workload.

Western Digital SATA in Argon Case

I tested a 500GB Western Digital Blue SATA SSD (WDS500G2B0B) in an Argon M.2 case. The drive is advertised to have sequential read speeds up to 560MB/s and sequential write speeds up to 530MB/s.

Here are the results of the test:

	Fio 4K – RAND Read	Fio 4K – RAND Write	Fio 4K – SEQ Read	Fio 4K – SEQ Write
Western Digital Blue SATA SSD	bw=34.6MiB/s	bw=9.7MiB/s	bw=100MiB/s	bw=77.6MiB/s

Toshiba NVME in an SSK Enclosure

I tested a 1TB Toshiba NVME drive (KXG50ZNV1T02) in an SSK Aluminum M.2 NVME SSD Enclosure Adapter (SHE-C325). The device is advertised to have a sequential read rate of up to 3,000MB/s and a sequential write rate of up to 2,100MB/s.

Here are the results of the test:

	Fio 4K – RAND Read	Fio 4K – RAND Write	Fio 4K – SEQ Read	Fio 4K – SEQ Write
Toshiba KXG5 NVMe	bw=35.0MiB/s	bw=87.7MiB/s	bw=87.7MiB/s	bw=87.5MiB/s

KingSpec SATA M.2 in an ORICO Enclosure

I tested a 256GB KingSpec SATA SSD (NT-256 2242) in an ORICO M.2
Enclosure for SSD (B08R9DMFFT). The drive is advertised to have
a sustained read rate of 500~550MB/s and sustained write rate of
450~500MB/s.

Here are the results of the test:

	Fio 4K – RAND Read	Fio 4K – RAND Write	Fio 4K – SEQ Read	Fio 4K – SEQ Write
KingSpec SATA	bw=35.1MiB/s	bw=18.8MiB/s	bw=100MiB/s	bw=87.2MiB/s

Kingston SATA M.2 in an ORICO Enclosure

I tested a 240GB Kingston SATA SSD (SUV500M8) in an ORICO M.2 Enclosure for SSD (B08R9DMFFT). The Kingston drive is advertised at up to 500MB/s read and 450MB/s write rates.

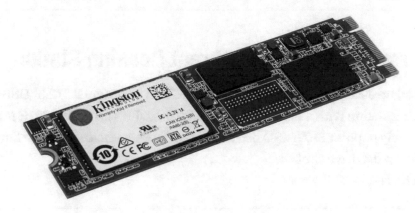

Here are the results of the test:

	Fio 4K – RAND Read	Fio 4K – RAND Write	Fio 4K – SEQ Read	Fio 4K – SEQ Write
Kingston SATA	bw=8.7MiB/s	bw=17.9MiB/s	bw=99.9MiB/s	bw=81.7MiB/s

Micron M500DC in a MASSCOOL External Enclosure

I attempted to test an 800GB Micron M500DC SATA SSD in a MASSCOOL 2.5" USB 3.0 external enclosure. ESXi did not see the device when I plugged it in.

	Fio 4K – RAND Read	Fio 4K – RAND Write	Fio 4K – SEQ Read	Fio 4K – SEQ Write
M500DC SATA/ MASSCOOL	Failed	Failed	Failed	Failed

Micron M500DC in a Sabrent Docking Station

I tested an 800GB Micron M500DC SATA SSD in a Sabrent 3.5/2.5" USB 3.0 docking station with a built-in cooling fan (EC-DFFN). The M500DC is an extremely popular SATA SSD drive, and the Sabrent enclosure has a fan in it to keep the drive cool.

The results of the test.

	Fio 4K – RAND Read	Fio 4K – RAND Write	Fio 4K – SEQ Read	Fio 4K – SEQ Write
M500DC SATA/Sabrent	bw=9.2MiB/s	bw=19.7MiB/s	bw=79.9MiB/s	bw=82.4MiB/s

Seagate IronWolf in a Sabrent Docking Station

I attempted to test a 10TB Seagate IronWolf NAS HDD (ST10000NE0004) in a Sabrent 3.5/2.5" USB 3.0 docking station with a built-in cooling fan (EC-DFFN).

When I tried to create a file system on the device, I received this message "Error: Connection timed out". I tried the same operation on an x64 ESXi server and received the same message.

	Fio 4K – RAND Read	Fio 4K – RAND Write	Fio 4K – SEQ Read	Fio 4K – SEQ Write
Seagate IronWolf	**Failed**	**Failed**	**Failed**	**Failed**

diskAshur M2 High-Security Drive

I tested a 1TB iStorage diskAshur M2 drive (IS DAM2-256-1000). The M2 is
a rugged and highly secure drive. I had previously tested its ruggedness by
throwing it off a two-story balcony and driving over it with a 3.8-ton truck.
For security it requires a passcode to be entered before the contents of the
drive can be read. If the wrong passcode is entered after five times, the
contents of the drive will be unreadable.

Here are the results of the test:

	Fio 4K – RAND Read	Fio 4K – RAND Write	Fio 4K – SEQ Read	Fio 4K – SEQ Write
diskAshur M2	**bw=8.5MiB/s**	**bw=18.8MiB/s**	**bw=97.7MiB/s**	**bw=85.9MiB/s**

Compiled Results for Local Storage

Table 10-2 shows the results of the storage device testing that I conducted, with the highest performance numbers for each type of storage bolded. There wasn't a storage device that consistently performed better than the others. This was to be expected as flash memory has different characteristics; some perform better reading than writing and handle sequential loads differently than random loads.

Note   These numbers shown in the following should be taken with a grain of salt; my testing methods were not highly structured, and I did not carry out the testing in a highly controlled environment.

Failed results in my testing should not reflect poorly on the device and are not indicative of the device being of poor design or quality as I am using these drives beyond their intended use case.

Table 10-2. Storage Testing Results

	Fio 4K – RAND Read	Fio 4K – RAND Write	Fio 4K – SEQ Read	Fio 4K – SEQ Write
Network Storage				
iSCSI on Player	bw=5.2MiB/s	bw=1.2MiB/s	bw=76.9MiB/s	**bw=101MiB/s**
NFS on Windows Server	bw=6.1MiB/s	bw=5.3MiB/s	**bw=94.2MiB/s**	bw=67.6MiB/s
QNAP	**bw=9.2MiB/s**	**bw=9.2MiB/s**	bw=82.2MiB/s	bw=21.5MiB/s
TS-431K				
Thumb Drives				
PNY Elite-X Fit	Failed	Failed	**bw=89.8MiB/s**	bw=7.1MiB/s
Samsung BAR Plus 128GB	bw=6.9MiB/s	**bw=16.5MiB/s**	bw=77.8MiB/s	**bw=69.1MiB/s**
Samsung BAR Plus 256GB	**bw=7.5MiB/s**	bw=12.9MiB/s	**bw=57.2MiB/s**	**bw=63.7MiB/s**
SanDisk Ultra Flair	**bw=35.2MiB/s**	Failed	Failed	Failed
Attached Drives				
Western Digital Blue SATA SSD	bw=34.6MiB/s	bw=9.7MiB/s	**bw=100MiB/s**	bw=77.6MiB/s
Toshiba KXG5 NVMe	bw=18.8MiB/s	**bw=87.7MiB/s**	bw=87.7MiB/s	**bw=87.5MiB/s**

(continued)

245

Table 10-2. (*continued*)

	Fio 4K – RAND Read	Fio 4K – RAND Write	Fio 4K – SEQ Read	Fio 4K – SEQ Write
KingSpec SATA	**bw=35.1MiB/s**	bw=18.8MiB/s	**bw=100MiB/s**	bw=87.2MiB/s
Kingston SATA	bw=8.7MiB/s	bw=17.9MiB/s	bw=99.9MiB/s	bw=81.7MiB/s
M500DC SATA / Sabrent	bw=9.2MiB/s	bw=19.7MiB/s	bw=79.9MiB/s	bw=82.4MiB/s
Seagate IronWolf	Failed	Failed	Failed	Failed
diskAshur M2	bw=8.5MiB/s	bw=18.8MiB/s	bw=97.7MiB/s	bw=85.9MiB/s

Summary

The most consistent performance I observed was when I used network storage. The next most consistent performance was using an attached drive. I was not surprised by this as VMware has invested a lot of time and effort in network storage and it is used by most of their customers. On the other hand, USB storage is only used by a fraction of their customers and is NOT used as a production file system that gets written to and read from extensively. There is also a wide variety in the quality of chips used by thumb drives, which affects their performance.

Based on the testing outlined in this chapter, I would suggest that if you cannot or do not want to use network storage, using an attached drive is a much better solution than using a thumb drive.

We have covered installing VMs and some of the aspects around what type of storage you should use. In the next chapter, we will have some fun and run a desktop on a VM.

CHAPTER 11

Virtual Desktop on ESXi

Benefits of Virtual Desktops

In this book so far, we have been discussing virtual machines (VMs), but there is an interesting subset of VMs that run desktop OSs instead of server OSs – virtual desktops. In this chapter, we will look at virtual desktops, discuss some of their benefits, and walk through how to create and access them.

I was in a unique position when virtual desktops first came on the scene at VMware. At the time, I was working in the training department and was one of the first people in the company to install the software that eventually became known as VMware Horizon – the heart of their virtual desktop infrastructure (VDI) technology. Soon afterward, I had the opportunity to develop and deliver the first courses for this product.

At first, I didn't understand why anyone would want to run a virtual rather than physical desktop. However, as I dove further into the technology and worked with the engineers who developed it, I began to understand its power and attraction. Horizon is now one of VMware's major product lines; they have an entire division solely dedicated to its development, sales, and deployment.

© Thomas Fenton and Patrick Kennedy 2022
T. Fenton and P. Kennedy, *Running ESXi on a Raspberry Pi*,
https://doi.org/10.1007/978-1-4842-7465-1_11

Virtual Desktop Infrastructure

The most basic form of VDI is laid out in Figure 11-1. This setup is composed of an ESXI host that runs desktop OSs, VMs, and the VDI clients that are used to connect to these virtual desktops over the network, thereby allowing the virtual desktops to be accessed from a remote location.

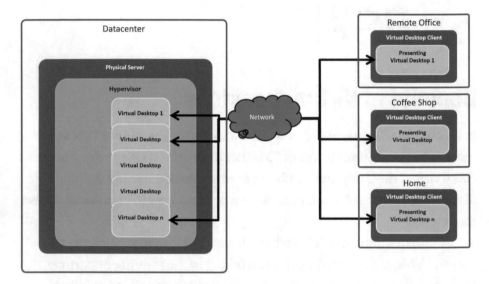

Figure 11-1. *Basic VDI Topology*

Although it is possible to access the virtual desktops directly using their IP address and Remote Display Protocol (RDP), unless you only have a handful of virtual desktops, you will want to use a connection server and a more sophisticated protocol to efficiently connect to them (see Figure 11-2).

A connection server (also known as a connection broker) authenticates users, entitles them to desktops, and performs other operations that assist with connecting users to virtual desktops. Most companies that supply VDI products, such as VMware Horizon, offer alternatives to RDP. These protocols are more performant and offer a greater level of functionality than RDP.

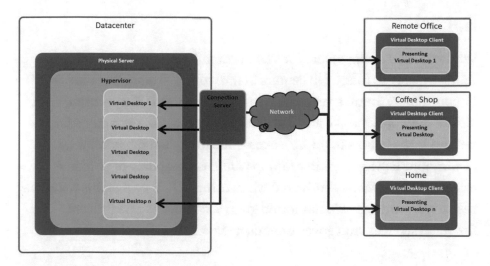

Figure 11-2. *Connection Server*

Cost Savings

When VDI was first introduced in the early 2000s, vendors used cost savings as a main selling point by using calculators that showed how much money you could theoretically save by deploying it. These calculators, however, took a lot of liberties with regard to how much it costs to purchase, maintain, and manage physical desktops. To be sure, if you ran and staffed a call center 24 hours a day, running VDI made a lot of sense from a cost perspective. For single-shift deployments, on the other hand, it was a bit of a stretch to justify the cost for anything above a task user.

But 20 years later, the cost savings for VDI is now valid for a couple of main reasons: the average price of servers has dropped dramatically, and the number of CPU cores and RAM in servers have increased equally dramatically. Twenty years ago, a dual-proc server with eight cores per proc and 128GB of RAM was considered the industry standard. On such a system, you could host between 50 and 70 task workers. Now, however, the standard server is a dual-proc server with 32 cores and as much as 956GB of RAM. A server such as this can host between 250 and 300 users. You can even have a GPU in the server that can be shared between multiple users.

Security

While the cost savings story for VDI eventually started to play out (as there are only so many call centers in the world), around this time the IT community found a very valid reason to embrace VDI: security. With virtual desktops, the OS, and the data that it accesses, remains secure behind locked doors in the datacenter, meaning that the possibility of someone leaving behind a laptop with customer data or personal information is greatly eliminated when using VDI. Based on the enhanced security it provides, VDI has found great acceptance in healthcare, financial services, and governmental agencies.

Business Continuity

Business continuity is another benefit of VDI. I was a sales engineer (SE) for VMware right around the time that a large hurricane hit the East Coast. Major cities were shut down for months, and people couldn't get to their offices to use their desktop computers. This disruption in work was so severe that it caused some companies to close – which really drove home the point that the desktop was a strategic asset that needed to be continuously accessible. The employees at the few companies that ran VDI were able to work from remote locations and were impacted by what was happening at their normal offices. These companies understood the value in remote accessibility of employees' desktops to ensure business continuity.

In 2020, there was a similar situation where, due to a pandemic, employees were unable to physically access their main places of employment. Working from home was no longer a simply nice option to have – it was government-mandated. While some employees were able to bring their laptops or small desktop systems to their home and continue to work, these systems had issues with security and manageability.

VDI became a very attractive option in this situation, and fortunately many of the obstacles that remote home access had early on (namely high-speed, reliable Internet) were removed.

Manageability

Maintaining and managing desktops has always been a painful proposition, and with VDI this aspect is greatly simplified. If a user is having an issue, for example, a technician can either shadow a user's session or log in directly to the desktop. When it comes time to install new applications, patch the system, or otherwise maintain the software, the technician can do all of this directly. In many cases, virtual desktops are cloned from a gold image, and only the gold image needs to be updated and then pushed out.

Data Locality

Apart from the more obvious benefits of VDI like security and manageability, one of the often-overlooked benefits of virtual desktops is data locality, that is, being as close to the data that needs to be processed as possible. Although data locality will never be an issue for a large portion of VDI users who only deal with common office documents that are quite small, there are cases where being close to the data can greatly affect a worker's productivity, such as when working with large databases, videos, high-resolution images, and CAD models that are usually stored on a discrete storage appliance.

For example, if you need to edit video files that are stored on a company's central storage repository, but you are located a couple of miles away, you could use a VPN to connect to this central storage from your home laptop (see Figure 11-3). Depending on how much data you are working with, it may become an exercise in frustration as the application may buffer the data due to the lack of bandwidth needed. Furthermore, if you have any jitter in your network, packets may need to be retransmitted.

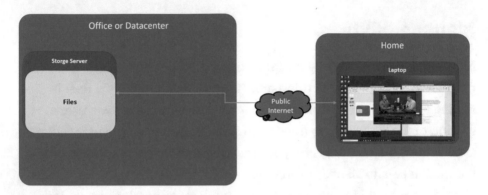

Figure 11-3. *Streaming Data*

A local system using remote storage data could end up consuming the entire bandwidth of your public Internet connection, making it impossible for others to use it.

Figure 11-4 provides an example of how you could transfer the files from a remote location to a local system. Depending on the size of the files, you may not be able to store them locally, or your local storage system may not be able to deliver the performance needed.

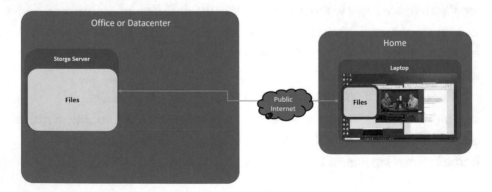

Figure 11-4. *Transferring Files*

File security (as discussed previously) may also be an issue. If multiple people are working on the same files, trying to keep track of them can be infuriating, and if a file gets accidentally deleted, it may take a considerable amount of time to recreate it. By connecting to a virtual desktop that is located close to the data, however, you can minimize network traffic as the remote protocol only uses a fraction of the bandwidth compared to streaming the storage (see Figure 11-5).

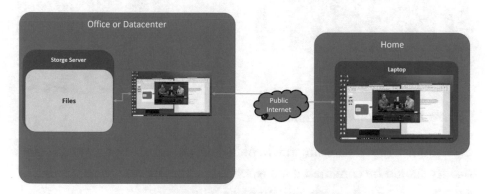

Figure 11-5. *Using a Virtual Desktop to Edit the Files*

Some VDI protocols allow multiple users to interact with the same virtual desktop (see Figure 11-6). This can save countless hours and avoid the frustration of trying to describe what others are seeing and trying to accomplish. VMware has implemented this in Blast with its session collaboration ability.

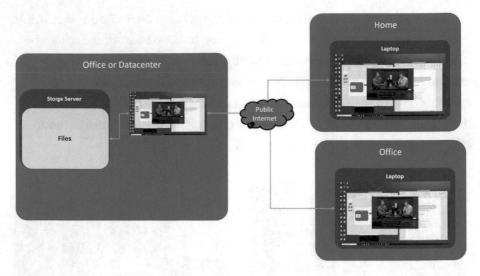

Figure 11-6.   *Collaboration*

In sum, when discussing the benefits of VDI, side benefits such as data locality should be considered along with the more obvious benefits like security, cost containment, and manageability.

Types of Virtual Desktop Users

Table 11-1 shows the classification of virtual desktop users. This classification helps to better identify the resources that the virtual desktops need based on the type of workers that use them.

Table 11-1. *User Types*

Classification	Workload	Resources Needed
Task Worker	Use one or two applications and are usually based in call centers.	Minimal desktop with one or two vCPUs, 2GB of RAM, and 32GB of storage. Companies may use Linux desktops to minimize costs.
Knowledge Worker	Use many different office applications as well as specialized applications. These are general office workers and corporate employees.	Full Windows desktop with a minimum of two vCPUs, 4GB of RAM, and storage appropriate for their use cases.
Power User	Engineers, content creators, and IT workers who use common office applications as well as specialized applications such as CAD/CAM, compilers, and other powerful applications.	Full Windows or Linux with a minimum of four vCPUs, 8GB of RAM, and storage appropriate for their particular use case.

Accessing Virtual Desktops

It's possible to access a virtual desktop from any device that supports the protocol that the virtual desktop uses. The following are some of the more popular types of clients that have been developed to connect to virtual desktops.

Media Redirection

Before discussing the different types of VDI clients, we need to first address a technology that is starting to come into play in the VDI world: media redirection. This is a technology that detects when certain applications such as web browsers, video conferencing, and other communication applications are redirected to run natively on the device where the VDI client is running rather than on the virtual desktop; that is, they are instantiated from the virtual desktop but run on the device itself. This is transparent to the user.

Figure 11-7 shows how, without redirection, browsing a website requires the application (in this case, a video website) to go from the website to the virtual desktop and then to the virtual desktop. This introduces latency into the transaction and consumes CPU resources on the host on which the virtual desktop resides.

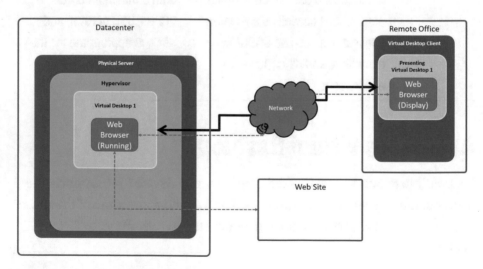

Figure 11-7. *Without Redirection*

Figure 11-8 shows how, by using redirection, a website can be accessed directly from the VDI client's hardware, thereby cutting down the network traffic, latency, and CPU usage on the virtual desktop and using the excess hardware capacity of modern VDI clients.

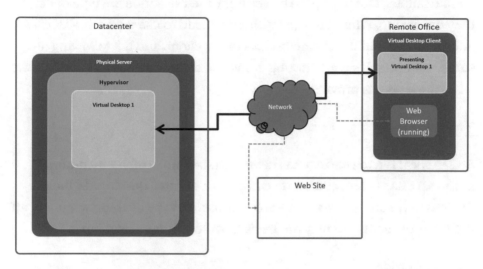

Figure 11-8. *With Redirection*

Figure 11-9 shows the output of Top (a process monitoring application). This shows that Zoom, a popular video conferencing application, is running on and consuming the resources of the VDI client after being instantiated and redirected from the virtual desktop.

```
                                                                Local Terminal
File   Edit   View   Terminal   Tabs   Help
top - 12:39:30 up 8 days,  3:16,  1 user,   load average: 1.26, 0.72, 0.49
Tasks: 280 total,   1 running, 207 sleeping,   0 stopped,   1 zombie
%Cpu(s): 12.7 us,   5.2 sy,   0.0 ni, 81.9 id,   0.0 wa,   0.0 hi,   0.2 si,   0.0 st
KiB Mem :  3838436 total,   1320016 free,    879912 used,   1638508 buff/cache
KiB Swap:  2303056 total,   2303056 free,         0 used.   2403840 avail Mem

   PID USER      PR  NI    VIRT     RES    SHR S  %CPU %MEM     TIME+ COMMAND
 138081 user      20   0 5258212  179456   93744 S  50.7  4.7   1:11.70 zoom
   8506 user       9 -11 1581244   15416   11088 S  15.6  0.4  53:46.56 pulseaudio
   6967 root      20   0 1182840  116808   80668 S   4.3  3.0  26:53.67 Xorg
```

Figure 11-9. *Redirected Application Running on VDI Client*

VDI Clients

Different classifications of clients have evolved over the years. Unfortunately, there isn't a strict standard for the names of these classifications, and it is up to the vendor to self-describe the type of client they are selling. When discussing clients, I tend to use the term *VDI client* and then spell out the characteristics of the client, and the following are some examples. It's worth noting, however, there is a lot of fluidity between what these clients provide.

Zero Clients

A *zero client* is a device that has been purpose-built using the minimal amount of hardware required to connect to a virtual desktop. As these devices only run firmware, they are considered to be the most secure of all the types of clients but may not be as flexible as other client types.

Thin Clients

Thin clients have been specifically designed to run as VDI clients. They usually have a low-powered and lower-cost processor and a minimal amount of RAM. They also only have enough storage to run an OS that has been designed to support VDI client software. Furthermore, because they run an OS rather than directly from firmware, they are easier to modify and may offer additional functionality than zero clients.

Thick Clients

Thick clients, or fat clients, have more powerful hardware than zero or thin clients and are purpose-built by vendors as repurposed PCs or laptops with an application installed on them that allows them to connect to a virtual desktop. Whereas thin or zero clients are very dependent on virtual desktops, a thick client may run some stand-alone applications such as office applications and may offer local storage.

Native Clients

Accessing a virtual desktop does not require a special device, and many companies allow – and may even encourage – end users to access their virtual desktops from a standard laptop or desktop. VDI vendors enable this functionality via an application that runs on Windows, Linux, macOS, or other operating systems (see Figure 11-10).

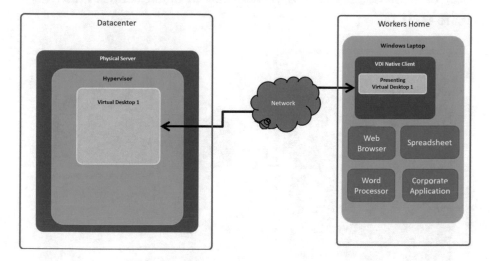

Figure 11-10. *Native Client*

Native clients may (depending on security requirements) allow integration features such as cutting and pasting from local applications to the virtual desktop.

Web Clients

With the advent of HTML5, web browsers soon became an attractive
way to access virtual desktops, and now all of the major VDI vendors
support web-based clients. While they may not have all the features of the
other clients listed previously, they do offer a very good user experience
and provide flexibility of access to a virtual desktop without requiring
a physical device or installing a native client. Many users who bring
their own devices (BYOD) prefer accessing via the web client as it does
not require them to install any additional software on their device. The
connection made between a web client and virtual desktop is shown in
Figure 11-11.

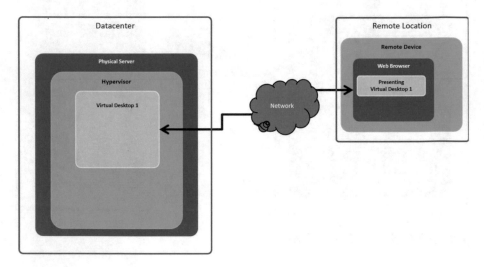

Figure 11-11. *Web Client*

All-in-One Client

For convenience purposes, many manufacturers have seamlessly coupled
a VDI client with a monitor. Not only does this clear up desktop space, it
also makes the device easier to maintain as it can be replaced as a unit.

Figure 11-12 shows an LG all-in-one device that was specifically designed for the healthcare sector. It has a built-in radio-frequency identification (RFID) reader for proximity-based, hands-free logon as well as other features that make it attractive to that market.

Figure 11-12. *LG All-in-One Device*

Mobile Devices

Tablets, cell phones, and other mobile devices can also be used to access virtual desktops. In fact, some VDI vendors even allow native gestures like "pinching" to be passed through to the mobile device. Some vendors support access to virtual desktops via web clients, while others have native clients specifically designed for mobile devices.

Being able to access a virtual desktop via a mobile device can be a freeing experience for users as they do not need to lug around a dedicated device. As a prime example, if a doctor is at an event and needs to access a patient's records, they can do so immediately from their cell phone and without needing to return to their office.

What a Remote Protocol Does

Before going further, I should explain what exactly a remote protocol does. In its simplest form, and as shown in Figure 11-13, a remote protocol takes the display from one system and shows it on another system; it also takes the keyboard and mouse from the local system and sends them to the remote system. This allows the user to interact with a remote system in the exact same way as a local system.

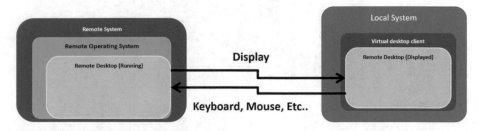

Figure 11-13. *Remote Protocol*

A remote protocol may also perform other functions such as encrypting the data stream for security, compressing the data stream to lessen the network requirements, passing the local machine's USB devices to the virtual desktop, printing from the virtual desktop to a locally attached printer, and a myriad of other services.

Connecting to Virtual Desktops

In this section, I will discuss some of the ways to connect to a virtual desktop. I will first use RDP as it is by far the most commonly widely available protocol. I will then connect to a desktop using X11, one of the first protocols used by Unix and Linux systems. Finally, I will use NoMachine (NX), a proprietary yet popular protocol used to connect to Windows and Linux desktops. I will be using a Windows 10 system to connect to Linux VMs.

Linux VMs

Windows is by far the most popular desktop OS; however, Microsoft has not released a public version of Windows that will run on a generic system with an Arm processor. However, the Linux community has fully embraced the Arm processor, and all the major Linux distributions have versions with desktop features. There are also many Linux distributions solely focused on providing a Windows-like desktop experience using Linux. In this section, we will look at installing the additional packages to our Linux VMs to make them suitable for desktop use.

Fedora

To use the Fedora VM, you can install a graphical desktop on it by following these steps:

1. Log in to your Fedora instance from the console.

2. Switch to root user, and then enter *sudo su.*

3. Install the GNOME desktop and GUI applications by entering

   ```
   dnf -y group install "Basic Desktop" GNOME
   dnf -y install LibreOffice
   dnf -y install xeyes
   ```

4. Disable the pcscd service by entering

   ```
   systemctl stop pcscd; systemctl disable pcscd
   ```

5. Start the graphics desktop by entering *startx.*

6. You will see a basic graphical desktop in your console. Click **Activities**.

7. Start a graphics terminal. In the search box at the top of the desktop, enter *XTerm*.

8. In the XTerm terminal, start a graphics application by entering */usr/bin/xeyes*.

9. Verify that the eyes follow the mouse.

10. Close XTerm.

Ubuntu

To use the Ubuntu VM, it will need a graphical desktop installed on it. Ubuntu has different desktops that can be installed, and the following are instructions for installing a basic GNOME desktop:

1. Log in to your Ubuntu instance from the console.

2. Switch to root user, and then enter *sudo su*.

3. Install the GNOME desktop and some applications by entering

```
apt install -y gnome-session gdm3
apt install -y libreoffice
apt install -y x11-apps
apt-get install -y gnome-terminal
```

```
apt-get install -y links2
apt-get install -y Firefox
```

4. Set the graphics desktop to start by default by
   entering

   ```
   systemctl set-default graphical.target
   ```

5. You will see a basic graphics desktop in your
   console. Restart the system by entering *Init 6*.

6. After the system boots up, log in to the GNOME
   desktop.

7. Click **Activities**.

8. Start a graphics terminal. In the search box at the top of the desktop, enter *terminal* and select **Terminal**.

9. In the terminal, enter */usr/bin/xeyes.*

10. Verify that the eyes follow the mouse.

11. Close xeyes.

12. Click **Activities**.

13. Start a graphics terminal. In the search box at the top of the desktop, enter *Firefox* and select **Firefox**.

14. From Firefox, navigate to *www.nomachine.com/ download/download&id=115&s=ARM.*

15. Download NoMachine.

NoMachine for ARM - arm64

Version:	7.6.2_3
Package size:	42 MB
Package type:	DEB
MD5 signature:	6a41e8e74b7241840d71c6372b5cf42c
For:	Dragonboard 410c (Snapdragon 410) running Debian GNU/Linux 8 arm64, Hikey 96 (Kirin 620) running Debian GNU/Linux 8 arm64, Odroid-C2 (Amlogic S905) running Ubuntu 16.04 arm64, Orange Pi Win Plus (Allwinner A64 quad-core ARM Cortex-A53) running Debian 8 and Ubuntu 16.04

Please note that NoMachine for Linux ARM software is in Alpha status.

Although your ARMv8 device may not be listed here, we encourage you to try the packages. Please consult the installation and configuration notes about Linux for ARM packages for more details about devices and specific distributions we have tested.

Download

16.   Install NoMachine by entering

```
sudo su
apt install -y nomachine
sudo dpkg -i nomachine_7.6.2_3_arm64.deb
```

Connecting to Fedora Desktop with RDP

RDP was the original protocol used with Windows machines. It was originally known as Terminal Services and was based on Citrix's MultiWin technology.

An RDP client is shipped with all Windows systems and can be launched from the Windows command line by entering *mstsc.exe*. RDP clients and servers have been developed for a wide variety of machines including Fedora.

Installing RDP Server on Fedora

To install an RDP server on a Fedora system, take the following steps:

1. Log in to the Fedora system using SSH or the console.

2. Install the RDP server, enable it, and open the firewall to it by entering

   ```
   dnf -y install xrdp tigervnc-server
   systemctl enable --now xrdp
   firewall-cmd --add-port=3389/tcp --permanent
   firewall-cmd --reload
   ```

Connecting to a Linux Desktop Using RDP

You can connect to the Fedora machine from a Windows machine by following these steps:

1. From Windows Start, enter *mstsc.exe*.

2. In the Remote Desktop Connection panel, enter the IP address of the Fedora system.

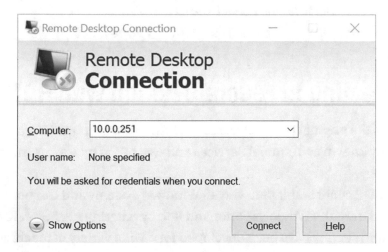

3.   Enter your username and password and click **OK**.

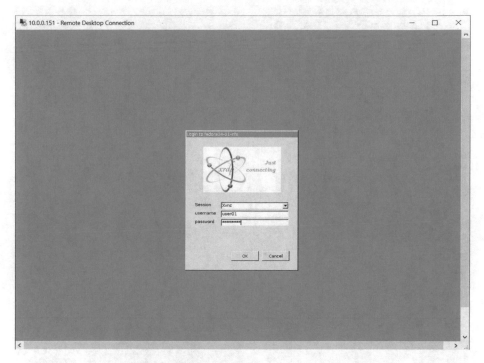

4.   After a short wait, you should receive a "Welcome to
     GNOME" message. Click **Take Tour**.

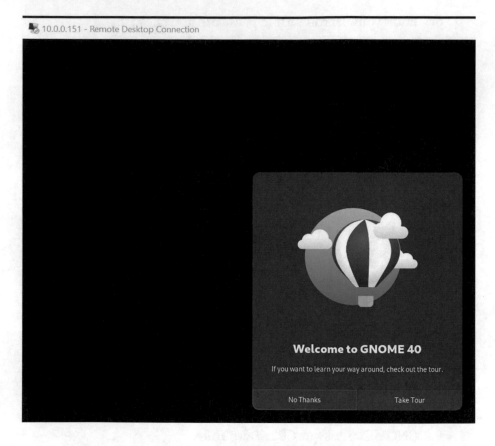

5. After the tour ends, start the word processor. In the
    Activities search box, enter *writer*.

6. You will see LibreOffice Writer in your console.

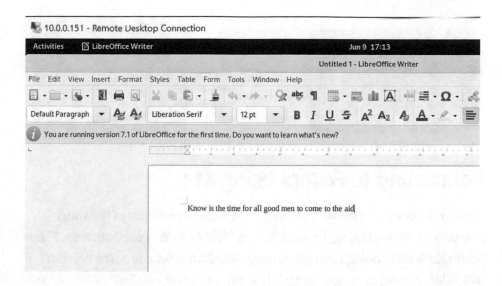

7. Work with Writer and then close the application and remote desktop windows.

X11

X11 was developed in the mid-1980s to provide a graphics framework for Unix machines that can either be used on a local monitor or over a network connection. It was designed from the start to allow more than one user to connect to a remote system. It is an open source project and has been ported to many other OSs.

X11 uses a client-server architecture, but the terminology is switched from what I have been demonstrating. The X11 client (xterm) runs on the remote system, and the X11 server runs on the system that is being used to access the remote system.

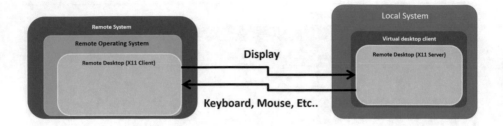

Connecting to Fedora Using X11

There are many X11 servers available for Windows; some of the more popular ones are Xming, Cygwin X, and VcXsrv. In this section, we will be using Xming. Although it is proprietary software, there is a free version available. Xming only acts as an X11 server, so I will use PuTTY to supply the communication to the remote system.

Although you can display an entire GNOME desktop using Xming over PuTTY, there are better tools such as NoMachine for doing this. In this section I will only show how to launch single applications using X11.

1. Download and install PuTTY on your Windows machine from www.putty.org/.

2. Download Xming from https://sourceforge.net/projects/xming/.

3. Install Xming with the Xming Setup Wizard.

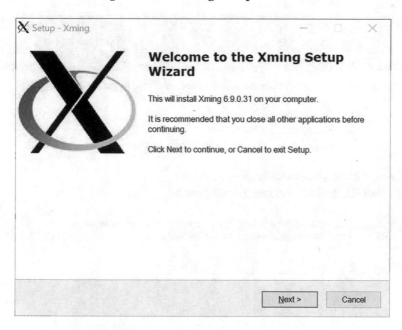

4. Launch Xming.

5. If asked by your firewall, allow Xming to
    communicate on a private network.

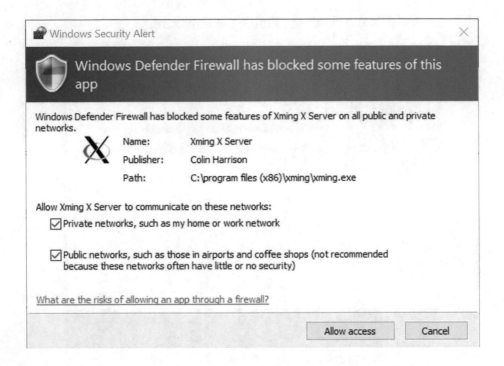

6. Xming will appear in your Windows system tray
    waiting for a connection from an X11 client.

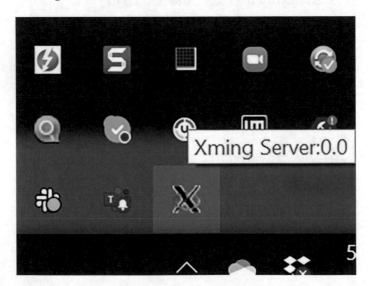

Once the Xming server is listening for an X11 client, a network connection will need to be established between the two, which you can accomplish by taking the following steps:

1. Launch PuTTY.

2. In the PuTTY configuration window, select **Connection ➤ SSH ➤ X11**.

3. Check the **Enable X11 forwarding** checkbox.

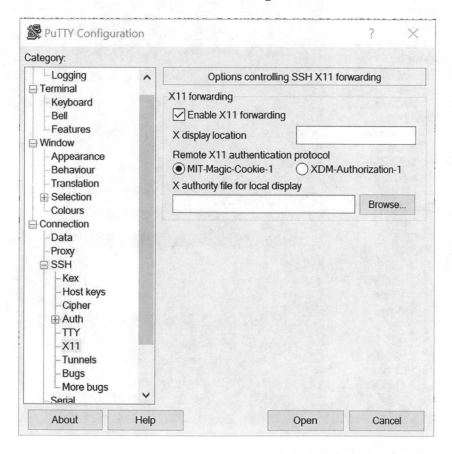

4. Select **Session**, and then enter the hostname or IP address of the Fedora system.

5. Enter a name in the **Saved Sessions** text box and click **Save**.

6. Select the session and click **Open**.

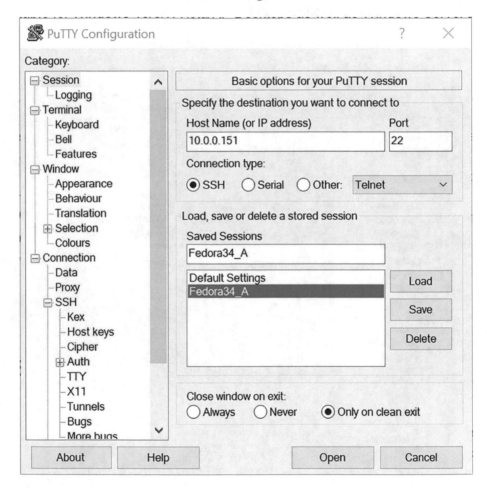

7. Log in to the system.

8. Start your X11 session and launch an application by
   entering

   sudo su
   Export DISPLAY=:0
   Xeyes

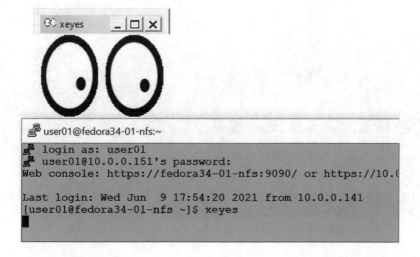

9. Close xeyes.

10. Start a spreadsheet and drawing program by
    entering

    libreoffice --calc &
    libreoffice --draw &

11. Work with the programs and then close them.

12. Install and launch the Firefox web browser by
    entering

    dnf -y install firefox
    firefox

13.   Work with the program and then close it.

NoMachine (NX)

NoMachine (NX) is a highly optimized proprietary software application that is used to access virtual desktops running on Windows, Linux, and macOS. We will be installing the free server and client, but there are also enterprise versions that include advanced features such as allowing multiple users to attach to the same session and running multiple virtual desktops from the same Linux system.

Connecting to a Virtual Desktop Using NoMachine

We will be using NX to connect from a Windows machine to your Ubuntu VM by taking the following steps:

1. Download the NoMachine package from

   www.nomachine.com/download/download&id=115&s=ARM

2. Transfer it to the Ubuntu VM using SCP.

3. From the console or using SSH, log on to the Ubuntu VM.

4. Install NX by entering

   sudo su
   dpkg -i nomachine_7.6.2_3_arm64.deb

5. Download and install NoMachine on your Windows System from www.nomachine.com/download/

6. Launch the NoMachine app.

7. Configure NoMachine to connect to your Ubuntu system.

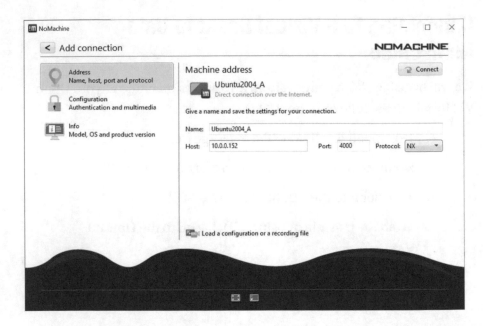

8.   Click **Connect** and log in to your Ubuntu desktop.

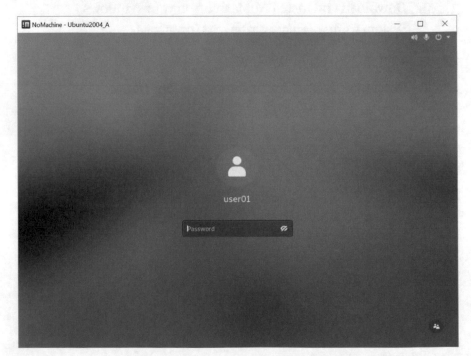

9. Open Firefox, Writer, and other applications from
    the Ubuntu desktop being displayed using NX (see
    Figure 11-33).

10. Close the NX application on your Windows system.

Changing Your Screen Resolution

For a long time, I could not figure out how to change the resolution of the
remote virtual desktop being displayed, but then I came across a blog
post by Cyprien Laplace titled "Setting Virtual Screen Resolution for ESXi
Arm VMs." In this article, Cyprien states, "Unfortunately ESXi for Arm
comes with a new, not final, version of the VMware virtual SVGA adapter,

and there is at the moment no driver available for Guest OSs." He then, however, goes on to say that you can change the resolution from the grub using its EFI GOP driver.

To paraphrase Cyprien's article, you put the resolution you want into the *GRUB_GFXMODE* variable in the */etc/default/grub* file and then update the system by entering the *update-grub2* command. After the system reboots, you will have the new screen resolution. Unfortunately, I didn't have time to test this, but I encourage you to try it if you need to change your screen resolution.

Summary

Linux offers many ways to connect to virtual desktops from a remote location, and I touched on a few of them in this chapter. They are all easy to set up and use, and if you need a secure yet manageable way to deliver desktops or individual applications to users, VDI is a technology to consider.

The reality is that the running three or four virtual desktops would only be applicable to a few niche use cases. You may want to set up a $100 Pi server in your house to allow guests to use your Internet and then delete and recreate the VM after they are finished. You may also just want a low-cost way to explore the power of VDI.

If you want to deploy a company-wide VDI solution, VMware and other companies have excellent and time-proven VDI products; however, they do not currently have an agent that works with Arm desktops.

Networking is one of the key components in a virtualized datacenter, and it can get quite complex. In the next chapter, I will give a high-level overview of how ESXi uses it and give you enough information so you can effectively use it in your environment.

CHAPTER 12

ESXi Networking

Virtual machines (VMs), like their physical counterparts, need to use network interface cards (NICs) and switches to connect to other systems and the Internet. But since it is impractical for each VM to have a physical NIC in a server, VMware has devised a scheme that allows physical NICs to be shared by VMs through the use of virtual NICs (vNICs), virtual switches (vSwitches), and port groups.

In this chapter, we will examine how VMs use both physical and virtual networking constructs, and we will also look at how to test the performance of a network.

Networking

Before discussing virtual networking, let's first take a look at the components that make up the infrastructure of a traditional physical environment.

To illustrate just one example, Figure 12-1 shows a topology in which all servers in a rack are connected to a top-of-rack (TOR) switch, and two racks are connected to each other via an aggregation switch (this allows the possibility of connecting additional racks). The aggregation switch can then be connected to other aggregation switches, a local area network (LAN), or a wide area network (WAN). This example is just one of many different types of networking topologies that can be used, but it demonstrates how different networking components can be used to interconnect systems.

© Thomas Fenton and Patrick Kennedy 2022
T. Fenton and P. Kennedy, *Running ESXi on a Raspberry Pi*,
https://doi.org/10.1007/978-1-4842-7465-1_12

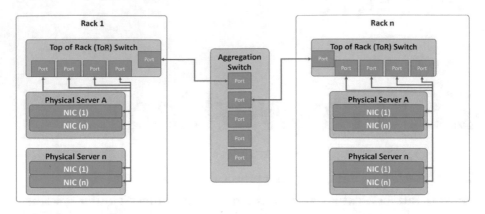

Figure 12-1. *Traditional Networking Topology*

When we initially set up an ESXi server, a virtual switch was automatically created, and the physical NIC on the server was attached to it. When we created a VM, a vNIC was created and attached to the virtual switch. This setup is shown in Figure 12-2.

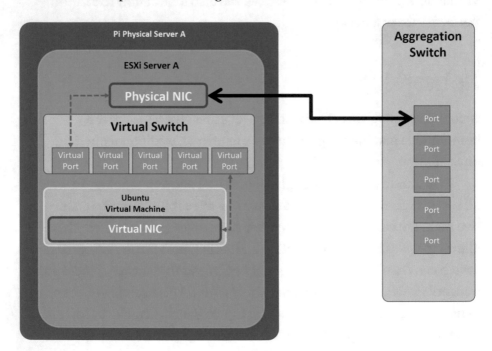

Figure 12-2. *ESXi Virtual Networking*

The components that make up a virtual network can be observed, created, and modified using the ESXi Host Client.

To see a high-level overview of *vSwitch0* (the switch that was automatically created as we installed ESXi), expand the **Networking** drop-down menu from the Navigator pane in the ESXi Host Client. Then, select **vSwitch0** and expand the **vSwitch topology** pane, and a graphic representation of the vSwitch will be shown (see Figure 12-3).

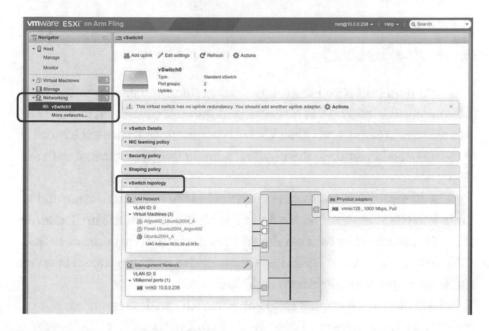

Figure 12-3. *vSwitch Topology*

Virtual Switch

vSwitch0 has two port groups: *VM Network* and *Management Network*, both of which were connected to a single *physical adapter* (see Figure 12-4) and were created automatically when we installed ESXi. The physical adapter is the NIC on the Raspberry Pi.

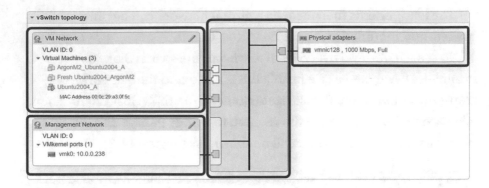

Figure 12-4. *vSwitch0*

Port groups allow you to group ports together, and each port can have different attributes. The VM Network port group is connected to the VMs that we have created, and these VMs can communicate with each other or to the outside world via the physical adapter that is associated with the vSwitch.

The Management Network port group is used to communicate and control the ESXi host, rather than the VMs that reside on it. The IP address of the Management Network is the address that is used to connect to the ESXi host via SSH or the ESXi Host Client. Active ports are shown in green, and inactive ports are displayed in white.

vSwitch0 is attached to a single physical NIC on the server, but a vSwitch can have more than one physical NIC, or it can be an *internal-only* vSwitch and not be attached to any physical NICs. An internal-only switch is useful in multitiered applications that only need VM-to-VM communication.

Figure 12-5 shows how vSwitches can be configured for multitiered applications. *Virtual Machine 2* (which contains an application such as a database that should not be accessed directly from the LAN) is connected to an internal-only vSwitch. *Virtual Machine 1* has two virtual NICs: one that is connected to the internal-only vSwitch and a second that is connected to a vSwitch that is associated with two physical NICs.

Both of these physical NICs are connected to different aggregation switches, which are in turn connected to the LAN. The dual physical NICs and aggregation switches provide redundancy in the case of a failure.

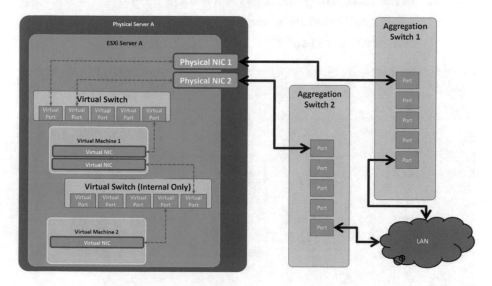

Figure 12-5. *Multitiered Application*

Creating a Virtual Switch

You can create a virtual switch using the ESXi Host Client. When creating a vSwitch, there are various options available, including

- Promiscuous Mode – Passes all the frames to the VMs on the switch; this is needed for firewalls, port scanners, WAN emulators, etc.

- MAC Address Changes – Allows traffic to the VM if the MAC address is changed by the guest OS.

- Forge Transmits – Allows VMs to pass network frames even if they do not match the MAC address of the vNIC.

In the following exercise, you will create an internal-only switch:

1. Log in to the ESXi Host Client as root.

2. In the Navigator pane, select **Networking**. Then
   select the **Virtual switches** tab, and click **Add
   standard virtual switch**.

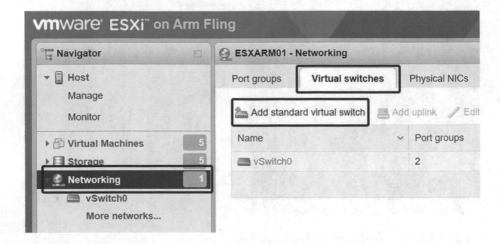

3. In the **vSwitch Name** text box, enter *InternalOnly0*.

4. Expand the **Link discovery** and **Security** drop-
   down menus and examine the options.

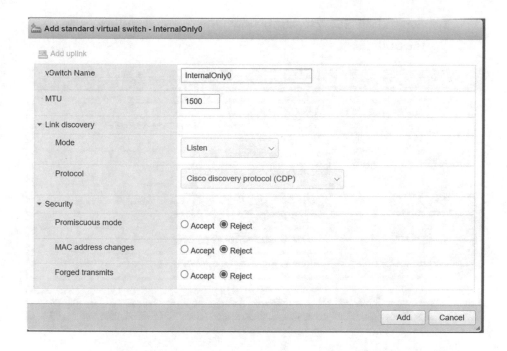

5.   Click **Add**.

Once a vSwitch has been created, you can then add port groups to it, and these port groups can have security attributes just like vSwitches. These attributes are inherited from the vSwitch by default.

In the following exercise, you will create a port group on the *InternalOnly0* vSwitch:

1.   Select the **Port groups** tab, and click **Add port group**.

2.   In the **Name** text box, enter *DatabaseToFrontend*.

3. Expand the **Security** drop-down menu and examine
    the options.

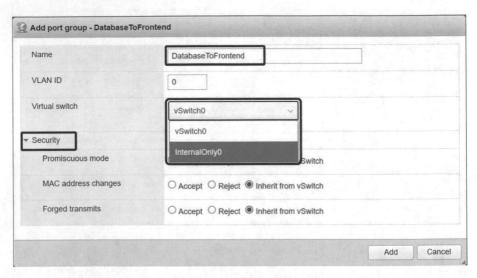

4. Click **Add**.

There is now a vSwitch with a port group that does not have a physical
NIC attached to it, but you can add a physical NIC if you wish.

If you decide to add a physical NIC to the switch at a later point in time,
the following are the steps to do so:

1. In the Navigator pane, open the **Networking** drop-
    down menu and select **More networks**.

2. In the right pane, click the **Port groups** tab, and
    click **DatabaseToFrontend**.

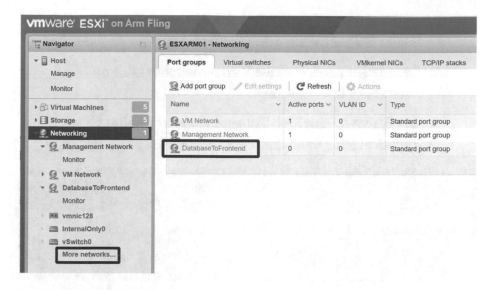

3. Verify in the diagram that it is part of the vSwitch and that it does not have any physical adapters attached to it.

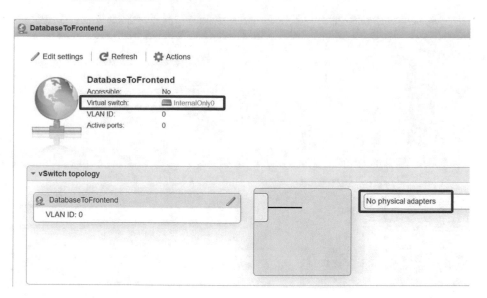

4. In the Navigator pane, select **More networks** again under the **Networking** drop-down menu.

5. In the right pane, click the **Virtual switches** tab, and then select **InternalOnly0**.

6. Verify that InternalOnly0 does not have any uplinks (physical NICs), and then click **InternalOnly0.**

7. Verify its settings and then click **Add uplink**.

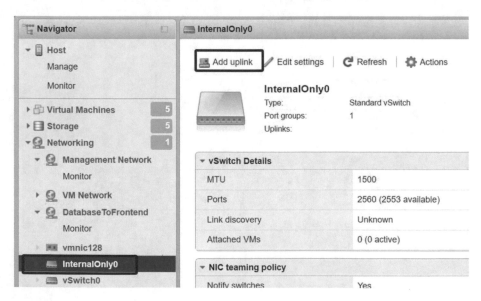

8. Verify that there are not any free physical NICs to add to it, and then click **OK**.

9. Click **Cancel**.

Physical NICs

The physical NICs on an ESXi host are detected automatically and can be used by the vSwitches on it. The ESXi Host Client can be used to examine and modify the attributes of the NIC.

In the following exercise, you will examine the attributes of the physical NIC:

1. In the Navigator pane, open the **Networking** drop-down menu, and then select **More networks**.

2. In the right pane, click the **Physical NICs** tab.

3. Verify the attributes of the NIC.

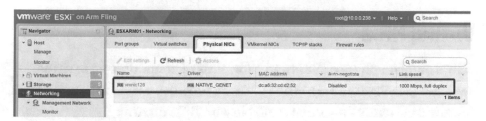

4. Click the NIC that is displayed.

5. Verify the details of the NIC.

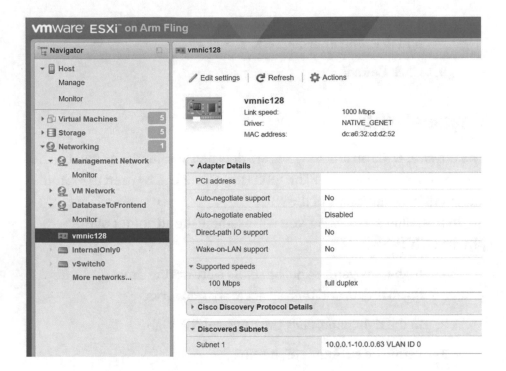

Virtual NICs

vNICs emulate physical NICs and allow VMs to communicate to virtual switches (see Figure 12-5). While VMware provides a wide variety of vNICs, there are currently only three available with ESXi on Arm:

- E1000 – An emulation of the Intel 82545EM Gigabit Ethernet NIC.

- E1000E – An emulation of the Intel 82574 Gigabit Ethernet NIC.

- VMXNET3 – This vNIC does not emulate an NIC but was designed by VMware from scratch for optimal performance for VMs.

The E1000 and E1000E vNICs can use standard OS drivers. As VMXNET3 does not have a physical counterpart, installing VMware Tools on the VM is required to obtain the driver for it. Although the OS on the VMs will report a maximum transfer rate, the actual limit is based on how much load the CPU on the host has and the physical network components.

Figure 12-6 shows how you can see and change the vNIC on a VM from the ESXi Host Client. This is the same panel that is used to see the vSwitch it is attached to. The MAC address is usually automatically assigned to the vNIC, but you can manually specify a MAC address if needed.

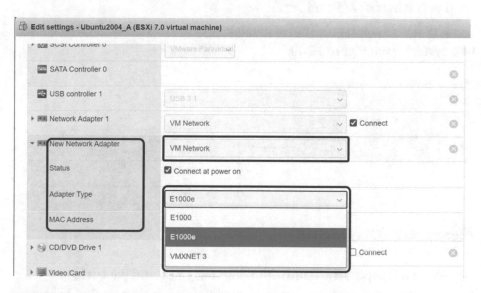

Figure 12-6. *vNIC Adapter Type*

Testing Performance of a Network

It is often helpful to measure how much network traffic can be passed between two systems and how cleanly that traffic can be passed. This information can be used for a variety of reasons, such as capacity planning, seeing how changes affect the system, or troubleshooting issues that you are having. There are many different tools that you can use to measure bandwidth, but the one I use the most is iPerf3 due to its ease of use and flexibility.

iPerf3

iPerf3 is the third rewrite of iPerf, which was first released in 2014. It was developed by Robert McMahon, Battu Kaushik, and Tim Auckland. It is free, widely available, and licensed under the BSD license. The home page for iPerf3 is https://iperf.fr/.

iPerf3 uses a server/client scheme to create an artificial load between two systems (see Figure 12-7).

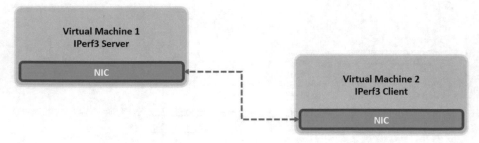

Figure 12-7. *iPerf3 Scheme*

iPerf3 will report the bandwidth, latency, jitter, and packet loss between two systems. The source code of iPerf3 can be downloaded and compiled on Arm machines, but as there are also precompiled packages of it for Ubuntu and Fedora Arm, we will be using those instead.

Using iPerf3 VM-to-VM on the Same ESXi Host

In this section, we will install iPerf3 on our Ubuntu and Fedora VMs. We will then use it to check the bandwidth between them (see Figure 12-8). In another section, we will check the bandwidth between a VM and a physical host (see Figure 12-11) and then use it to check the bandwidth between a VM and the ESXi host on which it resides (see Figure 12-15).

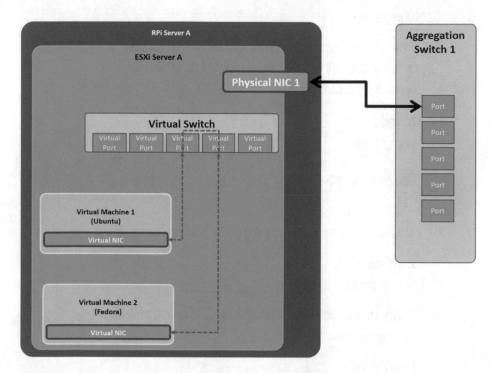

Figure 12-8. *iPerf3 on Two VMs on Same ESXi Host*

In the following exercise, you will install iPerf3 on two different VMs and use it to check the bandwidth between them:

1. Use SSH or the console to connect to your Ubuntu VM.

2. Install iPerf3 on the Ubuntu server by entering

   sudo su
   apt install iPerf3

3. Verify that iPerf3 was installed and check the version
    of it by entering

    ```
    iPerf3 -v
    ```

4. Obtain the IP address (you will use the IP address
    later) and start the iPerf3 server on the Ubuntu
    system by entering

    ```
    Ip add
    iPerf3 -s
    ```

5. Use SSH or the console to connect to your Fedora
    VM.

6. Install iPerf3 on the Ubuntu server by entering

    ```
    sudo su
    dnf install iPerf3
    ```

7. Verify that iPerf3 was installed and check the version
    of it by entering

    ```
    iPerf3 -v
    ```

8. Start an iPerf3 test by entering

    ```
    iPerf3 -c 10.0.0.152 -t 10 -i 5 -f g
    ```

In my case, this started the client system (*-c*) and connected to the
iPerf3 server (*10.0.0.152*); iPerf ran the test for 10 seconds (*-t 10*), showed
the results in Gb (*-fg*), and reported statistics every 5 seconds (*-i 5*).

The results show that the bandwidth between the two systems was
1.15Gbps (see Figure 12-9). The speed of the network was not limited by
the theoretical limit of the 1Gb virtual NIC on the VMs as both VMs were
on the same ESXi host. This is diagrammed in Figure 12-8.

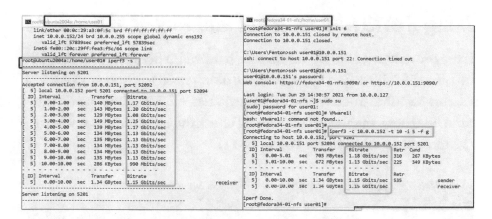

Figure 12-9. *iPerf3 results*

I then ran iPerf3 in the reverse direction by appending a *-r* to the command, and the results in Figure 12-10 show a slightly higher speed of 1.21Gbps.

```
[root@fedora34-01-nfs user01]# iperf3 -c 10.0.0.152 -t 10 -i 5 -f g -R
Connecting to host 10.0.0.152, port 5201
Reverse mode, remote host 10.0.0.152 is sending
[  5] local 10.0.0.151 port 52108 connected to 10.0.0.152 port 5201
[ ID] Interval           Transfer     Bitrate
[  5]   0.00-5.00   sec   718 MBytes  1.20 Gbits/sec
[  5]   5.00-10.00  sec   729 MBytes  1.22 Gbits/sec
- - - - - - - - - - - - - - - - - - - - - - - - -
[ ID] Interval           Transfer     Bitrate         Retr
[  5]   0.00-10.01  sec  1.42 GBytes  1.22 Gbits/sec  447         sender
[  5]   0.00-10.00  sec  1.41 GBytes  1.21 Gbits/sec              receiver

iperf Done.
[root@fedora34-01-nfs user01]#
```

Figure 12-10. *iPerf3 in Reverse Mode*

Using iPerf3 Between VM and Physical Machine

In the previous section, we verified the bandwidth between two VMs on the same ESXi host. The network traffic didn't need to go on any physical networking infrastructure (i.e., NICs, switches, etc.) as they were on the same ESXi host. In this section, we will check the bandwidth between a VM and a physical host (see Figure 12-11).

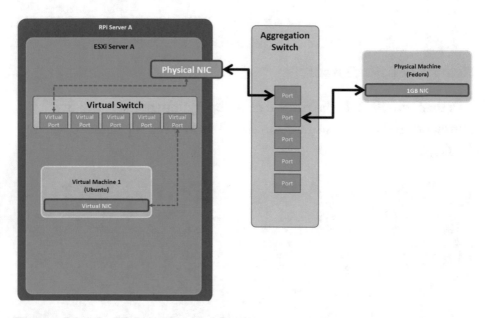

Figure 12-11. *VM to Physical Server*

I ran iPerf3 in forward and reverse modes. In both cases, due to the limitations of the physical hardware, the bandwidth was 0.90Gbps (see Figure 12-12).

```
iperf Done.
[user01@printserver01 ~]$ iperf3 -c 10.0.0.152 -t 10 -i 5 -f g
Connecting to host 10.0.0.152, port 5201
[  5] local 10.0.0.219 port 52978 connected to 10.0.0.152 port 5201
[ ID] Interval           Transfer     Bitrate         Retr  Cwnd
[  5]   0.00-5.00   sec   557 MBytes   0.93 Gbits/sec    0    776 KBytes
[  5]   5.00-10.00  sec   554 MBytes   0.93 Gbits/sec    0   1.02 MBytes
- - - - - - - - - - - - - - - - - - - - - - - - -
[ ID] Interval           Transfer     Bitrate         Retr
[  5]   0.00-10.00  sec  1.08 GBytes   0.93 Gbits/sec    0             sender
[  5]   0.00-10.00  sec  1.08 GBytes   0.93 Gbits/sec                  receiver

iperf Done.
[user01@printserver01 ~]$ iperf3 -c 10.0.0.152 -t 10 -i 5 -f g -R
Connecting to host 10.0.0.152, port 5201
Reverse mode, remote host 10.0.0.152 is sending
[  5] local 10.0.0.219 port 52982 connected to 10.0.0.152 port 5201
[ ID] Interval           Transfer     Bitrate
[  5]   0.00-5.00   sec   537 MBytes   0.90 Gbits/sec
[  5]   5.00-10.00  sec   534 MBytes   0.90 Gbits/sec
- - - - - - - - - - - - - - - - - - - - - - - - -
[ ID] Interval           Transfer     Bitrate         Retr
[  5]   0.00-10.00  sec  1.05 GBytes   0.90 Gbits/sec    0             sender
[  5]   0.00-10.00  sec  1.05 GBytes   0.90 Gbits/sec                  receiver

iperf Done.
[user01@printserver01 ~]$ ▄
```

Figure 12-12. *iPerf3 Results from VM to Physical Host*

Using iPerf3 Using the VMXNET3 Driver

In our previous test, we used iPerf3 with VMs that had E1000E vNICs. In this section, we will check the bandwidth between two VMs using the VMXNET3 vNICs on the same ESXi host.

To change from the E1000E to VMXNET3 vNICs, take the following steps:

1. Log into the ESXi Host Client.

2. Power off the Ubuntu VM.

3.   Select **Edit**.

4.   Expand the **Network Adapter 1**. Then, from the
     Adapter Type drop-down menu, select *VMXNET 3*.

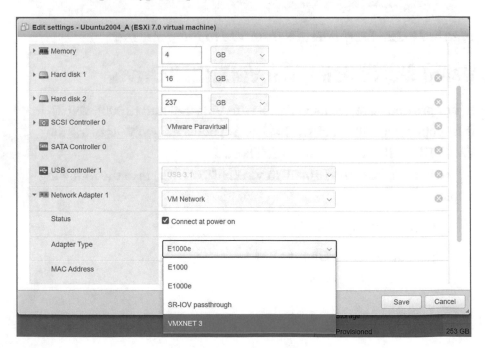

5. Click **Save**.

6. Start the VM.

Next, verify that the VM is using the VMXNET3 driver by taking the following steps:

1. Log into the Ubuntu VM.

2. Check the driver that was being used by entering

    sudo su
    `lshw -class network`

In my case, this showed that a VMXNET3 Ethernet Controller was being used and it had a capacity of 10Gbps (see Figure 12-13).

```
root@ubuntu2004a:/home/user01# lshw -class network
  *-network
        description: Ethernet interface
        product: VMXNET3 Ethernet Controller
        vendor: VMware
        physical id: 0
        bus info: pci@0000:0a:00.0
        logical name: ens192
        version: 01
        serial: 00:0c:29:10:ad:23
        size: 10Gbit/s
        capacity: 10Gbit/s
        width: 32 bits
        clock: 33MHz
```

Figure 12-13. *VMXNET3 Attributes*

I then created another Ubuntu VM as I did not install VMware Tools on the Fedora VM. I reran my iPerf3 test between the two Ubuntu VMs with VMXNET3 vNICs. The results showed that the bandwidth was 2.08Gbps (see Figure 12-14).

```
root@ubuntu2004a:/home/user01# iperf3 -c 10.0.0.148  -t 10 -i 5 -f g
Connecting to host 10.0.0.148, port 5201
[  5] local 10.0.0.131 port 48892 connected to 10.0.0.148 port 5201
[ ID] Interval           Transfer     Bitrate         Retr  Cwnd
[  5]   0.00-5.00   sec  1.24 GBytes  2.12 Gbits/sec    0   1.95 MBytes
[  5]   5.00-10.00  sec  1.18 GBytes  2.03 Gbits/sec  728   1.70 MBytes
- - - - - - - - - - - - - - - - - - - - - - - - - -
[ ID] Interval           Transfer     Bitrate         Retr
[  5]   0.00-10.00  sec  2.42 GBytes  2.08 Gbits/sec  728             sender
[  5]   0.00-10.00  sec  2.42 GBytes  2.08 Gbits/sec                  receiver

iperf Done.
```

Figure 12-14. *VMXNET3 vNIC*

The ESXi Host Client showed that the CPU cores on the Pi were at greater than 90% while the iPerf3 test was running (see Figure 12-15). This could be the reason that only 2Gbps was being transferred.

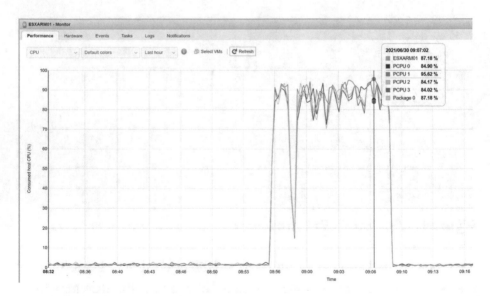

Figure 12-15. *CPU Usage*

iPerf3 on ESXi

For troubleshooting and planning, it is desirable to see what kind of bandwidth you can get to an ESXi host rather than the VMs that reside on it.

VMware discourages installing any third-party software on an ESXi host as it could have disastrous consequences that could interfere with the operation of both the hypervisor and the VMs that reside on it. That said, VMware included iPerf with ESXi 6.5, removed it in 6.7, but then added it back again in 6.7 U1. It is included in the x64 version of ESXi 7.0 but not with the ESXi on Arm Fling.

iPerf3 can be compiled from the source, and compiled versions can be downloaded from the Internet. I installed a precompiled version and ran it on my Pi ESXi host, and the following are the results that I recorded when I ran it from a VM on the ESXi host and from a physical machine.

When I ran it from/to an ESXi host to a VM with an E1000E vNIC, it reported 1.28Gbps (see Figure 12-16).

```
[root@fedora34-01-nfs user01]# iperf3 -c 10.0.0.238 -t 10 -i 5 -f g
Connecting to host 10.0.0.238, port 5201
[  5] local 10.0.0.151 port 56080 connected to 10.0.0.238 port 5201
[ ID] Interval           Transfer     Bitrate         Retr  Cwnd
[  5]   0.00-5.00   sec  1.15 GBytes  1.98 Gbits/sec    0   2.03 MBytes
[  5]   5.00-10.00  sec  1.17 GBytes  2.02 Gbits/sec    0   2.03 MBytes
- - - - - - - - - - - - - - - - - - - - - - - - - - -
[ ID] Interval           Transfer     Bitrate         Retr
[  5]   0.00-10.00  sec  2.32 GBytes  2.00 Gbits/sec    0             sender
[  5]   0.00-10.00  sec  2.32 GBytes  1.99 Gbits/sec                  receiver

iperf Done.
[root@fedora34-01-nfs user01]# iperf3 -c 10.0.0.238 -t 10 -i 5 -f g -R
Connecting to host 10.0.0.238, port 5201
Reverse mode, remote host 10.0.0.238 is sending
[  5] local 10.0.0.151 port 56084 connected to 10.0.0.238 port 5201
[ ID] Interval           Transfer     Bitrate
[  5]   0.00-5.00   sec   791 MBytes  1.33 Gbits/sec
[  5]   5.00-10.00  sec   734 MBytes  1.23 Gbits/sec
- - - - - - - - - - - - - - - - - - - - - - - - - - -
[ ID] Interval           Transfer     Bitrate         Retr
[  5]   0.00-10.00  sec  1.49 GBytes  1.28 Gbits/sec    0             sender
[  5]   0.00-10.00  sec  1.49 GBytes  1.28 Gbits/sec                  receiver

iperf Done.
```

Figure 12-16. *iPerf3 Results ESXi Host to VM Using E1000E*

When I ran it from/to an ESXi host to a VM with a VMXNET3 vNIC, it reported 2.01Gbps (see Figure 12-17).

```
root@ubuntu2004a:/home/user01# iperf3 -c 10.0.0.238 -t 10 -i5 -f g
Connecting to host 10.0.0.238, port 5201
[  5] local 10.0.0.152 port 57578 connected to 10.0.0.238 port 5201
[ ID] Interval           Transfer     Bitrate         Retr  Cwnd
[  5]   0.00-5.00   sec  1.18 GBytes  2.02 Gbits/sec    0   2.07 MBytes
[  5]   5.00-10.00  sec  1.16 GBytes  2.00 Gbits/sec    0   2.07 MBytes
- - - - - - - - - - - - - - - - - - - - - - -
[ ID] Interval           Transfer     Bitrate         Retr
[  5]   0.00-10.00  sec  2.34 GBytes  2.01 Gbits/sec    0             sender
[  5]   0.00-10.00  sec  2.34 GBytes  2.01 Gbits/sec                  receiver
```

Figure 12-17. *iPerf3 Results ESXi Host to VM Using VMXNET3*

When I ran it from/to an ESXi host to the physical system, it reported 0.94Gbps (see Figure 12-18).

```
[user01@printserver01 ~]$ iperf3 -c 10.0.0.238 -t 10 -i 5 -f g
Connecting to host 10.0.0.238, port 5201
[  5] local 10.0.0.219 port 58440 connected to 10.0.0.238 port 5201
[ ID] Interval           Transfer     Bitrate         Retr  Cwnd
[  5]   0.00-5.00   sec  561 MBytes   0.94 Gbits/sec    0   1.00 MBytes
[  5]   5.00-10.00  sec  560 MBytes   0.94 Gbits/sec    0   1.11 MBytes
- - - - - - - - - - - - - - - - - - - - - - -
[ ID] Interval           Transfer     Bitrate         Retr
[  5]   0.00-10.00  sec  1.09 GBytes  0.94 Gbits/sec    0             sender
[  5]   0.00-10.00  sec  1.09 GBytes  0.94 Gbits/sec                  receiver

iperf Done.
[user01@printserver01 ~]$ iperf3 -c 10.0.0.238 -t 10 -i 5 -f g -R
Connecting to host 10.0.0.238, port 5201
Reverse mode, remote host 10.0.0.238 is sending
[  5] local 10.0.0.219 port 58444 connected to 10.0.0.238 port 5201
[ ID] Interval           Transfer     Bitrate
[  5]   0.00-5.00   sec  560 MBytes   0.94 Gbits/sec
[  5]   5.00-10.00  sec  560 MBytes   0.94 Gbits/sec
- - - - - - - - - - - - - - - - - - - - - - -
[ ID] Interval           Transfer     Bitrate         Retr
[  5]   0.00-10.00  sec  1.10 GBytes  0.94 Gbits/sec    0             sender
[  5]   0.00-10.00  sec  1.09 GBytes  0.94 Gbits/sec                  receiver

iperf Done.
```

Figure 12-18. *iPerf3 Results ESXi Host to Physical System*

Summary

From their founding, VMware has recognized the importance of networking with regard to virtual infrastructure; their engineers have honed their implementation of physical networking components into virtual ones to a fine degree. VMware virtual NICs and switches and their TCP stack have proven to be rock-solid over the years. It is simple and intuitive to work with their virtual networking constructs.

Although I used iPerf3 to test the performance of VMs, physical machines, and even ESXi servers, there are other tools that can be used. These tools can be extremely helpful when troubleshooting performance problems, and every system administrator needs to be comfortable with them.

So far we have treated our ESXi host as an individual unit, but the reality is that it is extremely rare that you will see an ESXi host act as a single entity as the real power of virtualization comes into play when you have multiple ESXi hosts in an environment. vCenter Server is VMware's product that allows the management and monitoring of multiple ESXi hosts. We discuss it in the next chapter.

CHAPTER 13

Managing ESXi Systems with VCSA

In this book so far, we have concentrated on using the ESXi Host Client to manage our ESXi server primarily because it is a free tool that comes with ESXi. Although useful when managing a single server, the ESXi Host Client is seldom used in production environments as the real power of vSphere comes with clustering many ESXi hosts together under the management umbrella of vCenter Server.

In its early days, vCenter Server needed to be installed on a Windows Server system, but it is now also delivered as a virtual appliance known as vCenter Server Appliance (VCSA). As the VCSA is far more popular now, we will only be discussing it in this chapter.

vCenter Server has, up until recently, only supported x64 ESXi hosts – but vCenter Server 7.0 now supports Arm ESXi hosts as well. Despite the fact that the appliance is compiled for x64 and cannot be installed on an Arm ESXi host, it can be installed on VMware Workstation Player. Player is not an approved platform for vCenter Server, but it will work fine for our needs.

In this chapter, we will discuss the power of VCSA and explain how to install it. We will also walk through how to manage ESXi systems using the vSphere Client, the VCSA web-based interface, as well as ControlUp, a third-party product.

© Thomas Fenton and Patrick Kennedy 2022
T. Fenton and P. Kennedy, *Running ESXi on a Raspberry Pi*,
https://doi.org/10.1007/978-1-4842-7465-1_13

vCenter Server License

There are three common ESXi licensing options – *Essentials*, *Foundation*, and *Standard*.

Table 13-1 shows some of the capabilities of VCSA 7.0.

Table 13-1. *VCSA License*

	Essentials	Foundation	Standard
Maximum supported ESXi hosts	3	4	2000
Management server	☐	☐	☐
Built-in database	☐	☐	☐
Inventory server	☐	☐	☐
vMotion	*	☐	☐
vRealize Orchestrator			☐
vCenter High Availability			☐

All three licenses include the right to use a PostgreSQL database, which is installed when the appliance is installed. Other databases, such as Oracle and MS SQL Server, can be used with VCSA, but the PostgreSQL database has proven over the years to be able to handle the kinds of loads required of it.

- *VCenter Server Essentials* was designed for companies that are either small or are just starting to use virtualization; it only supports three ESXi hosts and is often bundled together with other licenses. The basic version of Essentials does not come with the ability to do vMotion, but the *Essentials Plus* version does.

- *VCenter Server Foundation* was also designed for smaller companies as it only supports four ESXi hosts. It does not come with a license for ESXi hosts, so they will need to be purchased separately.

- *VCenter Server Standard* was designed for companies of all sizes and supports up to 2000 hosts. It does not come with licenses for ESXi hosts, so they will need to be purchased separately. It does come with many features for availability and orchestration that make it enterprise-ready.

I know that I have not given the complexities of VCSA and vSphere licensing the attention that they deserve in this section, but to do so would take up the entire chapter. What I am attempting to do is give you a feel for the different licenses that are available for it. VMware has a sub-portion of their website entitled *VMware Licensing Help Center* that you can visit for more guidance. If after reading it and you still have questions, VMware or one of their many partners can help you determine the best license for your environment.

VMware provides a 60-day trial license for vCenter Server, which is what we will be using for demonstration purposes in this chapter.

Installing vCenter Server

Installing VCSA in the early days was a catch-22; it was installed as a virtual appliance, but you needed a VCSA to install a virtual appliance in the first place. To some extent, the ESXi Host Client made it possible to install a virtual appliance without a VCSA, but VMware provides an easier option by making it possible to install a VCSA on an x64 ESXi host from the installation ISO mounted on a Windows system. The version of ESXi that you installed (7.0) on the RPi will only work with VCSA 7 and will not work with the 6.x versions of VCSA.

Alternatively, and not widely advertised and not supported, VCSA can be deployed on VMware Workstation Player.

I will show you how to deploy it on an x64 ESXi host and on Player.

A VCSA can be deployed using the GUI or from the command line, but we will be using the GUI. This is a two-stage process: the first stage deploys the OVA file of the appliance, and the second stage sets up and starts the services of the newly deployed appliance.

In this section, I will show you the steps involved, regardless of whether you are going to install it on an ESXi host or Player, to prepare for a VCSA installation.

To prepare to install VCSA, complete the following steps:

1. Read the release notes for the VCSA to make sure that you meet all the system requirements (i.e., storage, network, compute capacity, etc.) for the install.

2. Download the latest VCSA 7.0 or newer appliance installer to your Windows system from `my.vmware.com` under *Datacenter & Cloud Infrastructure*.

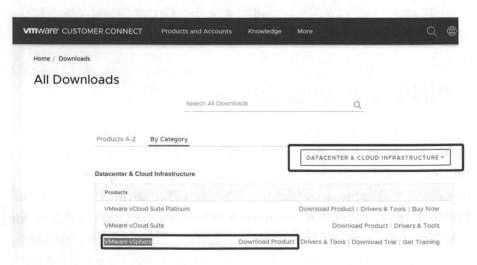

3. It is listed as *VMware vCenter Server*.

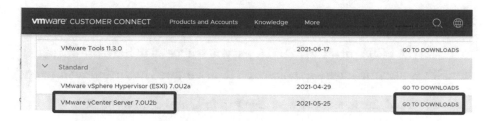

4. Click **Read More** and verify that you are
    downloading the file titled *VMware-VCSA-all-
    version_number-build_number.iso*. The ISO is quite
    large and will take a while to download.

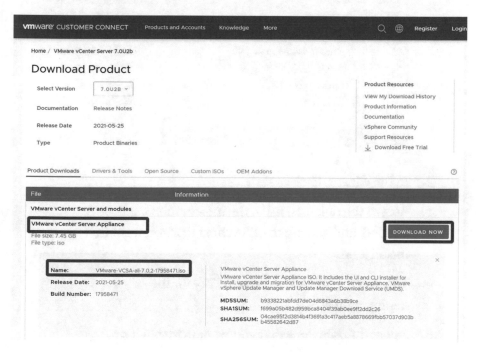

5. Mount the ISO as a CD. To do this in Windows 10,
    double-click it.

Installing vCenter Server on an x64 ESXi Host

To install the VCSA on an x64 ESXi host, you will need to have pre-installed the ESXi server and have a datastore on it (as outlined in the following steps).

1. Navigate to *vcsa-ui-installer* ➤ *win32* and double-click **installer.exe**.

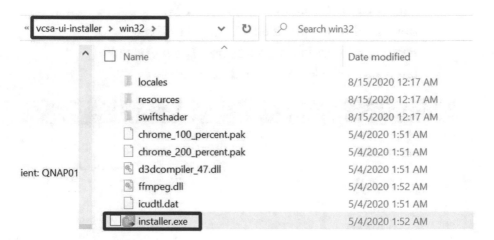

2. In the wizard, click **Install**.

3. Accept the defaults, fill in the information as needed, and specify the ESXi host that you want to install it on.

4. When you get to step 5, select **Tiny** for the deployment size.

5. Select the datastore that you want to install it on.

6. Set the networking information.

7. On the **Summary** page, verify your settings and click **Finish**. It can take up to a half hour to complete the first stage of the installation.

8. After the first stage has been completed, click **Continue**.

9. Accept the defaults and fill in the information as needed for the second stage.

    a. When asked to create a new single sign-on (SSO), call it *vsphere.local*.

10. On the **Summary** page, verify your settings and click **Finish**. It can take up to a half hour to complete the second stage of the installation.

11. After the installation has completed, make a note of the URL listed for the *vCenter Server Getting Started Page*.

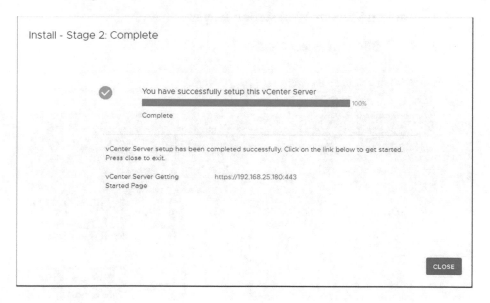

Install - Stage 2: Complete

✓   You have successfully setup this vCenter Server

▬▬▬▬▬▬▬▬▬▬▬▬▬▬ 100%

Complete

vCenter Server setup has been completed successfully. Click on the link below to get started. Press close to exit.

vCenter Server Getting   https://192.168.25.180:443
Started Page

CLOSE

12. Click **Close**.

If you installed the VCSA on an x64 ESXi server, you can skip over the next section.

Installing vCenter Server on VMware Workstation

If you do not have an x64 ESXi server installed, you can install VCSA on Player on a Windows or Linux system by following the steps listed in the following. If you do not yet have Player installed, I walked you through the steps to install it in a previous chapter. If you are using a system running macOS, you can use VMware Fusion to install and run vCenter Server.

To install the smallest VCSA available (Tiny), the system on which it runs will need to have the capacity to host two vCPUs, 10GB RAM, and 415GB of storage space for the VM. As Player can only run a single VM at a time, if you want to run a second VM, you will need to upgrade to VMware Workstation.

1.   Launch VMware Workstation Player.

2.   Click **File** and select **Open**.

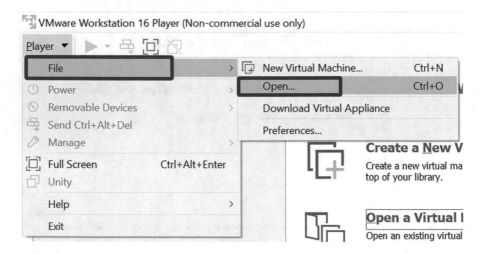

3. Navigate to the mounted ISO's *vcsa* folder and double-click ***VMware-vCenter-Server-Appliance***.

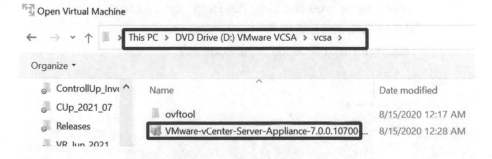

4. Accept the EULA and click **Next**.

5. Give the VCSA a name and click **Next**.

6. Select **Tiny vCenter Server with Embedded PSC** for the deployment size and click **Next**.

Import Virtual Machine

Deployment Options
   Select deployment options.

Deployment Options

Tiny vCenter Server with Embedded PSC
Small vCenter Server with Embedded PSC
Medium vCenter Server with Embedded PSC
Large vCenter Server with Embedded PSC
X-Large vCenter Server with Embedded PSC
Tiny vCenter Server with Embedded PSC (large storage)
Small vCenter Server with Embedded PSC (large storage)
Medium vCenter Server with Embedded PSC (large storage)
Large vCenter Server with Embedded PSC (large storage)

7. Click **Install**.

8. Accept the defaults and fill in the networking
    information (you can click the Help icon on the
    right of the text box to find out more about the
    information that needs to be entered).

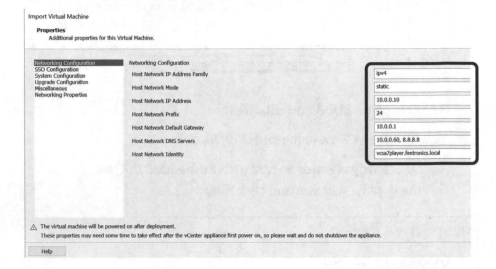

9. Click **Import**. The importation will take a few minutes to complete.

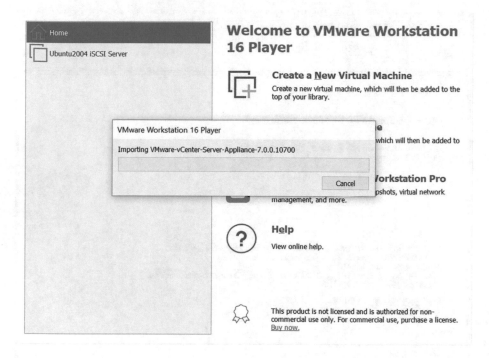

10. After the importation has completed, you will see
     the following screen.

11.   Press the **F2** key, and enter a root password.

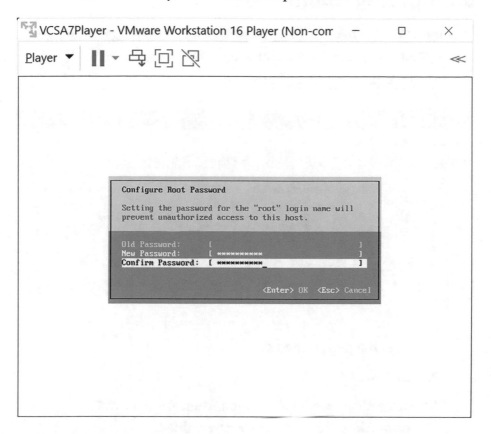

12.   Press **Esc**.

13.   From a web browser on the same network, enter the
URL that was given to configure the appliance. If you
get a message that the site can't be reached, wait a
few minutes, and then try again.

Configuring vCenter Server

After the VCSA has been installed, it will present a web page to configure it. At this point, follow these steps listed in the following:

1. In the web browser, click **Set Up**.

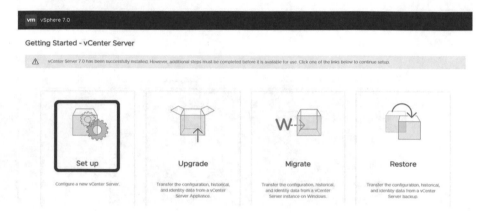

2. Enter the root password.

3. Click **Next**.

4. Verify the network information. Then, from the **SSH access** drop-down menu, select **Enabled**.

5. Click **Next**.

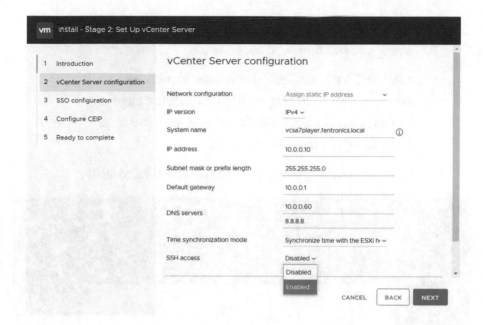

6. Set a domain name and password for your SSO
    domain, and then click **Next**.

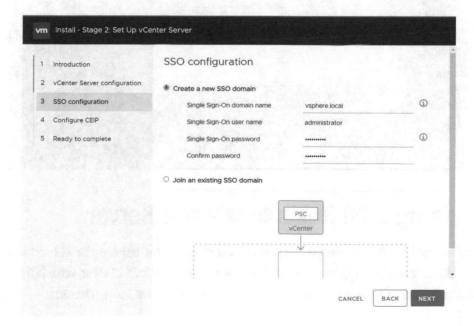

7.   Decline to join CEIP.

8.   Verify your settings and click **Finish**.

9.   Click **OK**. The installation can take 30 minutes to complete, and you may need to refresh the page to see its progress. Be patient until you see a message indicating that it has completed.

10.   Click the **vCenter Server Getting Started Page** URL.

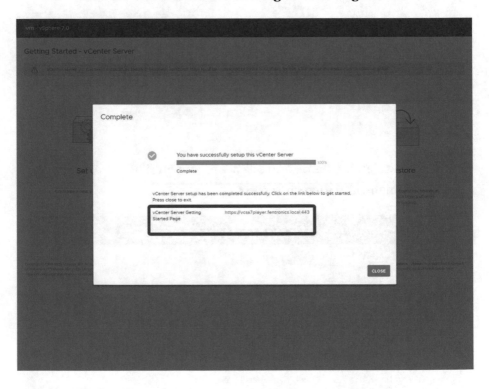

Adding ESXi Hosts to vCenter Server

After the VCSA is installed, you will need to add your existing ESXi hosts to it. vCenter has a topology where ESXi hosts are part of a cluster, which in turn is part of a datacenter, which in turn belongs to vCenter Server.

Figure 13-1 shows how vCenter Server (*vcsa7player*) has a single datacenter (Arm Datacenter), which has two clusters (Arm Cluster and Intel Cluster). All of these are logical objects that help with managing the objects (e.g., ESXi hosts, VMs, etc.) that are contained with them.

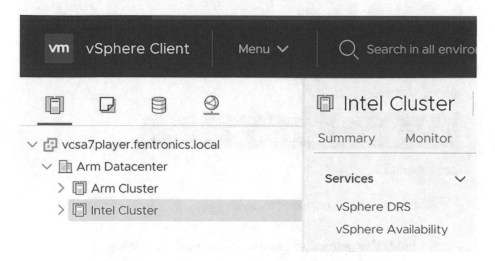

Figure 13-1. *Topography*

Both Arm and x64 ESXi hosts can be added to a VCSA; however, if you do so, you will want to create separate datacenters for them for management purposes.

To add an ESXi host to a VCSA, do the following:

1. In the web browser, click **Launch vSphere Client (HTML5)**.

← → C ⌂   ▲ Not secure | 10.0.0.17

vmware

Getting Started

LAUNCH VSPHERE CLIENT (HTML5)

Documentation

VMware vSphere Documentation Center

2. Enter the name and password that you previously set, and then click **Login**.

VMware® vSphere

administrator@vsphere.local

•••••••••

☐ Use Windows session authentication

LOGIN

3. In the navigation pane, right-click the name of your
    VCSA and select **New Datacenter**.

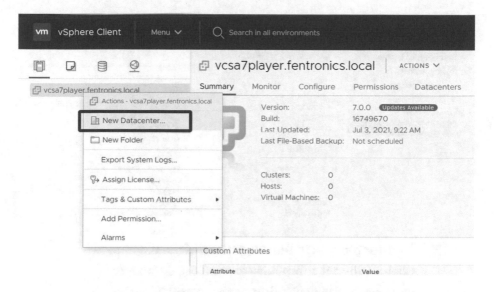

4. Enter a datacenter name and click **OK**.

5. Right-click the datacenter and select **Add Host**.

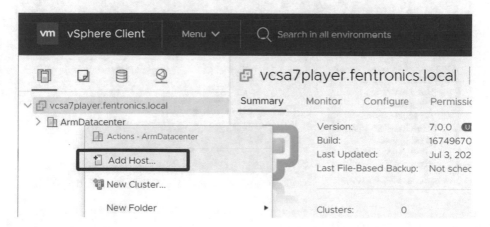

6. Enter the information asked for, verify the information that you entered, and click **Finish.**

7. Monitor the task in the lower pane of the vSphere Client. When it completes, expand the datacenter and host in the navigation pane to verify that the VMs that you previously created are shown.

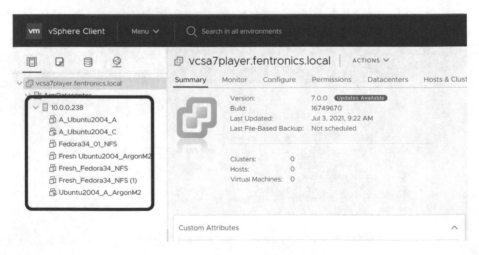

Managing ESXi Using vCenter Server

From an information and functionality standpoint, everything that was available in the ESXi Host Client is also available in the vSphere Client, but the vSphere Client has additional functionality in it as well. vCenter Server is a very powerful tool that is used to provide unparalleled business continuity, flexibility, and availability to servers. In the following section, we will provide a very basic overview of some of these features.

Note   As stated earlier, vCenter Server and the vSphere Client were designed to work with clusters of ESXi hosts, and to demonstrate the power of them, I will occasionally show a datacenter with a second ESXi host added to it.

Licensing

VMware licenses many of its features and products; for instance, the ESXi on Arm hosts come with a 180-day license, and vCenter Server has a 60-day trial license.

You can verify what is currently licensed in your environment by taking the following steps:

1. In the **Menu** drop-down, select **Administration**.

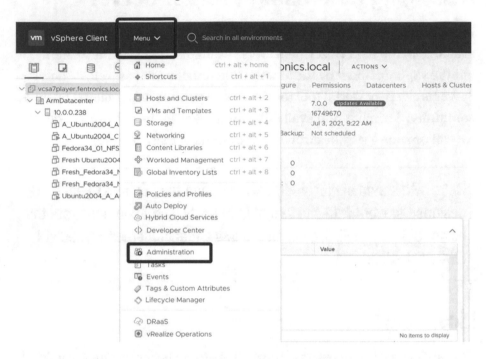

2. In the navigator, select **Licenses**.

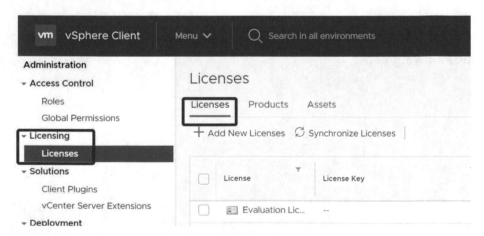

3. From within the **Assets** screen, select the **vCenter Server Systems** tab and verify that it has an evaluation license.

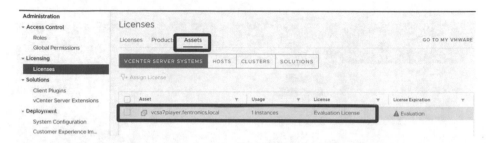

4. Select the **Hosts** tab and verify that it has an evaluation license.

Storage

All the storage that was created on your ESXi host can be seen using the vSphere Client. As vCenter Server was designed to host multiple ESXi hosts, shared storage devices like NFS shares and iSCSI targets can be accessed by multiple ESXi hosts simultaneously. This feature enables features like vMotion.

Figure 13-2 shows a datastore being shared between two hosts.

QNAP01_iSCSI01 | ACTIONS ⌄

Summary   Monitor   Configure   Permissions   Files   **Hosts**   VMs

Name ↑	State	Status	Cluster	Consumed CPU %
10.0.0.173	Connected	✓ Normal	NUC01	0%
10.0.0.21	Connected	⚠ Warning	Fentronics Clus...	34%

Figure 13-2. *Shared Datastore*

You can explore the storage with the vSphere Client by doing the following:

1. In the **Menu** drop-down, select **Storage**.

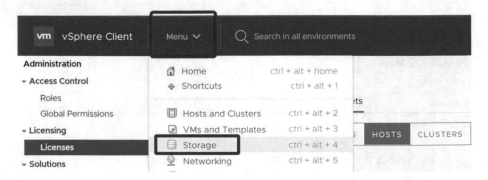

2. Verify that the **Storage** icon is underlined at the top of the navigation pane, and then expand the datacenter.

3. At the top of the main pane, select the **Datastores** tab.

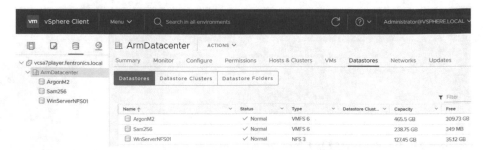

4. Verify that the datastores are shown and that the
    information (e.g., capacity, type, etc.) is all correct.
    For example, in my following screenshot, you will
    see that the *Sam256* datastore has an alert as it was
    running low on capacity.

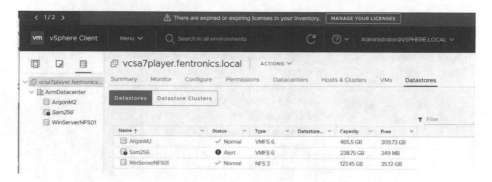

5. In the navigator, select one of your datastores and
    click all the tabs ending at **VMs**. Verify that the VMs
    that you created on the datastore are shown.

Networking

To explore networking using the vSphere Client, follow these steps in the following:

1. In the **Menu** drop-down, select **Networking**.

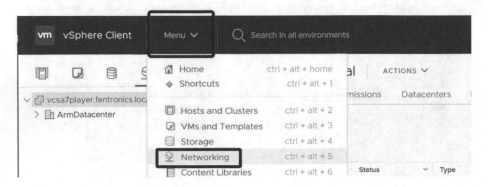

2. Verify that the **Networking** icon is underlined at the top of the navigation pane, and then expand the datacenter.

3. At the top of the main pane, select the **Networks** tab.

4. Verify that the networks are shown and information
    (e.g., type, hosts, etc.) is correct.

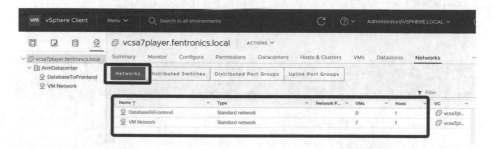

5. In the navigator, select **VM Network** and click all the
    tabs ending at **VMs**. Verify that the VMs that use the
    network are shown.

Virtual Machines

To explore VMs using the vSphere Client, do the following:

1.   In the **Menu** drop-down, select **VMs and Templates**.

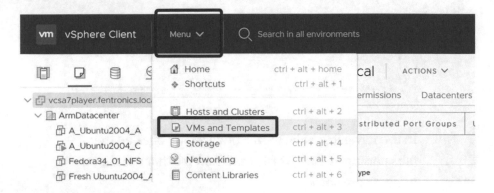

2.   Verify that the **VMs and Templates** icon is underlined at the top of the navigation pane, and then expand the datacenter.

3.   At the top of the main pane, open the **VMs** tab and select **Virtual Machines**.

4. Verify that the VMs are shown and all information
    displayed (e.g., state, status, etc.) is correct.

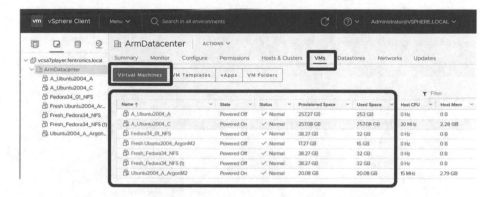

5. In the navigator, select one of your VMs and click
    through all the tabs.

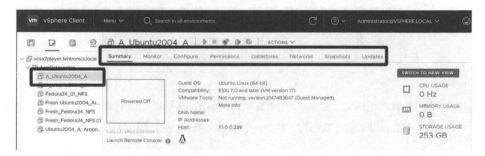

Cloning Virtual Machines

You can clone a VM with the vSphere Client. When using the ESXi Host
Client, we needed to manually copy the files to make a copy of a VM. You
can clone powered-on and powered-off VMs, but cloning a powered-
on VM will take longer. When cloning a VM, you can select a different
datastore for the VM.

To clone a VM using the vSphere Client, take the following steps:

1. In the navigator, right-click a VM and select **Clone ➤ Clone to Virtual Machine**.

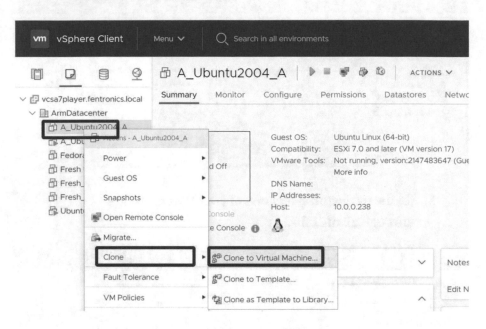

2. Enter the information for your cloned VM, accept the defaults, verify your settings, and click **Finish**.

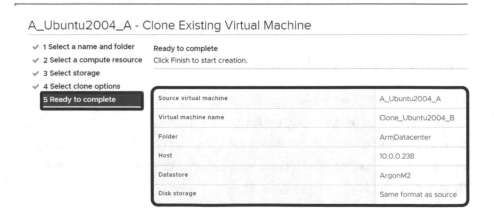

3. Monitor the task in the lower pane of the vSphere
    Client until it completes.

vMotion

The vSphere Client allows a VM to be transferred from one ESXi host to
another while it is still running – a very powerful tool from a business
continuity and availability perspective. This is perhaps the one feature
that enshrined VMware in the datacenter. An Arm-based VM cannot be
vMotioned to an x64 server.

In a production environment, you would set up a separate virtual
network to handle vMotion traffic. Since the RPi only has a single NIC, we
didn't set it up.

In the following example, I used vCenter Server with multiple ESXi
hosts.

To vMotion a VM, do the following:

1. In the navigator, right-click a running or powered-
    off VM and select **Migrate**.

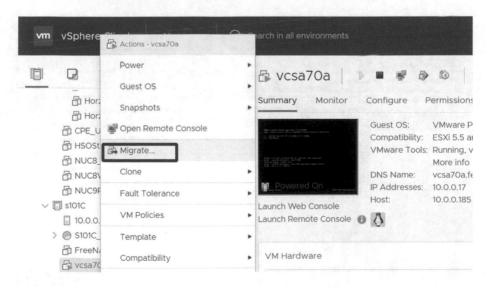

2.   Select **Change compute resource only** and click **Next**.

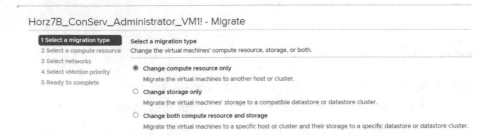

3.   Select the host that you want to migrate the VM to (all the hosts that the VM can migrate to will be displayed).

4.   Select the network that you want the migrated VM to use.

5.   Set the vMotion priority.

6.   Verify the information and click **Finish**.

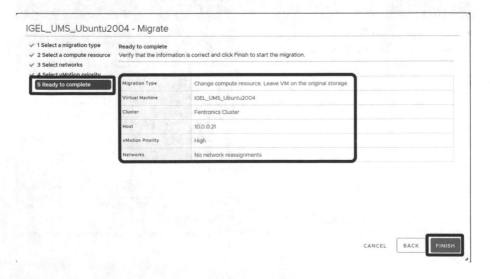

7.   Monitor the task in the lower pane of the vSphere
     Client until it completes.

Recent Tasks   Alarms

Task Name	∨	Target	∨	Start Ti... ∨	Status ↑
Relocate virtual machine		🗗 IGEL_UMS_Ubuntu2004		07/03/20... 11:44:23 AM	✓ Completed

Storage vMotion

The vSphere Client allows a VM not only to be transferred from one ESXi
host to another while it is still running, but it can also change the datastore
on which it resides. This allows storage to be maintained and taken off
lease or to have VMs moved off it for performance reasons. A VM can be
relocated from any datastore to another datastore; this includes migrating
from locally attached storage to network storage and vice versa.

To storage vMotion a VM, do the following:

1.   In the navigator, right-click a running or powered-
     off VM and select **Migrate**.

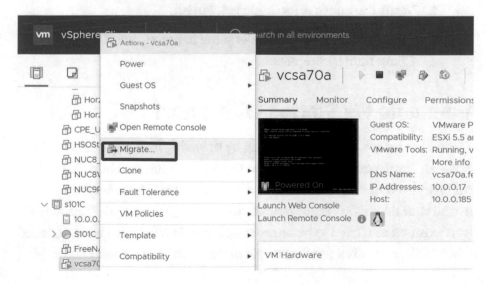

2. Select **Change storage only** and click **Next**.

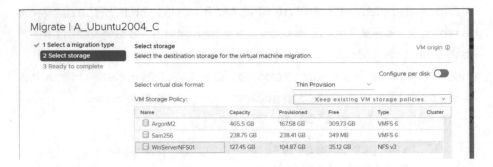

3. Select the storage that you want to migrate the VM to.

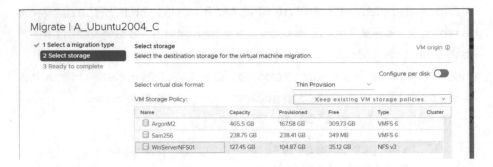

4. Verify the information and click **Finish**.

5. Monitor the task in the lower pane of the vSphere Client until it completes.

Automatic VM Startup with a Host

vCenter Server is a powerful tool, and by browsing its many features via the vSphere Client, you can start to grasp the power it has and how this power can be utilized in a datacenter. One example of this is its ability to start up and shut down VMs automatically with an ESXi host. This feature isn't used as much as it used to be as more advanced techniques have replaced it, but I still think it is a good example of the power of vCenter Server.

To have a VM start up with the host, follow these steps:

1. In the **Menu** drop-down, select **Hosts and Clusters**.

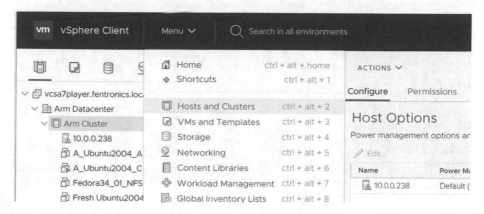

2. Verify that the **Hosts and Clusters** icon is underlined at the top of the navigation pane, and then expand the datacenter.

3. In the navigator, select an ESXi host, and then open the **Configure** tab.

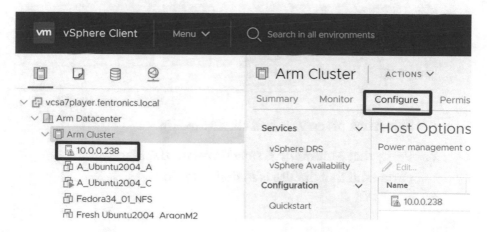

4. Expand **Virtual Machines**, select **VM Startup/Shutdown**, and then click **Edit**.

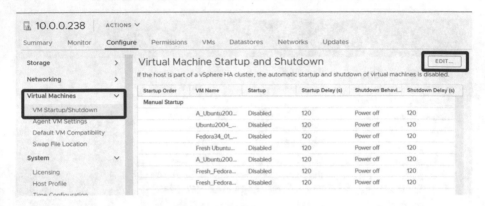

5. Select the **System influence** checkbox.

Edit VM Startup/Shutdown Configuration | 10.0.0.238

Default VM Settings

System influence	☑ Automatically start and stop the virtual machines with the system
Startup delay	120 ☐ Continue if VMware Tools is started
Shutdown delay	120
Shutdown action	Power off ˅

6. Select one of the VMs and click **Move Up**.

7. Verify that **Automatic** is now shown under Startup Order and that the VM is in that column.

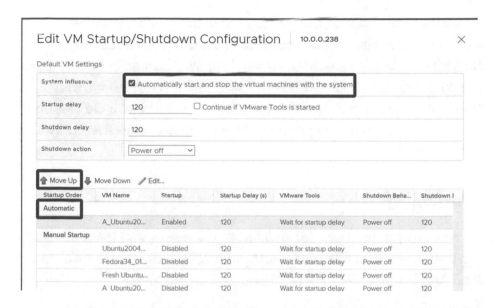

Using vCenter Server's automated startup and shutdown feature, you can gracefully shut down and restart a multitiered application in concert with an ESXi host. For example, you may want to have a VM that hosts a web application wait a few minutes after a VM that hosts a database starts up, and this feature allows you to do just that. If a VCSA is being hosted on an ESXi host, you can even set it to automatically initiate when a system starts up as these features do not rely directly on the VCSA.

Using Third-Party Products with VCSA

VMware realized early on that they cannot be all things to all people, and as such they actively promote an ecosystem of vendors to fill in the gaps and niches in their line of products. VMware has hundreds, if not thousands, of these vendors. If you have ever had a chance to visit VMworld, VMware's annual user conference, you would have seen a small sampling of VMware third-party vendors, ranging from software backup tools to massive displays by major hardware vendors.

At the time of writing this, I haven't seen any vendors who have explicitly stated that they support ESXi on Arm, but at the same time I haven't seen any that say that they don't support it either. In theory, since the ESXi host and vCenter Server use the same APIs to integrate with VMware products, as long as it doesn't directly interact with the VMs on the host, they should work just fine with ESXi on Arm as well as ESXi on an x64 ESXi host.

ControlUp

Third-party products provide a richness to VMware, and in this section, I will show you how one third-party product in particular, ControlUp Real-Time Console, enhances VMware's base products.

Note   As a disclaimer, at the time of writing this, I work for ControlUp as Technical Marketing Engineer, and I chose to use this product due to my familiarity with it.

Although I was fairly certain that many, if not most, third-party products would work with ESXi on Arm, I wanted to verify this to be true. I believe ControlUp was a good choice as I know that it is stable and uses APIs for deep integration with vCenter Server.

ControlUp is widely used to monitor and manage VDI environments. It has been around for over a decade, and in its early days it focused on Citrix VDI environments, that is, Citrix virtual desktops and the infrastructure on which they ran. As a vast majority of Citrix desktops run on vSphere, ControlUp from an early stage became familiar with the nuances of the integration of VCSA with third-party products. ControlUp now supports a wide range of VDI environments, including VMware Horizon. As discussed in an earlier chapter, Horizon desktops running on Arm are not supported, but we can still look at the Arm-based ESXi hosts and the VMs that run on them.

ControlUp Real-Time Console, like many third-party products for VMware, comes with a free trial license. It took me about five minutes to download and install the console on a Windows machine. I then added vCenter Server that was associated with my ESXi on Arm server to the console. Within moments, I saw the server and the VMs that were running on it.

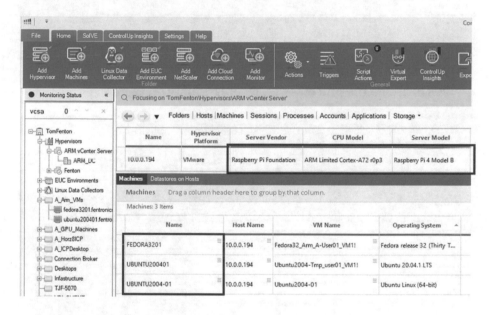

ControlUp obtains information about the VMs from vCenter Server, but one of its unique features is that it can also obtain information about what is happening inside a VM. It uses an agent to get this information from Windows machines and a Linux Data Collection (LDC) to obtain information from Linux systems. After setting up the LDC, I was able to see metrics from the VMs to gain deeper insight about them.

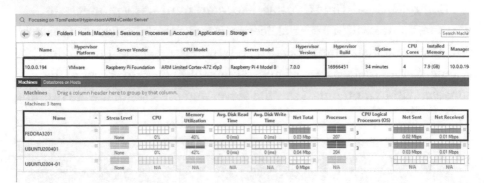

This included the processes that were running on the VMs.

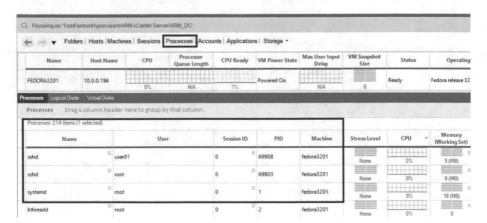

In one case, I found that the stress level was red due to disk latency. Upon investigating the issue, I found that this was due to the thumb drive that it was using for storage.

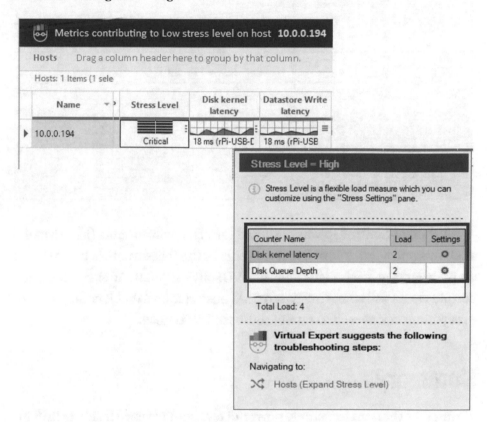

When running iPerf3 between two VMs on the same host, I monitored the network statistics in real time using the ControlUp dashboard.

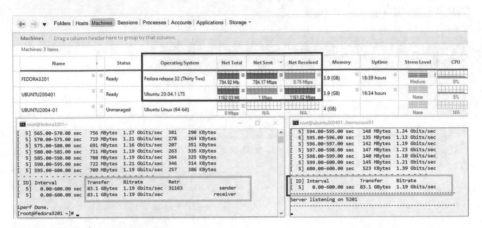

Although ControlUp was designed for VDI environments (i.e., virtual desktops and applications), it also monitors the infrastructure it is running on in order to give a holistic view of a VDI environment. After spending a couple weeks with the Arm-based ESXi hosts, I found that it could monitor everything on it as well as on my x64-based ESXi hosts.

Summary

vCenter Server is an extremely powerful tool, and we gave it short shrift in this chapter to stay within the scope of this book. One of its major powers is the ability to create scripts to programmatically work with and manage them via PowerShell using PowerCLI. A huge and enthusiastic community has formed around this and has come up with scripts to automate just about any task.

Although I was able to use Player to install and run VCSA, it does consume a fair amount of resources (two vCPUs and 12GB of memory), so make sure the system that you are using is equipped to handle the load that will be put on it.

By using the VCSA and its vSphere Client, you can clone a VM with just a few clicks and vMotion VMs to/from different hosts and different storage even as they are running, as well as perform many, many other operations that we didn't even touch on.

Most third-party products from the VMware ecosystem require vCenter in order to function. My tests with ControlUp Real-Time Console demonstrate that it can effectively monitor and manage the hypervisor and VMs that reside on it.

With vCenter Server installed and functional, you have the basis for a fully functional vSphere environment! From this environment, small as it is, you can begin to explore the power and capabilities of a virtualized environment and learn more about how it has enabled thousands of businesses great and small. In the next chapter, we will see how Arm is going to play with the datacenter of the future.

CHAPTER 14

The Future of ESXi on Arm

In this book, we have demonstrated how to get started with VMware on Arm. The future goes well beyond using VMware on a Raspberry Pi (Figure 14-1). While the capability may be relatively new, it is crucial for VMware's continued relevance in the market.

Figure 14-1. *Raspberry Pi Supercomputer at Oracle OpenWorld 2019*

© Thomas Fenton and Patrick Kennedy 2022
T. Fenton and P. Kennedy, *Running ESXi on a Raspberry Pi*,
https://doi.org/10.1007/978-1-4842-7465-1_14

The ecosystem for Arm servers is set to look a lot different from the traditional x86 servers that have dominated the past decade. Companies such as Amazon AWS with Graviton, Ampere with Altra, and Huawei with Kunpeng are bringing innovative servers competitive with the best x86 servers from Intel and AMD. What is more, instead of being lab projects of curiosity, the new processors are being adopted by major cloud providers. Today these processors make up a small fraction of the CPU cores that are used in the cloud, but they are steadily increasing.

Using Arm cores goes beyond general-purpose compute. While x86 has cringed to legacy infrastructure dominated by generations of backward compatibility, Arm is starting fresh tailoring its hardware to specific workloads such as cloud and high-performance computing (HPC). Indeed, in June 2020, Supercomputer Fugaku became the world's fastest supercomputer based on the semi-annual TOP500 supercomputer list published by TOP500.org. That accomplishment was due to custom Arm cores that are well tailored to the HPC market in a way that would be nearly impossible in the modern x86 market, with Intel's Knights Landing and Knights Mill being the most recent examples. There are several other Arm for HPC projects underway as of mid-2021 in other geographies. NVIDIA has already announced its "Grace" solution years early bringing an Arm CPU and GPU together (see Figure 14-2).

Figure 14-2. NVIDIA Grace Arm CPU and GPU as shared at NVIDIA GTC 2021

The next boom for Arm in the datacenter is by adding Arm as the infrastructure gateway to devices in the datacenter. Datacenter operators in modern environments face a fundamental challenge every day. Users that are running workloads may or may not be trustworthy. Even trustworthy users may download malicious code. As a result, datacenter operators are on a journey to separate the infrastructure and application layers in their environments. AWS Nitro was the leader in this space, but the rest of the industry is catching up.

Using a new class of device, currently called the DPU or data processing unit, datacenter operators are able to maintain a secure endpoint where services can be provisioned. Most current DPUs have Arm CPUs, memory, storage, high-speed networking, and security accelerators built in. They run their own OSs whether that is Linux like Ubuntu or, as with VMware's Project Monterey, VMware ESXi directly on the PCIe add-in card. With the major cloud providers adopting this operating model, VMware needs to put ESXi on DPUs to bring their customers a similar level of capability. DPUs generally are Arm-based, which means that without Arm support, VMware cannot continue to provide an operating model that matches the leading industry practices.

The high end of the datacenter space generally garners a lot of industry buzz, but as server average selling prices (ASPs) rise, volumes are constrained. The next megatrend is decentralization of compute from the large cloud datacenter. With 5G edge technologies focusing on latency-sensitive applications, there will be a need to build a larger set of edge computing devices to meet next-gen service requirements. Many services are sized on some simple metric such as one core per user, and so getting more cores to the network edge is important. Arm's portfolio of Neoverse cores as well as Arm's customer projects are building this higher core count and lower-power core for the edge.

Arm already dominates the edge being found in mobile devices, but is also behind a large number of IoT devices as traditionally mechanical-only devices such as water pumps become networked. Sensors are increasingly being added to devices and data streamed back to the cloud. As these devices proliferate, the data they generate becomes too costly from an IT and environmental perspective to bring back to large centralized datacenters. Instead, data must be sifted through and important insights brought back to the cloud when further investigation is needed. This work drives demand for Arm not just at the edge device and the datacenter but also in the infrastructure that connects the two extremes.

For VMware, the implication is straightforward: it must either bring ESXi and its suite of products to these 5G edge deployments or it will cede this enormous market to the Linux hypervisor, Kubernetes, and public cloud deployments. Strategically, VMware needs to support Arm as that will be a dominant processor architecture at the edge simply due to its lower cost per core.

Summarizing this point, Arm is making headway into the mainstream cloud computing and high-performance computing markets. Arm is the dominant architecture for the new DPU class of devices that will go into large servers as that operating model expands beyond public cloud providers in the next few years. Arm already is dominant for IoT and edge devices and has a core value proposition for the next generation of 5G edge computing infrastructure. While VMware may have introduced ESXi on Arm as one of its "Flings," the company is already behind Linux tools such as KVM supporting Arm and cannot miss this technology transition.

Key Challenges for the Future of ESXi on Arm

There are a few key challenges for VMware ESXi on Arm. One of the biggest is simply that Arm is a relatively open architecture. While Arm has gone a long way to standardize instruction sets recently and push initiatives such as SBSA to make Arm platforms more compatible, the flexibility complicates Arm support.

As a great example of this, an Arm SoC vendor may say that they have a large speedup due to adding a specific cryptographic acceleration instruction and logic. A virtual machine live migrating from one Arm host to another may face challenges if that same instruction is not present on the new host. When AMD EPYC started gaining traction in the mainstream x86 market, this was a common marketing point Intel highlighted to slow its competition. Between the two, AMD x86 is closer to Intel x86 than x86 is to Arm (Figure 14-3).

Figure 14-3. *AMD EPYC 7001, Cavium (Marvell) ThunderX2,*
Various Intel Xeons

Another challenge is availability. While servers from AMD and Intel
are available from almost every major server vendor, Arm servers tend to
have fewer vendors supporting them. As we are writing this book, there is
not a mainstream Dell PowerEdge, HPE ProLiant, Inspur N Series, Lenovo
ThinkSystem, or other platform from a major vendor outside of Huawei
that is Arm-based. Almost every server vendor has had a product that
involved Arm, but none, thus far, have shown a sustained commitment to
bring Arm servers to the enterprise datacenter for many generations.

VMware has its own challenges. ESXi on Arm is still considered a
"Fling" and is not officially supported for mainstream deployments.
When it does become mainstream, VMware will need to have a licensing
structure that makes sense. Arm has been growing in the public cloud
often because public cloud providers are discounting Arm offerings over
x86 counterparts. Applying the current VMware core and socket licensing
model to Arm servers would effectively price Arm out of competition with
x86 servers.

Finally, Arm has to overcome inertia. While availability and pricing
are critical elements to success, very few installations are completely
greenfield. In most deployments there is existing x86 infrastructure running
existing workloads. Getting IT organizations to adopt a new architecture is

a relatively slow process. AMD EPYC 7002 "Rome" (see Figure 14-4) in 2019 was a technically superior part to the 2nd Generation Intel Xeon Scalable "Cascade Lake" launched that same year. EPYC to Xeon is a comparatively small shift, and AMD had mainstream platforms launching with almost every major OEM. Still, it took many quarters for organizations to slowly adopt AMD's newest chips because of IT organization inertia.

Figure 14-4. AMD EPYC Rome in Socket

Finally, there is a manufacturing risk. Intel and its x86 Xeon processors (see Figure 14-5) enjoyed a near monopoly on the mainstream server market for years when Intel's manufacturing technology led the industry. Now, Taiwan's TSMC is producing the leading semiconductor manufacturing processes. If anything were to occur to change that balance either from a technical or a geopolitical trade perspective, the Arm ecosystem could be set back by several years.

Figure 14-5. *Intel Ice Lake Xeon in Patrick's Hand*

Life is filled with risks and challenges. It is worth noting that players in the industry are well aware of all of these, but they prevent Arm from becoming the #1 server architecture in 2021.

How to Get Involved

For those practitioners in the space, there are multiple avenues to get involved.

In this book, we have demonstrated how to get VMware ESXi running on a low-cost Raspberry Pi. While that is an excellent effort, there is a large gap between a Raspberry Pi and a mainstream server (Figure 14-6).

Figure 14-6. *Wiwynn Mt. Jade Ampere Altra 2U Hyper-scale Server*

If you want to trial a mainstream server with VMware ESXi on Arm, perhaps the best platform today is the Ampere Altra platforms currently sold by a handful of vendors (Figure 14-7). Soon, these will be joined by the Ampere Altra Max platforms with 128 cores per socket or 256 cores per server. These servers are roughly equivalent in cloud workloads to a mainstream x86 server. VMware has, at the time of this writing, started to make its VMware on Arm Fling capable of utilizing these servers. While availability may change, Oracle Cloud has announced a bare metal Ampere Altra offering for those who do not want to go through the procurement cycle. Also, we expect further support for AWS Graviton 2 and future generations as time progresses.

Figure 14-7. *Mainstream Dual-Socket CPU Options at the Start of 2021, AMD EPYC, Ampere Altra, and Intel Xeon*

A perhaps easier way to start using VMware ESXi on Arm in a next-generation proof-of-concept is to utilize an NVIDIA BlueField-2 DPU (and later) as these are listed as part of Project Monterey. They can be purchased today and offer a fairly standard Mellanox ConnectX-6-based dual 25GbE/100GbE (Figure 14-8) network path if the Arm cores are not being used in the data path.

Figure 14-8. *NVIDIA BlueField-2 DPU*

For those running 5G edge infrastructure, the Marvell Octeon 10 has been announced and is designed for 5G O-RAN applications. While 5G is entering the market as part of a standard telecom carrier and service provider offering, the promise of 5G is that it can be deployed in the enterprise and eventually displace WiFi (many years from now.) Octeon 10 VMware support has not been announced yet, but this is a very promising edge platform.

While writing this book, Intel has also jumped into the Arm DPU market with its Mount Evans IPU (see Figure 14-9). Intel, one of the biggest x86 proponents, is using 16 Arm Neoverse N1 cores on its infrastructure processor that is going after the same market as the NVIDIA BlueField line that is part of Project Monterey. Intel's choice of using Arm cores for this market was driven by a large cloud service provider, showing just how big the push toward Arm is. Since even Intel is capitulating to the Arm movement, it is wise that IT practitioners should take note.

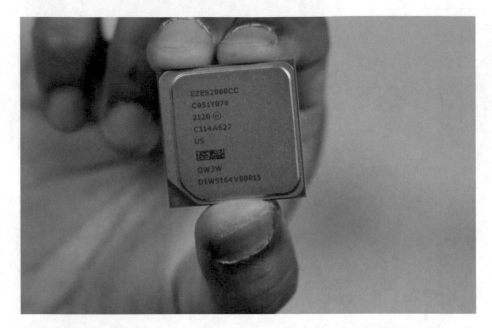

Figure 14-9.   *Intel Mount Evans Arm-Based ASIC at Intel Architecture Day 2021*

The easiest ways to get involved are to join the growing community working on ESXi on Arm. One can go to their local VMUG, check out the VMware forums, join the ServeTheHome Forums community, or even get out on various social media platforms. It is easy to get hands-on and learn for yourself but also to reach out and help others.

Final Words

We had two goals when writing this book:

- Give a high-level overview of the Arm processor history, how it's currently being used in the datacenter, and how it will be used in the future.

- Allow the reader to have hands-on experience installing, configuring, and using the most prevalent hypervisor in the datacenter – ESXi, using an inexpensive, Arm-based system, the Raspberry Pi 4 Model B.

Looking forward, Arm is going to be a bigger force in the datacenter. Arm processors are taking the form of both high-end datacenter chips that are competitive with their x86 counterparts and discrete components such as SmartNICs. We are starting to see multiple competitive offerings from a diverse set of vendors giving the market more confidence in Arm-based systems and components. Major customers are demanding Arm processors, thereby bringing forth a sense of inevitability to the growth of Arm not only in servers but also in the infrastructure and edge realms.

Two years ago, back in 2019, if someone would have suggested to us that they could purchase a new system that could run ESXi for under a hundred dollars, we would not have believed them, but the VMware ESXi on Arm Fling made this possible. Yes, the Raspberry Pi is limited, but it can, and people do run small workloads on it. More importantly, for the purpose of this book, it is a perfectly adequate, low-cost, entry point for working with and learning about ESXi and vSphere.

At the time of this writing, ESXi on Arm is still a Fling and not officially supported by VMware. We believe VMware sees the value of Arm in the datacenter and the value that ESXi, with its solid layer of abstraction and management, can bring to it. We also believe that as Arm becomes more relevant in the datacenter, the value that ESXi brings to it will become apparent. With this in mind, we fully expect ESXi on Arm to be a fully supported product sooner rather than later.

Now that you are armed (pun intended) with the knowledge that this technology transition is happening and how to work with VMware tools on Arm, you are in a unique position to be part of that future. Just as we built our knowledge on this subject from the community, we suggest that you also get involved with it. It may be by becoming a member of your local VMUG or participating in VMware forums and ServeTheHome Forums or the other online communities that have sprouted up around ESXi on Arm. Now is an ideal time to make an impact in the community while this transition is still in its infancy.

In closing, we would like to thank you for spending time with this book and for letting us share the knowledge and perspective that we have gained over the years.

Index

A

A64FX processors, 24

Amazon Web Services (AWS), 23

Application-specific integrated
circuits (ASICs), 28

Argon ONE case, 67, 68

Arm system

    computational storage, 33

        QNAP, 34, 35

        SoftIron, 33, 34

    ESXi, 20–22

    x64 systems, 18

B

Bare-bones script, 123

Build kits, 61

    Argon ONE case, 67, 68

    arm processor, 63

    Geekworm Armor Aluminum
Alloy Passive Cooling
Case, 70, 71

    low-cost naked
build, 64, 65

    M.2 case SATA drive, 69, 70

    Pi enclosure, 66, 67

    requirements, 61, 62

    storage devices, 66

3D printer, 72

    thumb drive, 63, 64

Business continuity, 252

C

Central processing unit (CPU)

    reserving server, 42, 43

    resource usage test, 44, 45

    VDI environment, 44

    vSphere client, 44

Cloud providers/arm servers, 23

Complex instruction set
computing (CISC), 18

Corporate sandboxes, 51

D

Datacenter, 1

    multitiered application, 2

    servers/operating
systems (OSes), 2

    server sprawl, 3

    three-tier architecture, 1, 2

Data processing unit (DPU), 357

Datastores

    host client

        detailed information, 122

        navigator pane, 122

© Thomas Fenton and Patrick Kennedy 2022
T. Fenton and P. Kennedy, *Running ESXi on a Raspberry Pi*,
https://doi.org/10.1007/978-1-4842-7465-1

Printed in the United States
by Baker & Taylor Publisher Services